Proliferation and Implementation of Prison Ombudsmen

Würzburger Schriften zur Kriminalwissenschaft

Herausgegeben von Klaus Laubenthal

Band 34

Sabine Carl

Proliferation and Implementation of Prison Ombudsmen

Comparative Analysis of the Prisons
and Probation Ombudsman for England
and Wales and the Justizvollzugsbeauftragter
des Landes Nordrhein-Westfalen

PL ACADEMIC RESEARCH

Bibliografische Information der Deutschen Nationalbibliothek
Die Deutsche Nationalbibliothek verzeichnet diese Publikation
in der Deutschen Nationalbibliografie; detaillierte bibliografische
Daten sind im Internet über http://dnb.d-nb.de abrufbar.

Zugl.: Berlin, Freie Univ., Diss., 2013

First Advisor: Professor Klaus Hoffmann-Holland, Freie Universität Berlin
Second Advisor: Professor Trevor Buck, De Montfort University, Leicester
Day of oral examination: January 24th, 2013

Library of Congress Cataloging-in-Publication Data
Carl, Sabine, 1985- author.
 Proliferation and implementation of prison ombudsmen : comparative analysis of the
prisons and probation ombudsmen for England and Wales and the
Justizvollzugsbeauftragter des Landes Nordrhein-Westfalen / Sabine Carl.
    pages cm. — (Würzburger Schriften zur Kriminalwissenschaft ; Band 34)
 Includes bibliographical references.
 ISBN 978-3-631-64559-8
 1. Ombudspersons—Germany—North Rhine-Westphalia. 2. Ombudspersons—
England. 3. Ombudspersons—Wales.4. Prisons—Law and legislation—Germany—
North Rhine-Westphalia. 5. Prisons—Law and legislation—England. 6. Prisons—Law
and legislation—Wales. 7. Criminal justice, Administration of—Germany--North Rhine-
Westphalia. 8. Criminal justice, Administration of--England. 9. Criminal justice,
Administration of—Wales. I. Title.
 KJC5630.C37 2013
 365'.66—dc23

                                                                                  2013033380

D 188
ISSN 1618-078X
ISBN 978-3-631-64559-8 (Print)
E-ISBN 978-3-653-03747-0 (E-Book)
DOI 10.3726/978-3-653-03747-0

© Peter Lang GmbH
Internationaler Verlag der Wissenschaften
Frankfurt am Main 2014
All rights reserved.
PL Academic Research is an Imprint of Peter Lang GmbH.
Peter Lang – Frankfurt am Main · Bern · Bruxelles · New York ·
Oxford · Warszawa · Wien
All parts of this publication are protected by copyright. Any
utilisation outside the strict limits of the copyright law, without
the permission of the publisher, is forbidden and liable to
prosecution. This applies in particular to reproductions,
translations, microfilming, and storage and processing in
electronic retrieval systems.

This book is part of the Peter Lang Edition
list and was peer reviewed prior to publication.

www.peterlang.com

Patri adhortatori,
marito fautori.

Acknowledgement

This doctoral thesis was approved by the Faculty of Law of the Freie Universität Berlin, Germany, in May of 2013.

First and foremost I would like to thank my doctoral adviser, Prof. Klaus Hoffmann-Holland. Not only did he agree to oversee my chosen topic of research, but he also continuously supported my work contributing to the academic discourse through journal articles and conference participation.

Heartfelt thanks also belong to my second adviser, Prof. Trevor Buck of the De Montfort University, Leicester, UK. I am especially grateful that he encouraged me to present at the 2012 Annual Conference of the Socio Legal Studies Association, where I came into first-hand contact with the British discourse on ombudsmen.

I would also like to thank my interview partners Roswitha Müller-Piepenkötter (Justizministerin des Landes Nordrhein-Westfalen 2005-10), Prof. em. Michael Walter (Justizvollzugsbeauftragter des Landes Nordrhein-Westfalen) and Olivia Morrison-Lyons (Assistant Ombudsman to the Prisons and Probation Ombudsman for England and Wales) for their voluntary participation in this study. I sincerely appreciate their most generous offer of both their time and unique insight.

Finally, I would like to thank the Hanns-Seidel-Stiftung for their financial and ideational support of my doctoral research via allotment of funds provided by the Bundesministerium für Bildung und Forschung. The opportunity to pursue this academic endeavor was greatly appreciated.

Content

Abbreviations

ABA	American Bar Association
ADP	average daily population
ADR	alternative dispute resolution
Art.	Artikel (article)
AV	Allgemeinverfügung (ministerial decree)
BIOA	British and Irish Ombudsman Association
BverfGE	Entscheidung des Bundesverfassungsgerichts (decision of the Federal Constitutional Court)
BverfGG	Bundesverfassungsgerichtsgesetz (Law on the Federal Constitutional Court)
CDU	Christlich Demokratische Union Deutschlands
DJT	Deutscher Juristentag (German Legal Association's Annual Meeting)
ECHR	European Convention on Human Rights
ECPT	European Committee for the Prevention of Torture and Inhuman or Degrading Treatment or Punishment
EctHR	European Court of Human Rights
EHRR	European Human Rights Reports
FCC	Federal Constitutional Court
FDP	Freie Demokratische Partei
GG	Grundgesetz (German Basic Law)
HM	His/Her Majesty
HMCIP	Her Majesty's Chief Inspector for Prisons
IBA	International Bar Association

IMB	Independent Monitoring Board
LJ	Lord Justice
MoJ	Ministry of Justice
MP	Member of Parliament
NGO	non-governmental organisation
NOMS	National Offender Management Service
NPM	National Preventive Mechanism
OPCAT	Optional Protocol to the Convention against Torture
PCA	Parliamentary Commissioner of Administration
PHSO	Parliamentary and Health Service Ombudsman
PSO	Prison Service Orders
SPD	Sozialdemokratische Partei Deutschlands
SPT	United Nations Subcommittee on Prevention of Torture and other Cruel, Inhuman or Degrading Treatment or Punishment
StVollzG	Strafvollzugsgesetz (German prison act)
UK	United Kingdom
UN	United Nations
US	United States of America
WWII	Second World War

Figures

Tables

A Introduction

Prisoners are denied their rights and lose their lives in prisons around the world every day. In England and Wales 60 to 100 people lose their lives in prison every year due to non-natural causes, which amounts to approximately one death every five days.[1]

As so called "total institutions", prisons are by definition closed environments designed to deprive the individual of a range of personal freedoms.[2] With the progressing renunciation of the death penalty, imprisonment constitutes the most severe form of state-imposed punishment for the commission of a crime. Thus, it is astonishing that "society as a whole is less than interested about what happens behind [prison] walls" leaving prisons to "operate outside the normal controls and processes of society".[3]

In spite of this societal disinterest, it is now commonly acknowledged that "[j]ustice does not stop at the prison doors" and that "[p]unishment and imprisonment have meaning [only] if, while maintaining the demands of justice and discouraging crime, they serve the rehabilitation of the individual by offering those who have made a mistake an opportunity to reflect and to change their lives in order to be fully reintegrated into society"[4]. To this end, the state must not curtail rights beyond what is necessary (freedom of movement, assembly etc.).[5] Yet, when- and wherever humans regularly exercise authority over others, unintentional as well as deliberate grievances of both petty and serious nature occur. These may concern anything from property to hygiene with issues escalating in significance pertaining to disciplinary matters possibly including instances of bodily harm.

---

1   Averages taken from the Inquest statistics of the last ten years – available from http://inquest.gn.apc.org/website/statistics/deaths-in-prison. In 2011 two prisoners were victims of homicide, 57 prisoners committed suicide and two prisoners died of other non-natural causes. North Rhine-Westphalian catalogues 20 to 45 inmate deaths per year over the last ten years (21 deaths in 2011, 12 of which are classified as suicides) – statistics available from
http://www.justiz.nrw.de/Gerichte_Behoerden/zahlen_fakten/statistiken/justizvollzug/index.php (all webpages last accessed August 15th, 2012)

2   Goffman (1961); Owers (2004), p. 109

3   Owers (2004), p. 109

4   Woolf/Tumim (1991), p. 411; Pope John II, Homily at "Regina Coeli" Prison in Rome during the Celebration of the Great Jubilee (July 9, 2000), in Holy Father Visits "Regina Coeli" Prison: "I was in Prison and You Came to Me", L'Osservatore Romano (English ed.), July 12, 2000 at p.1

5   Eady (2007), p. 266; Woolf/Tumim (1991), p. 411

It is only natural that "[a]dministrative law organizes a range of forms of redress" providing the prisoners with ample opportunities to make requests.[6] The majority of these grievances are resolved inherent to the system by the prison authorities. Yet, "one of the fundamental principles of human rights-compliant prison policy" is the provision of regular independent oversight.[7]

The high vulnerability and protective needs of prisoners are reflected by the fact that many key judgments of the European Court of Human Rights (ECtHR) have been in the area of prisoners' rights.[8] In fact, British prisoners have made more use of the European Convention on Human Rights (ECHR) than any other single group of people in Europe.[9]

While courts are the most wide-spread form of institutionalized, national, independent oversight bodies controlling the penal system, there exists also extra-judicial redress provided by Members of Parliament (MP), petition committees etc. These bodies reflect the extension of the term control from its traditional meaning of *contre-rôle,* implying the examination of already closed cases, to include guiding influence taken on cases prior to their closure.[10] The most significant of these forms of extra-judicial redress has been the Ombudsman movement as many countries have opted to include ombudsmen in their multi-pronged approach.[11]

Nowadays, the ombudsinstitution is acknowledged as an embodiment of the democratic yearning for the control of state sovereignty.[12] As "the office of the ombudsman has attracted limited academic [or public] attention", it may be prudent to mention that not all offices possessing the characteristics of an ombudsman actually carry the word ombudsman in their title; e. g. *Médiateur de la République, Defensor del Pueblo* or *Protecteur du Citoyen.*[13]

While the origin of the office itself can be traced back to Germanic tribes, the word ombudsman derives from the Swedish *ombuds* or *umbuds*, which translates as representative or agent of the people or a sub-group thereof.[14] This, of course, serves as a mere elucidation instead of fully-fledged definition of the term ombudsman. This study will show that any existing attempts at the latter are insufficient in precision and topicality. In fact, a new definition will be pro-

---

6   Bell (2006), p. 1278
7   Martynowicz (2011) p. 82; 70.1 to 70.7 of the European Prison Rules 2006
8   Here and in the following: Eady (2007), p. 266
9   Arnott et al. (2000), p. 5
10   Puchta (1986), p. 121
11   Bell (2006), p. 1278
12   Bauer (1964b), p. 5
13   Pearce (2005), pp. 110f; offices located in France, Spain and Québec respectively
14   Stuhmcke (2010), p. 162; Caiden et al. (1983), p. 9

posed which coins ombudsmen as public sector institutions designed to protect individual rights and defend the fundamental rights of democracy such as civil and human rights via the supervision of the executive. Ombudsmen are authorized by a parliament, a ministry or a subdivision thereof to independent investigation – either upon own initiative or upon receiving complaints from citizens – of an alleged part of the administration's acts, omissions, improprieties, and broader, systemic problems. Due to not being invested with any executive power, their only tools are personal authority, recommendations, annual and special reports and the media.

Ombudsmen have been considered a way of "fitting the forum to the fuss" and to remedy marginal defects in an overall sound system.[15] They were not designed specifically for prison purposes, but are said to be of a "cloth that can be cut into any form".[16] While the remit of many general ombudsmen includes penal matters, specialty prison ombudsmen as one of many adaptations of the original idea epitomise a concept that is neither widely known nor has been met with enthusiasm – in research or otherwise – befitting its importance.[17] It never was part of what has been described as "Ombudsmania" and outside of Britain – and possibly Canada or Northern Ireland – it would never be considered a feature of modern (prison) life.[18] Until 2007, prison ombudsmen exclusively existed in the common law world where they have been employed as mechanisms for penal control since the 1970s.

So far, the success of ombudsinstitutions has been the assumed reason for their spread – assumed because of the marked discrepancy between the frequency of use and the extent of existing academic research.[19] Ombudsmania has been identified as one reason for this lack of research. This does not mean that the need for evaluation has gone un-noted.[20] As Gellhorn puts it "[t]he Ombudsman has in recent years been so rapturously regarded abroad that his achievements have not often been evaluated. What he is supposed to accomplish is taken as the equivalent of what he has in fact accomplished".[21] Considering on the one hand the fact that ombudsmen hold the power to do much good and hide much evil[22] and on the other hand the truism that "few institutions work so well that

---

15   Buck et al. (2011a), p. 8; Anderson (1978), p. 243
16   Caiden (1983), p. 15
17   c.f. Gottehrer (2009), p. 5; Jacobs (2004), p. 300
18   Ascher (1967), p. 174; Gottehrer (2000), p. 47; Rowat (1968), p. xii; Seneviratne (2002), p. 29
19   Fuchs (1985), p. 19
20   Ayeni (2000), p. 16
21   Gellhorn (1966b), p. 239
22   Caiden (1983), p. 15

they cannot be improved"[23], it is all the more surprising that serious work has been few and far between[24]. Overall, "the current scientific patchwork of knowledge on the ombudsman is a far cry from being ideal".[25] This remains true despite the acknowledgement of ombudsmen as "an important object of comparative study that lies on the borderline between the disciplines of administrative law and public administration".[26] The same holds true for research done on prison ombudsmen. At a first glance the list of literature may appear long, but most of these essays do no more than call for the introduction of such an office.[27]

The lack of answers to the questions

- Do prison ombudsmen fulfil their purposes?
- Should they be recommended as penal oversight bodies and grievance mechanisms?
- And if so, how should they be moulded?

is an insupportable status quo in light of the human rights and rehabilitation requirements of prisoners, the severity of imprisonment as a form of punishment as well as the financial resources invested.

This study challenges the assumption of institutional success at the heart of the prison ombudsman spread. In order for success to trigger the spread, introducing state bodies would have to make a rational, level-headed choice to implement after proper consideration of what foreign penal oversight bodies would best suit both their local need and the already existing tableau. This assumption, however, has been never been researched let alone proven.

This study recognizes this deficiency, which ties in with Seneviratne's recent critique that "[the ombudsmen's] proliferation has occurred with little

---

23   Seneviratne (1994), p. 133
24   in depth work: Danet (1978), Male (2000), Fowlie (2005). Evaluation mentioned in: Holt (1980), Seneviratne (1994), Ayeni (1999), Aufrecht/Hertogh (2000), Male (2000), Fowlie (2005), Hyson (2006), van Roosbroek/Steven and van de Walle (2008). For the definition of success in ombudsman work see: Harrison (2004), Buck et al. (2011a)
25   Steyvers et al. (2009), p. 16
26   Bell (2006), p. 1279
27   Academic work mentioning prison ombudsmen at least in passing: Kühler (1970), Tibbles (1971), Taugher (1972), Fitzharris (1973), Münchbach (1973), Cromwell (1974), May (1975), Moore (1975), Williams (1975), Anderson (1975b, 1978, 1981a, 1983), Fulmer (1981), Barton (1983), Williams   (1984), Birkinshaw (1985), Johnson (1988), Selke (1992), Lesting (1993), Ryan/Ward (1993), Jacobs (2004), Lazarus (2004), Shaw (2004), Kretschmer (2005), Owers (2006), Alarcón (2007), Heskamp (2007-2008), Sanker (2007), Laubenthal (2008), Livingstone et al. (2008), Rotthaus (2008), Sapers/Zinger (2010). For work done on general ombudsman activities in prison see: Groves (2002, 2003), Fliflet (2009).

thought as to how they relate to each other, the civil justice system, or the administrative justice system".[28] The study aims to fill this research gap where the proliferation of prison ombudsmen is concerned by examining the why and how of the prison ombudsman spread across the borders of countries and legal cultures alike.

Thus, the research undertaken here is based on the questions

- How did prison ombudsmen evolve?
- What drives their spread?

which imply an enquiry into the needs state bodies seek to fill with the introduction of prison ombudsmen. However, the proliferation perspective only scrapes at the surfaces of the deeper underlying questions of

- How do such introductions proceed?
- What legal forms are employed?

which ask after the structures said state bodies utilize to meet their perceived needs. This research therefore contributes to the field by analysing the implementation of prison ombudsmen. The implementation perspective alone allows the identification of and constitutes proof of the occurrence of knowledge transfer.[29] The latter concept belongs to the realm of international relations, public policy, politics and sociology.[30] Accordingly, this study takes a comparative approach combining elements of the former with criminology, legal studies and administrative sciences.

In short, this study challenges the assumption that institutional success causes the spread of prison ombudsmen reasoning that the frequent introduction of executive prison ombudsmen makes a thorough examination process by state key-holders unlikely. This can be described in three hypotheses:

- Prison ombudsmen are only introduced during times of acute pressure on the host penal system.
- Their implementation happens via cross-fertilization.
- This frequently results in executive ombudsmen.

The technical terms used in these hypotheses (ombudsmen, prison ombudsmen, executive ombudsmen and cross-fertilization) will be defined and operationalized in the next chapter, which describes the current state of research. Subsequently, the methodology selected for the testing of the hypotheses as well as its

---

28   Seneviratne (2000b), p. 20
29   c.f. Evans (2009a), p. 246
30   Marsh/Sharman (2009), p. 269

application is explained in chapter C. Chapter D contains an analysis of the proliferation and implementation process of prison ombudsmen using the Prisons
Ombudsman for England and Wales and the Justizvollzugsbeauftragter des
Landes Nordrhein-Westfalen as the two primary examples. A conclusion comprising a compilation of research results, a critical analysis of this study's constraints as well as future research prospects in this field is presented in chapter
E.

B Current state of research

The current state of research operationalizes the technical terms used in this study. This operationalization entails three parts. First, the ombudsman concept is examined. This includes definitions and descriptions of both ombudsman *in generaliter* and executive ombudsman *in specialiter*. The operationalization of the technical term prison ombudsman comes next. The third section on learning process explains the concept of cross-fertilization.

I. The ombudsman as a concept

This study focuses on prison ombudsmen. In order to properly analyse their implementation modes, the term "ombudsman" must be operationalized by establishing as precise a definition as possible. Only a precise definition allows the identification of the aims against which to compare prison ombudsmen.

However, the availability of such a definition is historically impaired by the spread of the ombudsman idea, which, once it left its Scandinavian crib, may effortlessly be compared to a highly contagious disease aptly named Ombudsmania.[31] The sheer speed of this idea's diversification left academia struggling to keep up.[32] The resulting discrepancy between the factual proliferation of ombudsmen and their methodical academic assessment remains the source of many an academic disagreement on whether a new development was a valid extension or an off-shoot outside the conceptual borders. Indeed, no commonly accepted definition is currently available for the term.

The method applied in this study has led this researcher to examine multiple definitions and – when none was found to suit the purpose of this study – create a new one. This definition, which has already been outlined in the introduction, is based on an understanding of the ombudsman concept as a whole.

This section will therefore begin with a brief overview over the history of ombudsmen, which quickly reveals that the search for the conceptual borders cannot be limited to institutions bearing the ombudsman title. The grounded theory approach therefore required the researcher to look for common features, practice methods and expectations, all of which have facilitated the discovery of the plethora of technical terms describing ombudsinstitutions. Their categorization identified criteria for judging the inclusivity of the available definitions.

---

31   Ascher (1967), p. 174; Gottehrer (2000), p. 47; Rowat (1968), p. xii
32   Fuchs (1985), p. 19

When none was found to suit the purpose of this study, a new definition was created.

1. Short history

The method of administrative control is as prone to change over time as states and forms of government themselves are. Any method of administrative control set in stone is doomed to fail. This hypothesis is as old or new as Plato's *Politeia* VIII. Consequently, administrative control faces a constant process of adjustment. It therefore comes as no surprise that the ombudsman's roots reach back far in history. Forerunners can be found in the early history of Western Europe (e.g. the Roman tribune of the plebs[33]), the Middle East (the *kadi* during the Ottoman Empire[34]) and China (the control *yuan* during the Qin Dynasty[35]). How much these administrative control mechanisms really resembled what is now called an ombudsman is difficult to judge – especially, since the present-day concept is by no means well-defined itself.

It is much easier to pinpoint the origin of the term ombudsman.[36] In 1713 Charles XII, the Swedish king, exiled in the Ottoman Empire, installed as his proxy the *högste ombudsmannen*, whose duty was to ensure that the civil servants and judges acted in accordance with the law. In 1719 this "Supreme Ombudsman" evolved into the Chancellor of Justice. With the Swedish revolution and the consequent move to a limited monarchy in 1809, the Swedish Constitution created the office of the *Riksdagens Justitieombudsman*, who was directly responsible to the Parliament and, in contrast to his predecessor, was based on Montesquieu's model of the separation of powers. Ever since, the ombudsman's role and definition has proven difficult to place, which led Münchbach to consider it a *pouvoir neutre*, while Bauer went even further and defined the ombudsman as a separate "fourth power".[37] In any case, this Swedish ombudsman model was not an invention that took the world by storm.

The actual starting point of the worldwide spread of the ombudsman idea lies elsewhere. The crisis legislation in the 1930s and the growth of the state apparatus during the economic reconstruction after the Second World War (WWII) led many European citizens to perceive the administration as a potent, independ-

---

33   Ebert (1968), p. 9
34   Atalay (2000), p. 47
35   Owen (1993), p. 2
36   For a concise overview of the spread of the institution, see Ayeni (2000), pp. 20f
37   Münchbach (1973), p. 84; Bauer (1964a) p. 227 and (1946b), p. 3

ent power factor with them at its mercy and their individual rights at jeopardy.[38] Moore strikingly sums this up as the "ache-all-over-feeling of bureaucracy".[39] This feeling was only insufficiently counteracted by legal remedies since the judiciary throughout the ages has repeatedly been perceived as being in similar danger of institutional torpor.[40] Consequently, many European countries felt a need for administrative reform.[41]

Denmark reacted in 1955 by strengthening the role of its *Riksdag* as well as the legal guarantees of the individual's rights in relation to the administration.[42] The emergence of the modern welfare state was accompanied by a new concern for the protection of human rights and the growth of public education and participation.[43] As complaining may be considered one form of political participation[44], it comes as no surprise that the Danish reform included the implementation of an ombudsman scheme. This Danish Model, sculpted in a novel legal form, triggered the fast-growing popularity and consequent spread of the ombudsman idea with New Zealand (1962) as the first common law country and Norway (1963) as the first civil law country to implement similar institutions.[45]

It might be worthwhile to examine the spread of the idea more closely where the United States of America (US), the United Kingdom (UK) and Germany are concerned. The latter two are of particular interest in the context of this study's focus. The US stand out since this is where the concept of the ombudsman has undergone its most far-reaching diversifications.

The Danish Model spread to the UK in 1967 with the introduction of the Parliamentary Commissioner of Administration (PCA). The history of active academic interest dates back even further.[46] The one most remarked-upon change to the ombudsman idea made in the UK was the introduction of the so called "MP-filter", which forces the citizen to approach the PCA via the local Member of Parliament. This has limited the number and type of cases investi-

---

38   Matthes (1981), p. 12; Patterson (1959-63), p. 777; Bauer (1964b), p. 4
39   Moore (1986b), p. 70
40   Redeker (1967), p. 1298
41   Gregory/Giddings (2000), p. 2
42   Busck (1995), p. 23
43   Rowat (1985), p. 131
44   Hyson (2006), p. 11 and (2009a), p. 15
45   Note that although the date of introduction of the *Wehrbeauftragte des Bundesta*ges (German Military Ombudsman) in Germany in 1956 might give rise to the assumption that Germany was the first civil law country to implement a Danish model based ombudsman this would be a fallacy, since the *Wehrbeauftragte* was modeled on the Swedish - c.f. Schlaffer (2006), p. 87; Münchbach (1973), p. 85; Marti (1961), p. 178.
46   At least to the 1961 report by Justice, The Citizen and the Administration – c.f. Seneviratne (1994), p. viii; Chapman (1960), pp. 306; Gregory/Giddings (2000b), p. 21

gated. Since the introduction of the PCA the UK has introduced quite a few ombudsman-schemes (health service ombudsmen, local government ombudsman, prison ombudsmen etc.). Not all ombudsinstitutions are full members of the British and Irish Ombudsman Association (BIOA) due to its requirement of full independence manifested in a statutory footing. One of the members lacking this prerequisite is the Prison and Probation Ombudsman for England and Wales.

This marked interest in the ombudsman idea contrasts rather sharply with the situation in Germany. Although it was the first country outside Scandinavia to introduce an ombudsman[47], the German academic interest in the ombudsman concept may be called sporadic at best[48] and to this day, the concept remains largely unknown to the general public.[49] This might be due to the fact that the titles of the existing offices (*Wehrbeauftragte des Bundestages*, *Datenschutzbeauftragte* and the *Bürgerbeauftragte der Länder*) do not include the term ombudsman.[50] This in turn may be attributed to two key rejections of the concept: first in 1968 by the presidents of the state-parliaments (*Landtagspräsidenten*) based on the claim that the institution would impinge upon a long-standing constitutional body and second in 1973 by the *Enquete-Kommission* of the German parliament on "Questions of constitutional reform", which argued that the existing system of legal protection for citizens was almost perfect and did not require the introduction of an additional law court in the form of an ombudsman.[51] Interestingly, these rejections did forestall neither the introduction of the *Bürgerbeauftragte* for the Rhineland-Palatinate nor the much later introduction of the *Bürgerbeauftragte* for Mecklenburg-Western Pomerania, Schleswig-Holstein and the Free State of Thuringia after the fall of the Berlin Wall – all of which are clearly ombudsinstitutions.

The spread of the ombudsman concept to the United States during the 1960s was set against the background of the Vietnam War and the accompanying student protests, which together created a general sense of the overwhelming need for the protection of individual rights combined with the demand for regulation

---

47   The German Military Ombudsman - c. f Ayeni (2000), p. 2; Taylor (1984/1985), p. 152

48   Bauer (1964a and 1964b); Münchbach (1973); Wild (1970); Klasen (1991); Kretschmer (2005); Kruse (2006); Rotthaus (2008); Ritter (2009). Kühler (1970), p. 323 mentions the existence of a society called „Aktionsgemeinschaft Deutscher Ombudsman" in 1967, which was a small elite circle led by the Federal Minister of Justice at the time, Gustav Heinemann

49   In agreement: Kempf/Mille (1993), p. 195

50   Kruse (2006), p. 170

51   Kempf/Mille (1993), p. 195

of maladministration. [52] Unlike in Europe, this demand for regulation did not stop at the government only, but also extended to educational and corporate bureaucracies.[53] Warrington identifies the "unparalleled expansion in the density and range of contacts between citizens and governmental authorities, as well as between consumers and producers of public and private goods and services" as "the impetus behind the diffusion and diversification of the ombudsman".[54] It therefore comes as no surprise that the ombudsinstitutions introduced throughout the US were frequently appointed state, local government, university or newspaper ombudsmen, which differ greatly from the Danish Model.[55]

This extension of the ombudsman concept fits well with the US tradition of filling high-level government positions by appointment through the chief executive.[56] Rowat interprets this process saying that "the Americans loved the word but not the concept".[57] The "love" for the word, however, did not survive the 1970s feminist movement, which claimed that the term was not gender-neutral.[58] This resulted in a frantic renaming – especially in the private sector – which was expedited by the Corporate Ombudsman Association and lead to such appellations as ombud, ombuds, ombudsperson, ombudspeople, ombuddy and even the grammatically wrong ombudsmans.[59] Rowat blames "the casual way in which the word has been altered [to have] contributed to its disrespectful, 'dumbing down' usage."

The terms regularly used today are either ombudsman (with the plural ombudsmen or ombudspeople) or ombudsinstitution. The latter terms allow to avoid the complicated his/her constructions of the singular form to which some still react sensitively. The derived term ombuds is still favoured in the alternative dispute resolution (ADR) context of the private sector.[60]

Today the spread of the ombudsman concept is furthered by such highranking institutions as the Council of Europe, which welcomed the remarkable development the ombudsinstitution has taken at national, regional and local lev-

---

52   Thacker (2009), p. 67
53   Gadlin (2000), p. 37
54   Warrington (1999), p. 37
55   The Danish Model involves a parliamentary ombudsman with what has termed "soft powers" – c.f. Kucsko-Stadlmayer (2008), pp. 2, 44, 63
56   Tibbles (1971), p. 423
57   Rowat (2007), p. 43; in agreement Gadlin (2000), p. 40
58   A claim that was recently reiterated by LeBaron (2008), p. 4.; in disagreement, Seneviratne (2002), p.1 and Ayeni (2000), p. 2
59   Here and in the following: Rowat (2007), p. 45
60   Jessar (2005), p. 56; see also Alternative Dispute Resolution Act of 1996, 5 U.S.C. §573 (c)(3) (Supp. III 1997)

els in its member states.[61] It recommended introducing the institution to those states without an ombudsman as a contribution to parliamentary control, and to those states already in possession of an ombudsman it recommended to consider empowering existing ombudsmen further – especially in the context of human rights. This claim for the usefulness of general ombudsmen was reiterated in further detail as recently as 2005.[62]

2. Double function

The presented historical overview confirms Seneviratne's dictum that the proliferation of ombudsmen "has occurred with little thought as to how they relate to each other, the civil justice system, or the administrative justice system".[63] In face of the factual spillover of the ombudsman concept into the private sector, the idea that there might be a common denominator for public and private sector ombudsmen suggests itself. The search for a common denominator here commences with an examination of the primordial reasons for the creation of ombudsmen.

The previous section has identified the historical *raison d'être* of ombudsinstitutions to be twofold: On the one hand, the shift of power from the citizen to the state that accompanied the emergence of the welfare state caused a feeling of utter dependence on the state's superiority.[64] The consequent need for increased guaranties of individual legal rights necessitated the addition of further protective measures. On the other hand, the legislature traditionally in charge of the system of checks and balances for the administration delegated much of its power to the executive, which was increasingly perceived as an independent power factor.[65] This situation called for an augmentation of parliament's supervisory position as well as the solidification of the individual's legal rights in relation to the administration. The ombudsinstitution, now, was designed to cater to both purposes at once: the protection of individual rights as well as the defence of democracy as a whole via the supervision of the executive.[66] This phenomenon has sometimes been called the ombudsman's "double function".[67] The public

---

61   Here and in the following: Council of Europe (1985)
62   Council of Europe (2005)
63   Seneviratne (2000b), p. 20
64   Matthes (1981), p. 12
65   Frank (1975), p. 56; Busck (1995), p. 23
66   Busck (1995), p. 23; that the institution of the Ombudsman can contribute to the strengthening of parliamentary control is also opined by Council of Europe (1985).
67   Wild (1970), p. 8; Busck (1995), p, 23; Hopp (1993), p. 52

sector ombudsman's double function can be depicted as a conceptual core or nucleus as depicted in Figure 1.[68]

Figure 1: Conceptual core of the public-sector ombudsman

Private sector ombudsmen, as the historical overview has demonstrated, were created in comparable situations: During the 1960s the ever-increasing contacts between consumers and producers of public and private goods and services lead to a new demand for regulations safeguarding the rights of consumers – demands by students and employees quickly followed suit. In these private sector settings, an ombudsman may prove beneficial by handling individual grievances and improving the standards and practice of the respective sector or industry.[69]

It is therefore established that both, the public and the private sector ombudsman, hold a double function: redress of individual grievances and quality control.[70] It is self-evident that there is a gradation in the quality of the objectives of private and public sector ombudsman. The import of the defence of individual rights and democracy as a whole via the control of the administration carries weight unequalled in the private sector – where participation in any venture can be terminated in ways that participation in one's country cannot.[71]

To summarize: There exists a common groundwork for public and private sector ombudsman in that both share a double function. The latter takes on different specifications depending on the placement of the ombudsman within a

---

68   Carl (2012b), p. 212
69   See also Seneviratne (2000b), p. 19
70   Hopp (1993), p. 52; Matthes (1981), p. 17; according to Seneviratne (2002), p.8 the "search for defintions disguises the fact that there are 'significantly different interpretations of what exactly the Ombudsman's functions are' in the world community. The focus in the UK is on maladministration, whereas in some countries, the emphasis is on human rights". The double function, however, is basic to both.
71   Gadlin (2000), p. 44

specific sector. While private sector ombudsmen played a role in the discovery of this double function – which will become relevant in the further discussion – the focus of this study is on defining prison ombudsmen, which are public sector ombudsmen. Consequently, the further discussion only mentions private sector ombudsmen whenever necessary.

3. Features

The features[72] necessary for the successful work of an ombudsman derive from the double function and are (in approximate order of their importance):

- independence[73]
- impartiality[74]
- accessibility[75] (visibility, flexibility and informality)[76]
- accountability and transparency[77]
- confidentiality[78].

All these attributes must exist jointly for an ombudsinstitution to work effectively. Some concessions may be made concerning one or more of these features, but what may appear a simple gradation may eventually turn out to be a steep slope leading to a loss of faith in the ombudsman's capabilities.

The most important feature of all those listed by far is independence – three kinds of which may be distinguished: institutional, functional and personal independence.[79] Institutional independence means autonomy from the influence or control of the administrative branch the ombudsinstitution is charged to supervise. While full independence is impossible, this may be approximated by providing the strongest institutional basis possible that marks the ombudsman as an outside party in the eyes of any stakeholder. For public sector ombudsmen this recommends constitutional enactment.

Functional independence is achieved by ensuring the exemption of the ombudsman from all external pressures. While this can never be achieved in full, it

---

72 C.f. Buck et al. (2011a), p. 16, 51, 122 and Gregory/Giddings (2000), p. 5 which includes an extensive overview over the discussion of the essential features in the literature.
73 Oosting (1999), p. 1; Reif (2004), p. 399: Council of Europe (2005), p. 6
74 Council of Europe (2005), p. 6
75 Oosting (1999), p. 1; Reif (2004), pp. 404; Council of Europe (2005), p. 9
76 Council of Europe (2005), p. 9; Seneviratne (2000b), p. 23
77 Reif (2004), p. 407; Eklundh (2002), p. 14; Greggory/Giddings (2000), p. 6
78 Gottehrer/Hostina (2000), p. 410
79 c.f. Reif (2004), p. 399

14

may be attempted by implementing a strict policy of non-interference with the ombudsman's work as well as providing the greatest possible freedom in budgetary and personnel matters.[80]

The ombudsman is set apart from other institutions by the personal quality of the office which speaks to the outside world of the incumbent's approachability. This re-personalization is a key-factor of the ombudsman concept.[81] It heavily depends on the charisma of the office-holder. The background, knowledge, attitude, behaviour, and experience of the ombudsman constitute a certain personal authority, which manifests itself in the active and creative use of investigatory powers, a determination to uncover the truth and a willingness to adopt an open and frank attitude towards all those involved by listening to all sides of the argument.[82]

From the viewpoint of society, a decisive factor regarding the office-holder's personal authority is the impartiality of the ombudsman and any staff.[83] This personal authority is quite fragile and can be infringed or destroyed by both the introducing body and the office-holder. If the ombudsman's appointment is the result of marked politicization or a non-critical stance of the incumbent, impartiality and hence personal authority are difficult to achieve.[84]

In light of this, securing personal independence should be sought to achieve by providing the ombudsman with a fixed-term appointment only terminable for cause, a salary that reflects the ombudsman's high reputation as well as immunity from criminal and civil actions for any conduct undertaken in the proper exercise of official functions.[85]

---

80   c.f. Oosting, (1999), p. 8; Pearce (1992): "To have an Ombudsman makes a government look good. To underfund the office ensures that it is not too troublesome. After three years as Commonwealth Ombudsman I realised that no matter how strong a case for increased resources was put by the Ombudsman's office, nothing would be forthcoming from those who manage the Commonwealth's money. Why should the Executive finance a body that is going to call it to account as a result of complaints from members of the public affected by the Executive's decisions? Governments like to point to the fact that an independent person is available to review their decisions but they do not want that review body to be too powerful or too well known lest citizens be inclined to take frequent advantage of the office."

81   Hopp (1993), p. 63

82   Skinner (2006), p. 88

83   Oosting (1999), pp. 11-13

84   Oosting, (1999), p. 8

85   OSCE Human Dimension Seminar on Ombudsman and National Human Rights Protection Institutions, Consolidated Summary (Warsaw, May 25-28, 1998), p. 15, http://www.osce.org/odihr/44121 (last accessed June 6th, 2012). For a discussion of salary – c.f. Eklundh (2002), p. 15; Anderson (1978), p. 213. For a discussion of ap-

A well-secured independence of the ombudsinstitution is the foundation for its credibility. At the same time, the ombudsman does not exist in a void.[86] It would be naïve to deny the complex relations between ombudsman and surrounding institutions –all of which are influencing each other. The drawback of the ombudsman's independence may therefore be found in the absence of a political power base, which leaves the institution vulnerable to outside attacks.[87]

Another distinctive feature of the ombudsman is impartiality, which he shares with mediators – and which sets both apart from advocates.[88] The latter's distinctive feature is to defend one side against the other, while the ombudsman enters any investigation – be it triggered by either a complaint or an own-motion procedure – with a neutral mind only intent on discovering whether legality or practicality have been breached.

Accessibility, with its subspecies visibility, flexibility and informality, requires that the ombudsman may be approached without discrimination of the complainant, without major formalities and free of charge.[89] The latter is especially relevant for those who cannot afford courts and lawyers. In order to ensure visibility, the ombudsinstitution may decide to advertise its services via personal travel, the media, the internet etc. Flexibility means that the ombudsman should be left to decide which cases to investigate and which to reject as without merit. This is a necessary measure to ensure a speedy resolution of cases whilst avoiding an unnecessary increase in staffing and internal bureaucracy. The relative informality of the ombudsinstitution aims to increase approachability by lowering the threshold and may take many forms, e.g. accepting oral as well as written complaints.

The ombudsman's feature of accountability is shared with any and all public and private bodies to which resources are allocated. Where public sector institutions are concerned, there are three dominant perspectives on accountability identifiable in the literature, which imply three separate goals of accountability mechanisms[90]: The democratic perspective demands ombudsman accountability to effectively link government actions to the democratic chain of delegation, the constitutional perspective asks to prevent or uncover abuses of public authority and the learning perspective aims to make governments effective in delivering

---

pointment terms/tenure see Reif (2004), p. 400; Taugher (1972), p. 179; fixed-term appointments of two to seven years may now be considered a common standard, e.g. in the UK – c.f. Seneviratne (2008), p. 630.

86   Eklundh (2002), p. 13
87   Giddings (2000), p. 463
88   See section B I. 6. C) for an in-depth discussion of this point
89   Söderman (2004), p. 1; Council of Europe (2005), p. 9
90   Here and in the following: Kirkham et al. (2009), p. 614

on their promises. All three concepts of ombudsman accountability may be promoted simultaneously. What mode of expression the accountability of a particular ombudsinstitution takes depends on its legal basis. Accountability requirements may be met i.e. by providing special and annual reports or appearing in person in the media or before parliament.

Confidentiality as an ombudsman feature pertains to any information provided by either a complainant or a state agency.[91] This feature allows the ombudsman to lead *in camera* investigations in the three-sided relationship between ombudsman, complainant, and administration in the secure knowledge that if asked to do so the ombudsman may not disclose the information provided.[92] Any conflict with the accountability requirement may be resolved by eliminating all complainant-identifying information from the ombudsman's reports.[93]

4. Practice

The exact form of any ombudsman's practice depends on the institution's individual legal basis. Generally, ombudsmen are outfitted with the triad of investigation, recommendation and report.

At the beginning of any ombudsman's activity stands the investigation, which Gottehrer describes as

> [...] a jigsaw puzzle [...] except at the beginning, you don't know what the picture looks like, how many pieces exist, how they fit together and whether one or more pieces are missing. Your job is to figure it out. An investigation is like peeling away the layers of an onion and never knowing for sure whether you have peeled away the last layer.[94]

This process may be initiated either upon own-motion or by the reception of a stakeholder's complaint, where the stakeholder can either be the citizen in the case of general ombudsmen or a member of a specific group, e.g. a prisoner, for specialty ombudsmen.[95] The latter does not foreclose other available avenues of redress.[96] The investigation process is heavily influenced by the ombudsman's features. The reception of a complaint is shaped by the notion of informality and

---

91   Krent (2000), pp. 17f
92   Hyson (2006), p. 9
93   For further discussion of the confidentiality-feature see Gottehrer/Hostina (2000), p. 410
94   Baqwa (2000), p. 98
95   Not all ombudsmen are outfitted with the power of own-motion investigations. Especially in the UK, this has given rise to calls for the ombudsman system to be modified to include a „self-starting power", c.f. Giddings (2001), p. 1.
96   Abraham (2008), p. 5

depends on the ombudsman's accessibility. The own-motion investigation may be taken up at any point based on the ombudsman's flexibility. Any information the ombudsman obtains from the complainant or the administration is confidential. The process and outcome of the investigation depend on the ombudsman's independence.

As the ombudsman is personally in charge of establishing the factual basis of the case, the investigatory process takes on an inquisitorial fashion.[97] Some ombudsmen may resort to forms of ADR, such as mediation, shuttle-diplomacy etc. in their work.[98] The ombudsman himself, however, is neither an ADR measure nor a mediator.[99] The latter only facilitates the resolution of a conflict between the parties involved, whilst the ombudsman personally judges the situation at hand and presents a self-developed resolution in form of a recommendation.

Unlike a judge, who is limited by the statutory or legal context of an administrative action, an ombudsman may perform a non-legality review and look at substance and procedure of a decision.[100] The ombudsman may even criticize an administrative decision for unreasonableness.[101] Unlike a court's judgment that is only binding *inter partes*, an ombudsman's recommendation extends beyond the direct remedial power of placing a person in the position he or she would have occupied had a tort not occurred. The ombudsman may recommend that others in the same position be treated equally and that the legal or policy rules at the root of a problem be changed.[102] The latter is especially likely whenever a systemic investigation into patterns of recurring defectiveness of administrative action has been conducted.[103] Such a systemic investigation may be undertaken either based on a hunch and own-motion or be triggered based on the observation of similarity in in-coming complaints, which explains why the ombudsinstitution is sometimes compared to a watchdog.[104]

---

97   Seneviratne (2000b), p. 17; Abraham (2008), p. 4; Groves (2002), p. 196
98   Taylor (2000), p. 187; Abraham (2008), p. 4; but also note Skinner (2006), p. 98: "In Denmark and Sweden, the countries in which the ombudsman context was born, facilitating a settlement with a government body is not contemplated in the legislation and, as such, does not occur."
99   Abraham (2008), p. 3; Seneviratne (2000a), p. 590
100   Heede (2000), p. 90; Groves (2002), p. 187
101   Rowat (1985), p. 67
102   McLeod (2003), p. 64
103   For details on the advantages of systemic investigations, c.f. Buck et al. (2011a), pp. 133f; for an example of an empirical study on systemic investigations, c.f. Stuhmcke (2009)
104   Hill (1976), p. 13

Once the ombudsman discovers that the administration has acted unlawfully or unreasonably – be it on a single occasion or as a recurring pattern – the ombudsman applies the second tool, that of recommendation. In the case of the single occurrence the ombudsman will recommend a remedy, which could be anything from an apology to extensive *ex-gratia*-payment.[105] In the case of a recurring pattern, the ombudsman will recommend a change of policy to the legislature.

In most cases, the administration will comply with ombudsman recommendations.[106] Upon request, the ombudsman may even render assistance in developing new administrative practices.[107] This "gentle justice"[108] may well be the reason why the "close contact between Ombudsmen and agencies has not proven an irritant to agencies as 'familiarity, rather than breeding contempt, has bred co-operation'. The value of the office in providing a second look at decisions has been recognized as worthwhile".[109] Nevertheless, due to the non-binding nature of ombudsman recommendations, cases of non-compliance may occur.[110] This lack of enforcement powers has sometimes led to the institution being considered as "not powerful enough to warrant serious consideration".[111] Consequently, the alternative, namely to make an ombudsman's recommendation binding, has been much discussed.[112] Today, both academia and praxis believe the conjured threat of marginalization of the ombudsman to be a possible, but not a necessary consequence of the lack of enforcement power.[113] A compliance rate of 100% with the recommendations of the Parliamentary and Health Service Ombudsman proves that the inability to make binding decisions does not necessarily impair the ability to deliver substantive justice.[114]

Some voices caution that determinative powers could motivate the ombudsman to avoid lengthy investigations and tempt parties to assume adversarial tactics.[115] This would undermine the ombudsman's directive of discovering the source of a problem. In contrast, use of reasoned persuasion is believed to im-

---

105   Groves (2003), p. 136
106   For evidence of compliance, c.f. Buck et al. (2011b) p. 26
107   Groves (2002), p. 200
108   Chidiac (2004), p. 88
109   Groves (2002), p. 199
110   c.f., Buck et al. (2011a), p. 119; Hertogh (1998), p. 77; Abraham (2009), p. 29
111   Hill (1976), p. 14
112   Kirkham et al. (2008), pp. 518ff, 522, 530; Johnson (1988), p. 131f.; Smith(1998), p. 8
113   Kirkham (2008), pp. 254-6; Groves (2002), pp. 202, 205; Gottehrer/Hostina (2000), p. 410; Oosting (1999), p. 10
114   Abraham (2008), p. 2; Ebert (1968), p. 55; Owen (1993), p. 2; Gadlin (2000), p. 42
115   Groves (2002), p. 196

prove the fairness, factual grounding and quality of decisions, which will not only heighten their acceptability but also back-feed into the ombudsman's credibility.[116] It also allows the ombudsman to function as an end or break in the eternal chain of administrative control.[117] As such, the inability of the ombudsman to enforce recommendations might actually constitute strength rather than weakness.[118]

While the ombudsinstitution has no power to quash an administrative decision, it is empowered to publicize any criticism of the administration – either to its supervising organ, the media or both. [119] One of the great virtues of the ombudsman scheme lies in the fact that reason and persuasion are just as much in the ombudsman's arsenal as criticism and public embarrassment.[120] The publication format ranges from press releases to special and annual reports. The latter is usually of considerable length and contains a wealth of information on the office itself, its work and its constituents. It mainly serves two external purposes: that of providing information and rendering account.[121] Some internal significance may be attached to it for purposes of organization and reflection as well as the creation of an "institutional memory".[122] Special reports frequently are the result of own-motion or systemic investigation. Their length and depth varies depending on the severity and complexity of the examined problem. The special report is a tool employed whenever the ombudsman perceives the need to draw the attention of the legislature, public or media to a special problem. The publicity garnered by a special report can help to ensure proper consideration by the legislature and encourages the implementation of the ombudsman's recommendations.

5. Expectations

The expectations surrounding the work and achievements of ombudsinstitutions are as varied as the areas of application. There exists a list of expectations, both positive and negative, which apply to all public sector ombudsmen – thus warranting their description in this section.

---

116   Barbour (2002), p. 60; Sapers/Zinger (2010), p. 110
117   Ayeni (2000), p. 8
118   C.f. Kirkham (2008), p. 256
119   Rowat (1993), p. 127
120   Gadlin (2000), p. 42; Rowat (1985), p. 58
121   Jamieson (1997), p. 47; Hopp (1993), p. 56; Oosting (1998), p. 86
122   Oosting (1998), p. 90

a) positive

The positive expectations of the ombudsman's work may be divided into two separate domains: on the one hand, there is the expectation that an ombudsman will reduce costs and litigation while bringing systemic change. On the other hand, there is the expectation that the ombudsman will bolster the morale of civil servants and restore citizen's confidence in government and administration.[123] The former set of expectations focuses on external, easily measurable criteria; the latter set centres on internal – i.e. intra-personal amplified via intra-societal – change which is more difficult to quantify.

The expectation that the introduction of am ombudsinstitution will lead to cost reduction is based on the argument that courts themselves are too costly and only examine technicalities.[124] Avoidance of litigation therefore cuts court costs, frees resources within the administration formerly occupied with the handling of litigation thereby reducing the costs of administration, and forecloses the possibility of lost lawsuits, which reduces penalty fees. Obviously, the ombudsinstitution itself requires a budget as well. But here an objective case can be made to compare the associated costs and to then select and employ the cheaper method. Nevertheless, although this argument in favour of the introduction of an ombudsinstitution is frequently employed, no empirical data has been presented to prove the hypothesis.[125]

Another expectation tightly linked with cost and litigation reduction is that of systemic change.[126] By means of resolving individual complaints, an ombudsman office may not only be able to identify areas for increased operating efficiencies but may also discover patterns of recurring unfairness not readily noticeable to governmental and administrative agencies alike.[127] The expectation is that the ombudsman will then advise the agency on how to avoid injury in the future or even prompt an adjustment of laws and regulations. Owen points out that "[a] fundamental aspect of the systemic approach is a belief that public institutions, despite their size and complex responsibilities, are able and willing to respond to individuals in a fair way, on their own initiative".[128]

---

123 For the claim of cost reduction - c.f. Jacobs (2004), p. 301; for the claim to reduced litigation - c.f. Alarcón (2007), p. 594; concerning morale and confidence - c.f. Giddings (2000), p. 462; Gwyn (1968), p. 42

124 Kempf/Mille (1993), p. 197

125 Moore (1968b), p. 72; Brakel (1982), p. 131; Lesting (1993), p. 54; Owen (1993), p. 5; Kempf/Mille (1993), p. 197

126 Alarcón (2007), p. 594

127 Gwyn (1968), p. 41; Farrell-Donaldson (1999), p. 414

128 Owen (1993), p. 8

This demonstrates the strong interdependency of ombudsman and administration[129]: the belief held by the independent ombudsinstitution that public agencies are willing to respond fairly to the citizen is fundamental to restoring the citizen's confidence in administration. It creates a level of trust between citizen and state.[130] The same belief proves to the civil servants that the ombudsman will defend their decisions whenever correct, thereby bolstering their morale.[131] All this may be achieved in keeping with the general principle that it is the proper role of an ombudsman office to strive for the mutually acceptable resolution of a problem – rather than a finding of fault or proof of its absence.[132] Ascher underscores that the role of an external critic is to build for the future rather than to exhume the past.[133]

Although public ombudsmen are firmly located in the tradition of adversarial dispute resolution, any ombudsinstitution should attempt to provide informal mediation services wherever conducive to the solution of the case at hand.[134] Informal mediation frequently allows for a speedier resolution than a full investigation into the potential rights or wrongs while at the same time tending to result in greater satisfaction on all sides.[135] This form of dispute resolution coincides with the fact that the role of an ombudsman office is not designed to replace or oppose government decision-making. Rather, the office exists to assist the public service in becoming more aware of and responsive to the individual concerns of members of the public.[136] This may be called a soft approach or may let the ombudsman appear as a "toothless tiger" or "ombudsmouse", but, backed by the practice methods and qualities of the office-holder discussed above, it – may in fact result in a more smooth functioning of the public entity in its own right.[137]

The first legislative ombudsman for the City of Detroit, Marie Farrell-Donaldson sums up these positive expectations nicely when she reports:

> "There are many instances where the Detroit Ombudsman's Office has been instrumental in persuading a citizen not to take legal action against the city but, instead, allow the office to work with them to resolve their grievance against the government. [...] Not only has it saved the City money, but it has also resulted in an in-

---

129 C.f. Buck et al. (2011a), p. 122
130 Ebert (1968), p. 10
131 Hill (1976), p. 13
132 Owen (1993), p. 5
133 Ascher (1967), p. 176
134 Gadlin (2000), p. 42
135 Owen (1993), p. 5
136 Owen (1993), p. 8
137 Gregory/Giddings (2000b), p. 39

creased feeling of goodwill on the part of its citizens. Too many times, the only reason a citizen will file a lawsuit is when they feel no one is taking their claim seriously".[138]

b) negative

The negative expectations surrounding the introduction of an ombudsinstitution are just as pronounced as the positive ones. Here, a distinction can be made between the response to the above mentioned positive effects reminding that the Ombudsman is no panacea, versus the original negative expectations, which consist of a combination of administrative and political arguments.

The argument that the ombudsman is no panacea generally takes one of two forms. The first views the ombudsman only as a modern supplement to other existing controls of age-old democracies such as long-established institutions and guarantees: the ombudsman as one of several methods to gain redress for grievances.[139] The second argues *pro rata temporis* – that the ombudsman is not a once and for all solution, but requires just as much readjustment in terms of its fine-tuning as all other pre-and post-existent institutions in order to appropriately respond to the changing demands of the time. [140]

Although there are some minor additions, most of the original negative expectations are included in a list of six undesirable consequences compiled by Gwyn.[141] Hill denotes them as "supposedly" undesirable consequences, which hints at the ambiguous nature of some of these points.[142] The first undesirable consequence cited is that the ombudsman's presence increases civil servants' timidity in making decisions. This is indeed a negative consequence if it leads to unnecessary administrative delays. However, it has not been proven that this timidity goes beyond the general timidity inspired and checked by existing control mechanisms already present in any administrative hierarchy under the supervision of administrative courts (where those are absent, their function is usually assumed by MPs).[143] The second negative expectation in the list concerns the administrators' increased inclination to "cover" themselves by creating unnecessarily extensive records and "red tape" whenever an ombudsman is involved. Like the first point however, this expectation is not limited to the context of ombudsmen also usually takes effect as an administrative preventive

---

138 Farrell-Donaldson (1999), p. 413
139 Rowat (1985), p. 58; Oosting, (1999), p. 2; Busck (1995), p. 23; Patterson (1959-63), p. 781
140 Ebert (1968), p. 5
141 Gwyn (1968), p. 43
142 Hill (1976), p. 13
143 cf. Rowat (1985), p. 67

measure against any kind of control mechanisms. The third assumption, namely that ombudsmen tend to substitute their own judgments on complex policies for those of technical experts, although an unproven claim, is to be taken seriously as this clearly constitutes an over-stepping of institutional bounds. This may only be avoided by a clear-cut definition of the ombudsman's role, rights and duties and the selection of an office-holder willing to fulfil the role while facing its challenges. The fourth undesirable consequence, that the ombudsman's role as citizens' advocate promotes an adversary relationship with administrators who will create defences against him, is based on a mis-interpretation of the ombudsman's role as well as the independence of the office. This negative expectation can only become true in the case of a failing ombudsman-plan or an office misleadingly carrying the title. The fifth negative expectation states that because the ombudsman is not an administrator, any recommendations may be viewed as those of an idealistic and impractical outsider. This hypothesis is the most deserving of the title "supposedly undesirable" as the ombudsman is employed to provide exactly this fresh perspective.

The sixth argument is in so far different from the aforementioned points as it is focused on the political rather than the administrative aspects of the office: It holds that the ombudsman's existence may create a complacency which could distract policy makers from other needed reforms, a particularly concern wherever reforms of the administration and judiciary are concerned. The negative political expectation can be further extended and amplified by the argument that policy makers may themselves be aware of the need for reform but purposely conceal either the need thereof or their own inaction by implementing an ombudsman.[144] A similar scenario could be created in which the revelation of a severe case of maladministration or even the occurrence of an accident leads populace and media to take up a joint call for action. In both instances, the implementation of an ombudsman-scheme only serves as a public pacifier – easily disposable once the situation has calmed.[145] The ombudsman is introduced only as a pretence to improvement, to give the appearance of political intervention.[146] This is commonly referred to as symbol politics. The amount of mention this negative expectation finds in literature gives inkling as to the estimated threat this danger poses. However, neither the frequency with which this danger materializes has so far been studied nor has it been evaluated in how far this resem-

---

144   A fitting quote by the former Commonwealth Ombudsman, Dennis Pearce, may be found at supranote 79

145   Caiden (1983), p. xvii; others have called it a placebo – Burbridge (1974), p. 106; veil - Hopp (1993), pp. 4, 66, 68; cover-up Kirkham (2008), p. 254 or moral screen Jacoby (1999), p. 17

146   Reif (2004), p. 395; Kauß (1989), p. 22

bles the introductory scenario of other supervisory institutions such as committees, inspectors, inquiry boards and the like. Nevertheless, it seems convincing that whenever symbol politics is being practiced the situation is neither improved by the introduction of the ombudsman nor is the institution itself bound to find a supportive environment in which to succeed.[147] The negative expectation that the ombudsman may prove not to be effective may in some cases be valid. It is, however, no reason not to at least attempt the introduction.

The overview of the history, and features as well as the positive and negative expectations vis-à-vis the Ombudsman in general as detailed above provide the background framework for the process of categorization and definition that is to follow.

6. Categorization

The grounded theory research revealed the many different varieties of ombudsmen to coincide with a whole plethora of technical terms: public sector, private sector, traditional, classical, parliamentary, legislative, executive, specialty, single-subject, multiple-mandate, hybrid, organizational, corporate and advocate. Each conceptual adaptation of the ombudsman idea added further items to this list. Not all of these terms however truly describe different concepts of ombudsmen – some are even misnomers.

A process of thorough categorization is therefore unavoidable and involves the definition of all technical terms involved, the identification of synonyms and the elimination of any contradictory terms.[148] One approach to this effort would be to follow the historical order of the appearance of the technical terms. Another would be to sort them in pairs or groups. As the latter method allows for a more condensed and less convoluted discussion, by requiring less cross-referencing and cross-comparison with opposite and parallel models, this will be the approach taken here.

---

147 c.f. Oosting (1999), p. 8, who believes that, since media and citizens' campaigns for the implementation of policy "tend to be regarded as a nuisance", the ombudsman "can run the risk of marginalization within the spectrum of political and administrative concerns".

148 That this discussion will at the same time give an overview over the diversification and evolution of functions of ombudsmen is purely coincidental; c.f. Carl (2012b), pp. 206-10 and Gregory/Giddings (2000), pp. 8-15

a) Public and private sector

Until the ombudsman concept spread to the US, only public sector ombudsmen existed. When the US experienced its Ombudsmania, the result was the creation of ombudsmen not only within different parts of the public sector (such as the executive), but for the first time also within newspapers, universities and other institutions of the private sector. This gave rise to the need for a distinction between public and private sector ombudsmen.

Some authors hold that only public sector, legislative ombudsmen truly deserve their title and that the others "have been given the title of the Swedish institution only through (flagrant) misuse of language, to ease tensions and appease public opinion".[149] While the call for a restricted use of the term ombudsman has been echoed many times, the fact has to be acknowledged that the title has irreversibly spread to the private sector.[150] Even Rowat, a staunch defender of the ombudsman title, conceded in 2007 that the term was already too entrenched in areas outside the legislative scheme for there to be any use in trying to restrict it.[151] Nevertheless, the ombudsman schemes of some nations including New Zealand and Malta prohibit the use of the ombudsman title pending permission by their federal ombudsman.[152] In New Zealand, the unauthorized use of the Ombudsman title is even liable to a fine.[153]

The reason for the attempted restriction of the title was the honourable intention to avoid confusion as to an ombudsman's extent of powers and independence within their respective usership. In the public sector this refers to citizens or specific subgroups such as prisoners while in the private sector it means consumers, customers and their specific subgroups such as readers etc. The varying extent of power and independence is the biggest difference between public and private sector ombudsmen. While most public sector ombudsmen are external complaint-handling mechanisms with extensive powers of investigation and recommendation as well as considerable independence, private sector ombudsmen are dispute resolution mechanisms where powers and independence may be lacking from both a legal and/or factual viewpoint.[154] This, however, is a very strong generalization to which exceptions clearly exist. Some public sector executive and specialty ombudsmen raise much doubt as to the extent of their powers and independence while some private sector industry ombudsmen have

---

149   Hadi (1977), p. 334
150   Frank (1975), p. 55; Owen (1993), p. 2; Hyson (2006), p. 8
151   Rowat (1985), p. 182 and (2007), pp. 48f
152   Giddings (2000), p. 467; Reif (2004), p. 53
153   See provision 28 A of the Ombudsman Act 1975
154   Reif (2004), p. 53; this is emphasized by Seneviratne (2000a), p. 590

relatively strong powers and independence.[155] All ombudsinstitutions should strive to come as close to the ideal of the classical ombudsman as possible.[156]

Overall, both public and private sector ombudsmen as well as the subgroups thereof are well-established. The public sector ombudsmen encompass traditional classical, parliamentary, legislative, executive, multiple-mandate, hybrid, specialty and single sector ombudsmen. The private sector ombudsmen include the so-called corporate, organizational and advocate ombudsmen. A pristine specimen of the public sector is the Danish *Folketingets Ombudsmand*; while a good representative in the private sector is the British Financial Ombudsman Service.

b) Traditional, classical, parliamentary, legislative, executive

These five terms date back to the beginning of the spread of the ombudsman idea. In this context, "classical" does not refer to the first office ever to be called ombudsman.[157] Instead it alludes to the ombudsman model which became "classical" in the 20th century in Europe: a parliamentary ombudsman with only "soft powers" investigation, recommendation, reporting that conforms to the Danish Model.[158] "Classical" ombudsmen are distinguished by their statutory independence from governmental control, their power of investigation and their authority to publish findings, whilst only being empowered to issue recommendations and not to quash expert administrative decisions.[159] They are firmly located within the tradition of adversarial dispute resolution with their only ADR-resembling element being the fact that they cannot enforce the implementation of their recommendations.[160]

"Classical" ombudsmen exist at all levels of government: local, regional, national, international and supranational. Examples for international ombudsinstitutions may be found with the United Nations, the World Bank, the International Monetary Fund and the World Health organization. An example for a supranational "classical" ombudsman is the European Ombudsman, who is "very much in the mainstream of classical 'governmental Ombudsmen with general jurisdiction over administrative conduct'".[161]

155　Discussed in greater depth in sections B I. 2. and 3. respectively
156　Seneviratne (1994), p. 6
157　The Swedish "högste ombudsmannen". For an explanation of the Swedish and the Danish Ombudsman Model c.f. above at B I. 1.
158　Oosting (1999), p. 2; Kucsko-Stadlmayer (2008), p. 63
159　Rowat (1993), p. 127f; Gadlin (2000), p. 38
160　Gadlin (2000), p. 42
161　Gregory/Giddings (2000), p. 9

Yet, not all "parliamentary" ombudsmen are "classical" ones – particularly those, who do not only have soft, but "strong powers". An example would be the *Pučki pravobranitelj*, the Croatian Defender of People's Rights: a national, parliamentary ombudsman entitled to challenge the constitutionality of laws and the constitutionality and legality of regulations at the Constitutional Court to protect the constitutional and legal rights of citizens.[162] Still, all "parliamentary" ombudsmen are "legislative" ombudsmen – at least as long as one considers ombudsmen instituted by local and regional governments to be "parliamentary" in a wider sense as well. The terms are therefore nearly synonyms.

"Traditional" refers to the Scandinavian ombudsman idea, instituted with the Swedish office and exported in its Danish form. "Traditional" and "classical" are therefore mostly synonymous. Since "legislative" is the most inclusive of the above-named terms it will be the term used in the further discussion.

The following figure[163] was designed to ease the understanding of this section further:

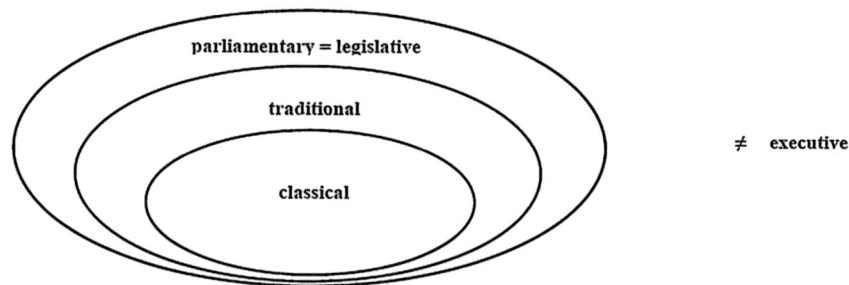

Figure 2: Different kinds of ombudsmen

The executive ombudsman is – beside the private-sector ombudsman – the most influential American mutation of the ombudsman concept. Wyner defines the executive ombudsman as "a centralized complaint-handling officer, who has been appointed to office and who serves at the pleasure of an elected or appointed chief executive".[164]

These two facts are the pivotal points for any criticism on the executive variation of the ombudsman concept. Firstly, although on the first glance it may seem convenient that the non-legislative establishment allows for a speedy crea-

---

162   Kucsko-Stadlmayer (2008), p. 136; for other examples of „strong powers" see p. 63
163   Carl (2012b), p. 208
164   Wyner (1975), p. 10

tion of the office – since the whole process of legislation may be cut – it also affords an equally fast abolishment should the ombudsman prove inconvenient. Secondly, whenever the people who appoint the ombudsman are the same people who run the administration, the ombudsman ceases to be independent. This decreases both the effectiveness and legitimacy of the ombudsman work and may in the worst case lead to a phasing out of the institution.[165] Reigrotzki describes this time of defunct existence and slow abolition stating that a crippled ombudsman robbed of his powers is worse than none.[166]

Throughout the history of executive ombudsmen, this politically and personally dependent position has repeatedly led to the refusal of the ombudsman title.[167] Rowat in particular has stressed the extension of the term to the executive variant as a downgrading of the ombudsman concept.[168] Whether this is actually true warrants some discussion.

As executive ombudsmen differ from legislative ombudsmen only where their legal basis and not where their practice procedures are concerned, the entire argument hinges on the question whether legislative ombudsmen are in fact more independent than executive ombudsmen. This, however, has repeatedly been called into question. Most recently, Buck et al. underscored the delicacy of the balancing act required from any parliament attempting to fulfil its combined roles of guaranteeing the ombudsman's independence and, at the same time, scrutinizing and supporting both the ombudsman and the administration.[169] The tension inherent to "officer of Parliament schemes weakens the argument that the legislature is the best vehicle through which to secure the ombudsman's independence" as – comparable to one of the objections raised against executive ombudsmen – it demonstrates that it "requires careful management" due to potential instability.

This argument attacks the fundament of the acclaimed greater legislative independence. Other approaches emphasize that executive ombudsmen may at least achieve *de facto* independence and that to the extent that they are indeed dependent, this dependence must not necessarily be a weakness.[170] Strong sup-

---

165 Burbridge (1974), p. 104; Thacker (2009), p. 70

166 Reigrotzki (1968), p. 7

167 Rowat (1985), p. 182; Seneviratne (1994), pp. 13f ; Gottehrer et al. (2000), p. 357; Abedin (2011), p. 10

168 Rowat (1985), p. 182 and (2007), pp. 48f . For early critique of Rowat's stance see Adamoleku (1984), p. 227

169 Here and in the following: Buck et al. (2011a), p. 158

170 For the mistake restricting the independence of legislative ombudsmen – c.f. Reigrotzki (1966), p. 39; for the de facto independence of executive ombudsmen – c.f. Reif (2004), p. 401

port by the chief executive, e.g. the mayor or governor, outfits the executive ombudsman with an additional power that creates the threat of repercussions for the failure to implement recommendations.[171] Kimweri called this phenomenon the "hidden club behind the door".[172] Whilst this club may also be wielded by legislative ombudsmen with strong parliamentary support[173], it will never create faster impact than when brandished by one (or maybe two) men – in this case the ombudsman and the chief executive.

Even those strongly emphasizing independence as a minimum characteristic of ombudsmen agree that "extraordinary Ombudsmen can and have overcome weak legislation".[174] Then why should they not be able to overcome their weak administrative modes of establishment? An explanation for Rowat's historic repudiative stance may be found with Mamadouh et al., who highlight that "[…] institutional transplantations are often perceived as failed attempts to reproduce the original model, even if they were a significant step in the right direction in the search of better and more efficient institutional system".[175]

The combined force of these arguments leads this researcher to accept executive ombudsmen as a legitimate variation of the ombudsman concept. In light of the double function of public sector ombudsmen this appears to be the most consistent decision. Like legislative ombudsmen, executive ombudsmen assist in the protection of individual rights as well as the defence of democracy as a whole via the supervision of the executive. In their own ways, both legislative and executive ombudsmen contribute to the improvement in the quality of administration.[176] While legislative ombudsmen stimulate fair procedures, executive ombudsmen contribute with the stimulation of faster and better services.[177] Examples for executive ombudsmen are the British Waterways Ombudsman and the Tanzanian Permanent Commission for Enquiry.

---

171 In agreement Thacker (2009), p. 69

172 Kimweri (1993), p. 44

173 on which legislative ombudsmen are dependent – c.f. Abedin (2011), p. 5. The extent of this dependency becomes apparent when both a former Minister of Justice and a current ombudsman jointly consider a statutory footing a mere shift of the dependence from the administration to the parliament – c. p. 11 of the interview conducted on February 7th, 2012 with the former Minister of Justice, Roswitha Müller-Piepenkötter and p. 33 of the interview conducted on April 25th, 2012 with the Justizvollzugsbeauftragter des Landes Nordrhein-Westfalen, Prof. Michael Walter. Buck et al. (2011a), p. 158 go so far as to consider the expectation of parliamentary neutrality naïve.

174 Gottehrer (2009), p. 5

175 Mamadouh et al. (2002), p. 5

176 Ultimately in agreement: Buck et al. (2011a), p.161

177 De Asper y Valdés (1999), p. 232

c) Organizational, corporate, advocate

The Ombudsman Association created the term organizational ombudsman and uses it to define all non-legislative ombudsmen.[178] Rowat argues that this is a meaningless distinction as legislative ombudsmen are just as much part of an organization and thus "organizational".[179] In addition, Gadlin's definition of organizational ombudsmen as private sector ombudsmen who "address the complaints, conflicts and concerns of people who are voluntary participants in the organizations they are part of" is redundant since the private sector with organizations such as universities, newspapers and corporations knows only voluntary participants.[180] Hence Gadlin states that all private sector ombudsmen are organizational ombudsmen and all organizational ombudsmen private sector ombudsmen: a tautology. This confirms Rowat's judgment that the term is indeed inane.

The corporate ombudsman's duty is to settle disputes within a business corporation. The complainants are either exclusively internal (employees) or, if they happen to be external (customers), they are not part of a system of subordination dependent on the company and thus may take their business elsewhere. The corporate ombudsman serves pending the goodwill of the company's management and, as a company subset, is part of the private sector. The use of the popular ombudsman term only adds to the "packaging" in order to be more readily accepted by the public.[181] This has no influence on the corporate ombudsman's main objectives, which are peace within the company and the latter's favourable public image. A more accurate title emphasizing the position's internal role might be mediator or works council; the external role would be better met by the titles liaison officer or customer service desk. Nevertheless, the corporate ombudsman constitutes a valid subspecies of the private sector ombudsman.

The term advocate ombudsman is an oxymoron. Even according to the broad ombudsman definition of the American Bar Association (ABA), an ombudsman has to be impartial.[182] Yet, an advocate is a person who pleads a case on someone else's behalf and is thus clearly partisan. Consequently, a per-

---

178   http://web.mit.edu/negotiation/toa/TOAintro.html (last accessed June 6th, 2012)

179   Rowat (2007), p. 46

180   Gadlin (2000), p. 44

181   Hyson (2009b), p. 6

182   "An ombuds is a person who is authorized to receive complaints or questions confidentially about alleged acts, omissions, improprieties, and broader, systemic problems within the ombuds's defined jurisdiction and to address, investigate, or otherwise examine these issues independently and impartially." American Bar Association (2001), p. 3

son/office can only be either ombudsman or advocate.[183] The ombudsman also is no champion of minority groups seeking to change public policy, but is instead in an equidistant position between citizen and government – equally concerned with the protection of both parties' rights.[184] The Norwegian Commissioner for Children, who in a survey conducted by De Asper y Valdés stated the non-neutral conduct of investigations by calling itself primarily a client's advocate, is correctly not carrying the title of ombudsman.[185]

d) General, specialty, single subject

Like public and private sector ombudsmen or legislative and executive ombudsmen, the terms discussed in this section are opposites. Unlike these terms however, general and specialty ombudsmen do not constitute categories of their own. Instead, they are better described as subgroups. General and specialty ombudsmen exist in both the public sector (prison, health service, military) and the private sector (newspaper, university, company). They can be either legislative or executive ombudsmen.

It is important to note that a specialty ombudsman is not a deputy appointed by the general ombudsman inside the general ombudsinstitution for a specific subject (as it is the case for the *Defensor del Menor* who is appointed by the Spanish *Defensor del Pueblo* for complaints from or about minors).[186] The specialty ombudsinstitution is established as a self-contained legal entity with a separate legal basis laying out its powers.

There has been much discussion in the past about the advantages and disadvantages of an appointing general as compared to specialist ombudsmen.[187] The points in favour of the general ombudsman are in short that it is easier for citizen to address all their complaints to a single institution and that the general ombudsman is better in handling complaints that involve more than one agency. Moreover, although the Council of Europe acknowledged in 2005 that there is no objection in principle against the practice of appointing ombudsmen for specific fields or groups, it cautioned that although specialty ombudsmen can be a useful addition to general ombudsmen, excessive proliferation might interfere with the functioning of a general system for the protection of human rights.[188]

---

183   A fact that seems to have been overlooked by the American Bar Association (2001), p. 2.; in agreement with the author: Tibbles (1971), p. 245
184   Moore (1968a), p. 245
185   De Asper y Valdés (1999), p. 250
186   See also Reif (2004), p. 35
187   Shaw (2004), p. 124; Reif (2004), p. 35
188   Council of Europe (2005), p. 11

However, depending on the size of the public sector any general public sector ombudsman risks becoming an unwieldy bureaucracy.

On the other hand, both the subject-specific expertise of specialty ombudsman incumbents and the opportunity for a government to demonstrate its commitment to guarantee the protection of distinct groups (such as minors, prisoners, handicapped etc.) speak in favour of introducing this ombudsman variety. The perception of the members of the targeted group can be a relevant factor in this consideration. This point is elucidated by the head of a Swedish inmate council who considers the Swedish general ombudsman a valuable, but somewhat remote, ally, who is "not nearly as strong as we would wish".[189] This perception could be different for a specialty ombudsman for Swedish prisons. In praxis, the trend today appears to have shifted from the "establishment of specialty offices with a well-defined and vulnerable constituency"[190] towards the "integration of public sector schemes"[191]. Exemplary for this stands the British effort to unify the public sector ombudsmen in England and Wales into a "one-stop shop".[192]

According to general linguistic usage, any single subject ombudsman, also known as single sector or single purpose ombudsman is a specialty ombudsman. The latter term extends to a two- and possibly even to a three- or four-subjects ombudsman depending on the relative size of the subjects. Examples of a single-sector and a two-sector specialty ombudsman are the Ombudsman for the Canadian Royal Mounted Police and the Prisons and Probation Ombudsman for England and Wales.

e) Multiple-mandate, hybrid

Further developments in the ombudsman diversification process are so called hybrid and multiple -mandate ombudsinstitutions.[193] The latter first became popular when Portugal established its Provedor de Justiça in 1975. The term "multiple-mandate" describes ombudsinstitutions usually at a national level of government having a special mandate for the protection of human rights for ex-

---

189   See Raphael (1975), p. 57
190   Gottehrer et al. (2000), p. 359
191   Giddings (2001), p. 1; Kirkham (2010), p. 326
192   Buck et al. (2011b), p.27
193   For a critique of this development, see Reif (2004), p. 395

ample, or the surveillance of the democratization process.[194] These institutions essentially represent a general ombudsman with a specified additional mandate.

The "hybrid" ombudsman constitutes an extension of the multiple-mandate concept to the private sector. In scientific literature, the term is generally used to refer to either an ombudsman with an additional focus on human rights or anti-corruption[195], or a hybrid public-private sector ombudsman, which would be an ombudsman for an entire industry/service sector created by legislation[196]. An example for this variant is the British Pensions ombudsman, who by statute is imposed on the pensions industry of both the public and private sectors.[197]

7. Definition

The categorization process established the terms public and private sector, legislative (which encompasses the terms classical, traditional and parliamentary), executive, corporate, general, specialty (including single-subject), multiple-mandate and hybrid ombudsman as valid variations on the ombudsman concept. These terms will be used to judge the inclusivity of the available definitions.

Their compatibility with the purpose of this study depends on their being suitable definitions of prison ombudsmen. As the latter are firmly set within the public sector, the most precise definition possible is one that expresses the modern understanding of a public sector ombudsman. The core of this modern understanding is the double function of protecting citizens' rights and defending democracy by exercising control over the executive.

A short explanation of the socio-historical reason for the lack of a universally accepted definition will precede the discussion of a sample of available definitions. Due to their unsuitability for defining prison ombudsmen, a new definition will be created.

a) Existing definitions

The publications of such big organizations as the International Bar Association (IBA), the International Ombudsman Institute and the International Ombudsman Association afford a multitude of ombudsman definitions. This diversity, however, is not due to continuing refinement of the term, but rather expression of the

---

194 Note that even before the invention of the human-rights ombudsman the scope of examination of classical ombudsmen already extended to human-rights, c.f. Kucsko-Stadlmayer (2008), p. 60.
195 Reif (2004), p. 7
196 Reif (2004), p. 43; highly in favour of this concept Cameron (2001), pp. 549
197 See Seneviratne (2000b), p. 15

existence of "two opposing camps", whose views have evolved over the course of the last 60 years: on the one hand, those in favour of the political ombudsman concept and on the other hand, those in favour of a broad application of the ombudsman term. [198] The former group is older and has slowly evolved from being defenders of the classical ombudsman only to include all those in favour of a public sector ombudsman idea – with some potential disagreement left where executive ombudsmen are concerned. The second view is represented by the private sector ombudsmen, who since their creation fought for recognition as part of the ombudsman family. The intercourse between the two groups is historically tense at best. Stieber puts it this way: "there is a certain distance, sometimes verging on disdain, […] which is often verbally reflected by some version of you-are-not-a-real-ombudsman".[199] This schism is the reason why no single definition has ever met with universal acceptance or even acknowledgment.

The resulting multitude of definitions makes any attempt to fully reproduce the grounded theory-led examination of available definitions illusory.[200] Instead, two definitions have been selected based on their representativeness. The intent is to give an introduction to the most frequently used, and therefore most influential definitions.

The definition most commonly cited throughout the international development of the concept stems from the IBA.[201] Here, the ombudsman is defined as

> "an office provided by the constitution or by action of the legislature or Parliament and headed by an independent high level public official who is responsible to the legislature or parliament, who receives complaints from aggrieved persons against government agencies, officials and employees or who acts on his own motion, and has power to investigate, recommend corrective actions and issue reports".[202]

The wording of the definition itself suggests the attribution to the group defending the public sector ombudsman. The definition was drawn up at the time when the Swedish ombudsman idea clothed in its Danish form was beginning to spread around the world.[203] Consequently, it fails to encompass all the subsequent transformations of the idea (such as private sector ombudsmen). It also

---

198   Gadlin (2000), p. 38
199   Stieber, p. 52-53; see also LeBaron (2008), p. 15. Over the course of history both sides have incorporated minority-opinions such as the view that only classical ombudsmen deserve the title, see Rowat (1985), p. 182.
200   Definitions are available from: Anderson (1975a); Ayeni (2001); Gellhorn (1966a); Hansen (1972); Hill (1976); Reif (2004); Thacker (2009). For a recent discussion of some of them – c.f. Carl (2012b), p. 205f, 210ff
201   Kucsko-Stadlmayer (2008), p. 5
202   Allen (1974), p. 1078
203   Kucsko-Stadlmayer (2008), p. 2

excludes executive ombudsman, which at that time were already springing up across all parts of the US and were felt to be a weaker version of the legislative ombudsman. Their exclusion is more readily understood if one takes into account the fact that the authors of the IBA definition never endeavoured to draft a scientific definition but rather intended their definition as a recommendation for international politics – consequently aiming for the ideal of legislative ombudsmen.[204]

The definition most frequently cited by those in favour of the inclusion of private sector ombudsmen was published in 2001 by the ABA:

> "An ombuds is a person who is authorized to receive complaints or questions confidentially about alleged acts, omissions, improprieties, and broader, systemic problems within the ombuds's defined jurisdiction and to address, investigate, or otherwise examine these issues independently and impartially".[205]

This definition is obviously much broader than the IBA's definition, which is partially due to its authors' historic knowledge of the extension of the ombudsman concept. Indeed, it was rather the intent of the ABA to create a definition that includes all ombudsmen. The disadvantage of this inclusivity is diminished accuracy. In fact, the ABA's definition has been described as "vague and virtually meaningless".[206] The definition is indeed so broad that it not only includes misnomers such as advocate ombudsmen, but also bestows the title of ombudsman on any mother settling her children's disputes.[207] What the ABA definition does define is better called a mediator or arbitrator, both of which already exist in the public and private sector.

Consequently, the breadth of the ABA definition and the narrowness of the IBA definition make both unsuitable for the purpose of defining prison ombudsmen via the expression of the modern understanding of a public sector ombudsman represented in the double function.

b) New definition

Since no definition expressing the modern understanding of a public sector ombudsman represented in the double function exists, a definition suitable to the focus of this study had to be designed. The definition on which to base this study should include the criteria: the ombudsman's double function, its legal basis and its practice.

---

204   Allen (1974), p. 1078
205   American Bar Association (2001), p. 3
206   Rowat (2007), p. 47
207   Carl (2012b), p. 210

A definition encompassing all these aspects would be a conglomerate of previous attempts and might read:

A public sector ombudsman is an institution, which for the purpose of the protection of *individual rights* and the defence of the fundamental rights of *democracy* such as civil and human rights via the supervision of the executive, is authorized by a parliament, a ministry or a subdivision thereof (*legal foundation*) to independent investigation either upon own initiative or upon receiving complaints from citizens of an alleged part of the administration's acts, omissions, improprieties, and broader, systemic problems and whose only *tools*, due to not being invested with any executive power, are personal authority, recommendations, annual and special reports, and the media.

This definition encompasses all public sector ombudsmen be they legislative or executive, specialty (single-subject) or general, with or without any multiple mandate or hybrid function.

A taxonomy illustrating the results of this section's discussion is shown in Figure 3.[208]

Figure 3:

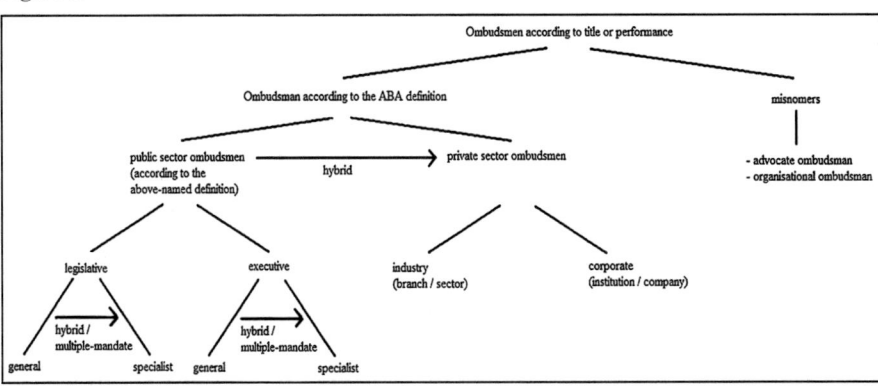

Taxonomy of ombudsmen

II. Prison Ombudsmen

There are two kinds of ombudsmen operating within prisons: general and specialty ombudsmen. The remit of general ombudsmen frequently extends to pris-

---

208   This taxonomy has been developed in Carl (2012b), p. 215ff – c.f. for a comparison with previous attempts at visualizing categorization.

on administration, which may result in overlapping jurisdictions.[209] General ombudsmen may be useful to prisoners but usually receive few complaints from prisoners, which may be due to such diverse things as accessibility (MP-filters, literacy problems of the prisoners), publicity and trust in the ombudsman's capabilities.[210] Raphael quotes an inmate council describing them as "not nearly as strong as we would wish".[211] However, generally the term "prison ombudsmen" refers to specialty ombudsmen. Specialty ombudsmen may take an infinite amount of different forms. The first to exist was the Military Ombudsman established in Sweden in 1915. At the height of Ombudsmania, the U.S. contributed heavily to this category, introducing ombudsmen to such different fields as newspapers, universities and prisons.[212]

As established in section B I. 6. d), specialty ombudsmen may exist in both the public and private sector. They operate as self-contained legal entities established by means of a separate legal basis laying out their individual powers. Depending on their mode of establishment, public sector specialty ombudsman have to be categorized either as legislative or executive ombudsmen. Their legal basis can be anything from an administrative act to a constitutional embedding causing them to sport a great bandwidth of both stability and independence. All kinds of possible legal bases may be found when it comes to prison ombudsmen, which especially in the North America are sometimes referred to as corrections or jail ombudsmen.

The purpose of this section is to operationalize the term "prison ombudsman" by means of a thorough analysis of these specialty prison ombudsmen. This will then serve as the groundwork for a grounded theory-driven examination of the question whether there is any need or demand for this institution within the prison sector – not only despite the existence of courts but also in light of the availability of other complaint channels. In a next step, the preconditions necessary for the well-functioning of this institution will be studied. This includes an examination of the legal basis, the available methods and tools and the challenges and expectations the institution faces. Finally, this section will be rounded off with an overview of the prison ombudsmen in existence today.

---

209 See Seneviratne (2010), p. 13
210 See Anderson (1978 and 1981b); Fliflet (2009); Senviratne (2010);
211 Raphael (1975), p. 57
212 Anderson (1981), p. 264

1. Demand

The question whether there is demand for a Prison Ombudsman can only be answered after recalling the justifications for and purpose of punishment, as well as the aims of the criminal justice system. These are not the same as the aims of sentencing, which constitutes only one part of the criminal justice system.[213] The rationales for punishment tend to be rather universal and their discussion and development takes place in an international context. In England, they are summarized in the following list: deterrence, rehabilitation, incapacitation, desert, social theories, and reparation or restoration.[214] Combining these terms in his *Vereinigungstheorie* (unification theory), the German Roxin agrees that the purpose of punishment is not one single objective. Instead, a) the threat of punishment inherent in the criminal law is justified by its general-preventive effect (positive: ensuring the population's trust in the legal order; negative: deterring them from committing crimes); b) sentencing to punishment is justified by its retributional effect and c) the enforcement of sentences is justified by its special-preventive effect (positive: rehabilitation and re-socialization of the offender; negative: protection of the population from the offender).[215] This unification theory is codified in § 46f of the German penal code, the *Strafgesetzbuch*. § 2 I of the German prison act called *Strafvollzugsgesetz* (StVollzG) explicitly names rehabilitation and re-socialization as the goals of all penal activity. Number three of the UK Prison Rules states the purpose of the training and treatment of convicted prisoners to be to encourage and assist them to lead a good and useful life[216]. Similar legal explications may be found across the globe.

Rehabilitation and re-socialization need an environment conducive to the betterment of the individual offender.[217] This requires a setting where the prisoner may learn or re-learn his or her functional role in society and discover his or her status as a legal person (*Rechtssubjekt*). Beneficial to this learning process is an environment respectful of human rights. Their observation is not only required by international and domestic law but conveys the strong message that everyone, regardless of their circumstance, race, social status, gender or religion

---

213 Ashworth (2010), p. 71
214 c.f. Ashworth (2010), p. 78ff
215 Roxin's unification theory (1966), pp. 378, 383 and (1997), p. 54f (§3 Rn. 36ff) is a so called preventive unification theory (p. 57) that excludes any form of vengeance or retribution. Although this theory is wide-spread in academia, the judicature still adheres to the so called retributional unification theory, c.f. Krey (2001), p. 50.
216 See the Prison Rules or for details Loucks (2000), p. 22
217 Wagner (1976), p. 243 considers legal protection t be conducive to resocialization and warns that this may only work if this legal protection is not merely theoretical but can be experienced.

is to be treated with respect and dignity.[218] Hoffmann agrees stipulating that the prisoner

> "shall not be degraded by the treatment to the level of a mere object, but instead shall achieve reintegration as a legal person. This touches upon the tension between the correctional aim and human dignity. It shall be demonstrated that the human dignity on the one hand creates an obligation for treatment, while the treatment concept may on the other hand signify specific limitations to the prisoner's freedom (curtailment of fundamental rights)".[219]

Observing human rights standards does not guarantee releasing a more responsible citizen, but at least it increase the odds thereof. Art. 6 and 7 I of the Human Rights Standards state that "[e]veryone has the right to recognition everywhere as a person before the law. All are equal before the law and are entitled without any discrimination to equal protection of the law".[220] This holds equally true for prisoners as imprisonment curtails no rights beyond the necessary (restriction of freedom of movement, assembly etc.).[221]

In his report on the 1990 English prison disturbances, Woolf concludes not only that explanations for grievances are necessary, but also that an independent grievance procedure should be available as an *ultima ratio*.[222] Giving prisoners the opportunity to complain is one expression of recognizing prisoners as persons before the law. Orderly complaining is part of the everyday culture and serves such functions as the attainment of explanations or revisions of decisions. It is necessary to rehearse these mannerisms because of the prisoner's isolation from society.[223] In total institutions like prisons, complaining also serves as a safety-valve allowing for the release of pent-up frustration and as such may avert more severe reactions such as prison revolts or riots.[224]

Besides an orderly complaint process, human rights also necessitate the existence of an institution providing systemic control of the prison service charged

---

218 Here and in the following: Sapers/Zinger (2010), pp. 104; Lazarus (2004), p. 3: "while punishment limits human rights, the extent of limitation should depend on the purpose of imprisonment, which in turn should link to background theory for the justification of punishment."
219 Hoffmann (2003), p. 207 – own translation
220 Also of interest may be Art. 25 I „Everyone has the right to a standard of living adequate for the health and well-being of himself and of his family, including food, clothing, housing and medical care and necessary social services, and the right to security in the event of unemployment, sickness, disability, widowhood, old age or other lack of livelihood in circumstances beyond his control."
221 Eady (2007), 266; Woolf/Tumim (1991), p. 411
222 Woolf/Tumim (1991), p. 26; in agreement: Neudek (1991), p. 709
223 Heskamp (2007-2008), p. 522
224 Woolf/Tumim (1991), p. 17; Goffman (1961)

with ensuring that in the best case no human rights violations occur and in the worst case they are investigated independently. This role corresponds with the double-function of ombudsmen pertaining to the supervision of the executive. A prison ombudsman could therefore independently perform the task of a human rights guarantee in prisons.

However, there are already many authorities both external and internal to the prison service, which are responsible for prisoners' complaints. The demand for a prison ombudsman can only be confirmed if the existing institutions were found to be insufficient. Woolf defined a set of criteria which acceptable grievance channels must meet to prove of merit:

- be straightforward. The prisoner must be able to understand and operate it;
- be expeditious. In many situations, unless this is the position, the remedy which it provides may come too late. There must therefore be appropriatetime limits;
- be effective. It must be capable of providing the remedy which is needed;
- be independent. And it must be seen to be so.[225]

a) Internal grievance channels

Internal grievance channels available to prisoners are the prison administration itself, prison boards and inmate councils.

aa) Administration

The prisoners may complain to those in the chain of command above the warden, such as the superintendent, the governor of the prison, the head of the department of corrections and the minister in charge of corrections.[226] That latter usually is either the Minister of Justice or the Home Secretary. The advantage of complaining to those in the administration who actually work within prison is their in-depth knowledge of the day-to-day occurrences of prison life. They also have a higher potential for easy accessibility and fast action. Whether these theoretical advantages also exist in reality depends heavily on those involved.

Either way, those within the administration will always be identified with the establishment and seen as biased.[227] This is easily verified when one consid-

---

225 Woolf/Tumim (1991), p. 414
226 Anderson (1983), p. 138; c.f. Douglas (1984), pp. 156; Fitzharris (1973), p. 33: "an important prisoner complaint concerns this practice of referring the prisoner's letter back down the chain of command. Often this means that the investigation is conducted, the response prepared, or, at the very least, the answer interpreted, by the very person against whom the complaint is lodged (emphasis in the original)."
227 Johnson (1988), p. 125

ers that the first duty of the called-upon officers is of course to their superiors.[228] The effectiveness of the Governor and the state legislators is also critically impaired by the fact that they have to rely on the agencies complained about as their source of information, and have a tendency to protect their administrators.[229]

Besides these problems there are also three internal factors that deter prisoners from using internal complaint channels. First, inmates may wish to avoid being labelled a troublemaker[230], which may have consequences for their parole.[231] Second, they may realize that he or she will have to intimately co-exist with both the officer taking the complaint and the officer complained against for the rest of the prison term. Third, inmates may fear being ostracized from inmate social groups because of peer-pressure not to fraternize with the prison guards and administration. All of this leads Jacobs to conclude that "[t]he impartiality of an outside agency is needed to collect and investigate inmate grievances".[232]

bb) Prison boards

Prison boards exist in many countries and have a tradition that predates WWII.[233] These boards are independent of the administration. The members are citizen volunteers charged with two objectives – one external to the prison, one internal. The first relates to the public and pertains to increasing both citizen involvement in the penal system as well public interest in and knowledge about prisons.[234] The second, internal objective is the control function and demands that the board members satisfy themselves as to the state of the prison premises, the administration of the prison and the treatment of the prisoners.[235] This purpose is fulfilled via the conduct of regular and irregular visits and/or inspections of the premises.

Although the objectives of all prison boards are alike, their names as well as their organizational link-ups differ greatly. In Germany they are called *Anstaltsbeiräte* and according to §163 StVollzG assist the head of the prison; in the UK they are called Independent Monitoring Board (IMB) and are appointed and

---

228 Tibbles (1971), p. 426; Fitzharris (1973), p. 33: "many prisoners contend that the department cannot be expected to investigate itself dispassionately. Others claim that the department only tries to 'cover itself' to make itself look good at any cost."
229 Moore (1968b), p. 98
230 For a description of the negative effects for a prisoner labeled as „litigious" see: Shaw (1999), p. 10
231 Here and in the following: Matheson (1982), p. 271
232 Jacobs (2004), p. 299
233 Gerken (1986), p. 10
234 Selke (1992), p. 93; Owers (2006), p. 86; Gerken (1986), p. 17f and 20
235 Gerken (1986), p. 18

guided by the Secretary of State according to Number 77 of the Prison Rules; in Maine, US, they are referred to as Boards of Visitors and are appointed by the Governor.[236]

As a complaint channel, prison boards have some advantages compared to the administration. They are outsiders and since they have to visit the prison frequently and are charged with hearing prisoners' complaints, they potentially provide easier accessibility. Yet, the legal framework usually leaves the determination of the frequency of their prison visits to the board members.[237] It has also been reported that only one or two members were charged with hearing complaints and did so while touring the prison with a guard.[238] The social composition of the boards equally impacts on perceived and real accessibility and impartiality.[239] The latter is also endangered by the board's responsibility to make recommendations to and confer with the head of prison – a situation that may easily lead the members to perceive themselves as "part of a team".[240]

Thus, the impact and quality of the prison boards depends on the individual effort and involvement of the board members and may be severely curtailed by their reporting agency.[241] It therefore comes as no surprise that prisoners assume the boards to side with the administration, while staff regards them as uninformed and superficial.[242] Although in some countries the prison boards publish annual reports, their dissemination and coverage in the local media is poor and the impact negligible.[243] This might be partially due to the board members misjudging the purpose of the confidentiality laws applying to them, which is limited to the protection of individual rights, but not intended to prevent any outside communication.[244] Overall, these prison boards have at best been declared able to enhance their influence and impact and at worst referred to as "a totally ineffective [...] method of oversight" and "watchdogs howling into empty space".[245]

---

236   http://www.maine.gov/corrections/facilities/msp/mspBoVisitorsNew.htm (last accessed June 6th, 2012)

237   IMB members, however, meet at the prison once a month according to Prison Rule Number 76

238   Douglas (1984), p. 156

239   Maguire (1985), p. 143

240   Maguire (1985), p. 145

241   Woolf/Tumim (1991), p. 309

242   Johnson (1988), p. 127; Maguire (1985), p. 143

243   c.f. Gerken (1986), p. 260f

244   c.f. Gerken (1986), p. 258

245   Schäfer (1985), p. 143; Selke (1992), p. 93; Eady (2007), p. 269

cc) Inmate councils

Inmate councils are comprised of prisoners elected by their fellow inmates and are intended to create democratic involvement in internal decision making.[246] In the US and Germany, inmate councils have been operating for some time. In UK prisons, inmate councils do not exist out of fear of butting prisoners against staff that might lead to an uprising and "industrial action" such as a refusal to work. However, there is now a pilot project: Parkhurst Prison Council at HMP Isle of Wight.

Prisoners may address their complaints to these inmate councils. They are always on site and available. But as the inmate council cannot make binding recommendations and has no power of publicity, they only ever operate as effectively as the superintendent or head of prison permits.[247] There are two ways an inmate council may intercede: either it takes up the complaint and tries to negotiate a change of practice or it may act as an intermediary.[248] Both possibilities involve turning to the superintendent or head of prison who makes the decision. The prisoner is therefore still dependent on the goodwill of the administration. The only advantage in this scenario over complaining directly to the administration is the chance that the inmate council may take up the complaint adding its pull within the prison to the inmate's cause.

b) External grievance channels

Selke holds that

> "[t]he prison system is the only public organization permitted to operate with little or no independent scrutiny from the outside. There are usually rationalizations about the dangerousness inside the walls or the disruption to security that might result from the intrusion of outsiders. These justifications, however, only serve to illustrate the degeneration that has been allowed to take place in prisons due at least partly to the absence of accountability. It is no surprise that as prison conditions became worse, there is more defensiveness on the part of correctional officials to deal with 'outsiders', and thus the cycle continues. As the prisons become further insulted [sic] from scrutiny and less accountable, the deterioration is likely to hasten".[249]

Nevertheless, there are external grievance channels providing scrutiny. Those are parliamentarians, parliamentary committees, the crown, general ombudsmen, non-governmental organizations (NGO), churches, the media, European and international authorities as well as courts.

---

246   Here and in the following: Douglas (1984), p. 155
247   Johnson (1988), p. 129
248   Douglas (1984), p. 155
249   Selke (1992), p. 92

aa) Parliamentarians; parliamentary committees; monarchs and other heads of state

Prisoners may also turn to their monarchs or heads of state, parliamentarians and/or petition committees. In some countries complaints can also be made to the parliamentary committee of legal affairs.[250] Prisoners, as part of the parliamentarians' constituency, may address them with their complaints. In the UK there is a strong tradition of complaining to one's MP. While the possibility also exists in Germany, it is not nearly as common. This may be due to the differences in the parliamentary culture and election systems with the focus in the UK being on the candidate, whereas the system in Germany is more partisan in nature.

In addition, not all elected representatives are equally engaged and efficient in their work on behalf of constituents – especially prisoners.[251] The question of the impartiality applies in so far as members of the governing party tend to champion the administration.[252] Also, the aptitude for handling complaints may differ greatly between parliamentarians. Anderson holds that

> "[w]hile it is a legitimate objection to the lawmaker [...] that his judgment may be impure, the more frequent occurrence is that the legislator simply makes no judgment at all. He receives a complaint which he has neither the time nor the ability to evaluate, and passes the complaint on to the agency which has been accused. Ironically, others may interpret this abdication of judgment as an expression of judgment".[253]

Even engaged, conscientious elected representatives are often ineffectual as they have to rely on internal files of public bodies in their decision making. Access to files may be frequently denied leaving them in no position to see through the veil of official secrecy.[254] Although in parliamentary countries access to information may be forced by official parliamentary questioning, the investigation is carried out by the department against which the complaint has been made and they reply by the Minister is that of his/her department.[255]

This does not imply that it is impossible for a parliamentarian to succeed in resolving the constituent's complaint. If that where the case, the tradition of com-

---

250　Woolf/Tumim (1991), p. 11; e.g. in Germany prisoners may petition the Bundespräsident (federal president) with their clemency pleas according to Art. 60 II GG. Overall, petitions to monarchs and heads of state play only a minor role.

251　Gregory (2000), p. 33

252　Frank (1975), p. 56; Rowat (1993), p. 130

253　Anderson (1968), p. 150

254　Gregory (2000), p. 33

255　Here and in the following: Frank (1975), p. 56

plaining to one's elected representative would have ceased. However useful facilitating relief in an individual case may be, the amount of complaints handled by an individual member of parliament usually prohibits the identification of underlying systemic problems. Where they are uncovered, the parliamentarian's time is often insufficient to pursue the broader implications of individual complaints.[256]

Prisoners may also turn to parliamentary committees. In federal states such as Germany, prisoners may turn to either the *Bundes-* or *Länderparlamente* depending on the matter concerned. There are several drawbacks to this complaint channel, however. Complaints may only be made in writing, a problem these committees frequently share with the parliamentarians, and have to be addressed to an anonymous board with constantly changing membership.[257] The work of these committees tends to be slow, which excludes all short-terms prisoners from utilizing this channel and prohibits the involvement of the committee in matters of every-day-life. Although these committees do receive complaints from prisoners, the quantity recorded stands in no proportion to the prisoners' need for external complaint channels. Consequently, parliamentarians and parliamentary committees are not an ideal external complaint channels for prisoners.[258]

bb) General ombudsmen

Another avenue open to prisoners' complaints are general ombudsmen, which can be of a legislative or executive nature. In Germany, some federal states employ *Bürgerbeauftragte*, while the UK has the national Parliamentary and Health Service Ombudsman. All of these general ombudsmen may be addressed by prisoners with their complaints. While complaints to them frequently have to be made in writing, some general ombudsmen also accept complaints to be made via email, by phone or in person. Usually prisoners are at least barred from using the first and last option, but some may complain over the phone.[259] While the

---

256 Moore (1968b), p. 99
257 Kempf/Mille (1993), p. 197
258 in agreement (with further details): Kreft (1953), p. 127
259 The *Bürgerbeauftragte* for the Rhineland-Palatinate visits one prison per year. During the visit prisoners may complain in person (Annual Report/*Jahresbericht* of the *Bürgerbeauftragte* 2009, Drs. 15/4357). However, due to the multitude of prisons the purpose of the visit has to be considered primarily inspectorial. By no means can this be considered an adequate grievance channel for all prisoners. Especially, for prisoners sentenced to short sentences the availability of this measure is purely a matter of chance.

latter constitutes an option for illiterates, it still excludes all those not in command of the national language. Both groups are over-represented in prison.

General ombudsmen will handle complaints assiduously and may make recommendations to the prison administration, the Minister and/or parliament. They publish annual reports and have access to the media. Consequently, the recommendations of general ombudsmen are usually taken seriously by the administration.

However, in the UK, Germany and many other countries prisoners' complaints have never formed a major part of the general ombudsmen's caseload. In Germany, the *Bürgerbeauftragte* for the Rhineland-Palatinate received 5141 complaints in total in 2009, of which 3897 were admissible. 14.71% (573) of those admissible were prison-related.[260] In 1992, before the introduction of a specialty ombudsman for prisons the UK, the PCA registered 15 cases, 2 of which he investigated in depth.[261] In 2009/10 the PCA received 67 complaints against the HM Prison Service; none of these cases was accepted for investigation.[262] The low complaint rate is due to the PCA's singular situation that all complaints have to pass through the "MP-filter". This means that they have to be forwarded by the prisoner's MP to the ombudsman. This is a strong disincentive for prisoners driven by the same reasons as their reluctance to complain to their MPs directly.

There are two more disadvantages for prisoners complaining to general ombudsmen: The terms of references of some general ombudsmen such as the PCA only assign them the task of discovering maladministration in the application of laws and rules regulating the prison life. They are not permitted to consider whether those same regulations are themselves unjust or unfair or applied unjustly or unfairly.[263] The second disadvantaging factor is time. The *Bürgerbeauftragte* of the Rhineland-Palatinate resolves prisoners' complaints on average within six to seven weeks.[264] The PCA only gives a "substantive response" to 78% of the inquiries within 40 days. Indeed, out of those inquiries which were followed up on through an investigation only 65% were concluded within 12 months.[265] This excludes short and medium term prisoners from complaining to

---

260 Annual Report/*Jahresbericht* of the *Bürgerbeauftragte* 2009, Landtag Rheinland-Pfalz, Drs. 15/4357, p. 6
261 C.f. Seneviratne (1994), p. 43
262 C.f. PHSO Annual Report 2009/2010, p. 49
263 Ryan/Ward (1993), p. 41
264 Telephone Interview on December 1st, 2010 with Mr. Schöpflin, who is the administrator responsible for prisoners' complaints within the office of the *Bürgerbeauftragte* for the Rhineland-Palatinate.
265 C.f. PHSO Annual Report 2009/2010, p. 47

the PCA. The PCA's diligent work, however, is rewarded with an impressive rate of 99% compliance with the recommendations made.[266]

Overall, the general ombudsmen leave much to be desired in terms of accessibility, remit and speed. The former general ombudsman of Denmark, Lars Nielsen, agrees, saying that the lengthy procedure connected with his work causes his office to be of limited use to individual prisoners: "What prisoners need to protect their rights are not people to write letters to, but someone they can contact immediately if something happens."[267]

cc) NGOs, pastoral caregivers and the media

Prisoners may also turn to NGOs, pastoral caregivers and the media. NGOs and the media both do not have any on-site representative. Instead, prisoners may contact them via mail or phone. There are big organizations like Amnesty International and comparably smaller organizations active on a national or even local level like the Howard League in the UK. NGOs frequently have a long-standing tradition of dedication to prisoners' causes and have a better understanding of prison life. In Germany, §153 StVollzG even prescribes the interaction of prison administration with NGOs.[268]

The media regularly feature articles on convicts, crime and sometimes prison matters, as for example the *Bild* in Germany or the *Sun* in the UK. However, the media especially are only interested in the most serious and controversial cases and their involvement is usually solely due to commercial interest: "crime sells". The media tend to take sides without having any special insight into prison matters or access to relevant information. Their coverage of the situation is spotty at best.[269]

Most states allow for pastoral care within their prisons with the only differences being which denominations provide the pastoral care and how many hours the pastoral caregivers are available for.[270] Where they are on site during all working hours, such as in Germany, all prisoners – not only those of their denominations – may turn to them for advice or complaints. Since the pastoral caregivers tend to be relatively unrestricted in their movements throughout the prison and prisoners are usually allowed to visit them, their accessibility is much higher than that of NGOs and the media. However, not all prisoners may wish to seek assistance from a caregiver linked to a particular religion.

---

266   C.f. PHSO Resource Accounts 2009/2010, p. 5
267   Raphael (1975), p. 57
268   For details see: Schäfer (1985), p. 15
269   Rowat (1993), pp. 130
270   Fitzharris (1973), p. 29

The handicaps of complaining to NGOs, pastoral caregivers and the media are all alike: their availability is too unpredictable to constitute a reliable external complaints mechanism, their inquiries lack the force implicit in a statutory or political mandate, and they fail to contribute to the general improvement of administrative organization and procedure.[271] At best they are useful to raise awareness for prisoners' needs while at worst they can detract from the likelihood of the success of a complaint by alienating the administrative channels the complaint will inevitably have to pass.

dd) European and international authorities

Prisoners may also turn to the European Court of Human Rights established by the European Convention of Human Rights and the European Committee for the Prevention of Torture and Inhuman or Degrading Treatment or Punishment (ECPT).

Under the ECHR, prisoners in those countries which are signatories to the convention may complain to the ECtHR concerning aspects of their treatment.[272] British prisoners have made more use of the Convention than any other single group of people in Europe.[273] Many key rulings of the ECtHR are related to aspects of prison life. The biggest deterring factor is the amount of time necessary to achieve a court ruling, which can take up to six years and as such disqualifies the ECtHR from being a useful external grievance mechanism in matters concerning day-to-day-life.

The same holds true for the ECPT, which organizes visits to places of detention, in order to assess how persons deprived of their liberty are treated. After each visit, the ECPT sends a detailed report to the State concerned. This report includes the ECPT's findings, recommendations, comments and requests for information. A detailed response to the issues raised in the report is requested. During these visits prisoners may approach the members of the delegation. Due to the sporadic nature of these visits to the member countries, let alone the individual prisons, complaining to the ECPT is not an adequate external grievance mechanism. Although the ECPT provides a prisoner the occasion to complain in person, those visits are not frequent enough to provide a serious avenue for individual redress. In fact, this is also not the conceptual intent behind the idea of the ECPT, which is strictly limited to systemic oversight and/or systemic administrative change.

A similar concept based on a twin-pillar approach comprising the UN Subcommittee on Prevention of Torture and other Cruel, Inhuman or Degrading

---

271   Moore (1968b), p. 72
272   Here and in the following: Johnson (1988), p. 128
273   Here and in the following: Eady (2007), p. 266; Arnott (2000), p. 5

Treatment or Punishment (SPT) and National Preventive Mechanisms (NPM) exists on an international plane as well.[274] In those states that have ratified the Optional Protocol to the Convention against Torture (OPCAT) – such as the UK and Germany – the SPT examines conditions of daily life in places of detention.[275] SPT members talk in private with people in custody, without the presence of prison or other staff or Government representatives. Their work is governed by strict confidentiality and they do not give out names or details. However, their efforts – like those of the ECPT – are only directed towards systemic change.

Article 17 of the OPCAT obligates the state members to set up one or several independent NPMs for the prevention of torture at the domestic level.[276] Mechanisms established by decentralized units, e.g. the German Länderparlamente, may be designated as NPM for the purposes of OPCAT if they conform to OPCAT provisions. While general ombudsmen for example may be designated as NPM, those are not ideal external grievance mechanisms as has been elucidated above.[277]

Overall, due to their accessibility, remit and speed as well as their focus on systemic change rather than individual grievance relief, the European and international authorities discussed here do not suffice to satisfy the prisoners' need for an external complaint agency.

ee) Courts

The last of the external grievance mechanisms to be employed by prisoners are the courts. Courts everywhere play a major role in the correction of administrative and governmental shortcomings and abuses.[278] However, the traditional concerns about the use of the normal court system also apply to prisoners' complaints. Despite the fact that in light of recent democratic changes courts have undergone serious reform in many places, some of their more problematic features have remained untouched.[279] They only offer ex-post-factum-review and are costly, protracted, adversarial and, due to their formality, difficult to ma-

---

274 Evans/Haenni-Dale (2004), p. 20
275 Here and in the following: http://www2.ohchr.org/english/bodies/cat/opcat/index.htm (last accessed June 6th, 2012)
276 To be found at http://www2.ohchr.org/english/law/cat-one.htm (last accessed June 6th, 2012)
277 c.f. Fliflet (2009), p. 7
278 Frank (1975), p. 56
279 c.f. Ayeni (2001), p. 41; Eady (2007), p. 266

noeuvre for the legally non-educated public.[280] In common law countries they are also bound by precedent.

All these concerns are very relevant to prisoners' complaints. Additionally, there are also some concerns unique to the prison situation. Throughout the past, courts have proven reluctant to hear prisoners' complaints – justifying their non-interference with the separation of powers.[281] Whenever they have taken on prison related cases, they have proven rather deferential to the prison administration.[282] The latter goes hand in hand with their reluctance to visit prisons. Even in Germany where there exists a court chamber (*Strafvollstreckungskammer*) exclusively charged with hearing cases brought forth by prisoners, on-site visits by judges are a rare occurrence. This limits the judges' insight into the every-day-prison life forcing them to rely on information supplied by the prison administration.

The general reluctance in the past to hear prisoners complaints has been ascribed to the fear of "opening the floodgates" to hundreds of disgruntled prisoners presumed to have nothing better to do than to make things difficult for prison staff.[283] This view however seems to be receding as courts realize their duty to safeguard the rights of all citizens, irrespective of their status.[284] Douglas holds that "the limitation of cost and the need for legal aid serve effectively to prevent most 'vexatious' actions from reaching the courts".[285] This statement is possibly problematic, but should be interpreted *in dubio pro spiritu rectore* to only refer to those prisoners' complaints obviously without merit – and not all those where the prisoner has a righteous cause for complaint about some small, every-day-life or singular occurrence of maladministration whose rectification is cumbersome to the administration. In the latter case, exploiting the prisoners' restriction of funds would be reprehensible and not worthy of a prison administration in a rule of law state.

Nevertheless, the observation that the costliness of the courts frequently poses a serious challenge to prisoners is correct.[286] Even for an average citizen,

---

280 Kempf/Mille (1993), p. 197; Owen (1993), p. 11; Frank (1975), p. 56; Abraham (2008), p. 4; Cromwell (1974), p. 55; Ayeni (2001), p. 41; Owers (2006), p. 86; Morris/Henham (1998), p. 348; Taugher (1972), p. 177; Moore (1968b), p. 72
281 Fitzharris (1973), p. 22
282 Douglas (1984), pp. 160; Heskamp (2007-2008), p. 552; Dünkel/van Zyl Smit (1991), p. 728
283 Here and in the following: Douglas (1984), p. 160
284 In the UK the House of Lords clarified the extent of the courts' responsibility in prison matters, c.f. Woolf/Tumim (1991), p. 412.
285 Douglas (1984), p. 160
286 Frank (1975), p. 56

the cost of legal action is a potent deterrent.[287] If one takes into consideration the clear over-representation of the uneducated, poor, foreign or socially disadvantaged within prison, it is easily understood why the necessary funding for legal action as an external grievance mechanism is not forthcoming.

Another problem not unique to prisoners but which hits them especially hard is the limitation of court remit.[288] Like all citizens being party to court proceedings, prisoners may perceive the court to rule against them – despite their cause being just and their being victim to administrative maltreatment. Courts are only concerned with the manner in which a decision is reached not its merits or fairness and may be precluded from hearing appeals either by law or technicalities of form, time, standing, jurisdiction, nature and extent of interest, the character of the administrative act, and the wording of statutes.[289] The review of administrative acts may be limited to such questions as to whether the administration acted within its powers and on grounds of substantial evidence. Regardless of the outcome, prisoners will often consider themselves the weaker party, who has been unjustly treated – first by the administration and then also by the court.

Even in those cases where the court rules in favour of the prisoner, it can only provide an ex-post-factum-review – meaning: a court only intervenes once an abuse, or alleged abuse, has already occurred.[290] This is of course true for all grievance mechanisms. Yet, there are significant differences as to the time elapsed between the act underlying the complaint and the intervention of the grievance mechanism. While on-site mechanisms are generally faster than off-site grievance channels, courts have a tendency to be particularly slow. Thus, prisoners sentenced to short sentences have limited or no access to court review.[291] The length of elapsed time makes a difference in so far as alternative methods of resolution such as a simple apology, explanation or mediation may be impossible due to a prolonged festering of ill-will on both sides.

The uncertainties, practical difficulties and delays of litigation, therefore, present a palpable barrier to the straightforward and expeditious resolution of

---

287   Kempf/Mille (1993), p. 197

288   For a description how the US Prison Litigation Reform Act (Publ. L. No. 104-134, §§801-10, 110 Stat. 1321-66 to 1321-77 (1996) codified as amended in scattered sections of 18 U.S.C., 28 U.S.C., and 42 U.S.C.) has helped in narrowing the scope of prison reform litigation from systmic problems to individual violations only, please see Heskamp (2007-2008), p. 530.

289   Here and in the following: Frank (1975), p. 56; Owen (1993), p. 11; Kempf/Mille (1993), p. 197

290   Owers (2006), p. 86

291   Owers (2006), p. 86

complaints.[292] Especially in cases of minor problems and every-day concerns, the time-consuming and costly court review does not meet the prisoner's need which would be better met by some quick informal review of lesser problems.[293] In cases of severe or systemic maladministration or continued infringement on constitutional rights this barrier obviously has to be overcome in order to facilitate a court ruling, thereby setting a precedent in common law countries, against future incidents. In some countries, like Germany, the problem of court costs at least is mitigated by the availability of legal aid.

Another problem is the so called contempt of the court, which means that due to the lack of legal enforcement measures, court rulings may be ignored by the administration.[294] Selke reports that especially "court rulings having to do with overcrowding and violence are typically ignored [in the US] through appeals and claims that the funds simply do not exist to comply with court decisions".[295] This sort of behaviour may only be contested by prisoners wherever their constitutional or human rights are infringed.

Courts and their stakeholders also face some problems of their own. Large quantities of prisoners' complaints have the capacity for clogging the courts.[296] The handling of prisoners' complaints binds human, monetary and time resources. All of these have to be provided by the courts' stakeholders, which are ultimately the taxpayers. It is in their interest to research alternatives that are less costly by either being faster, or more efficient or both. Overall, courts are thus not an ideal external grievance mechanism for prisoners' complaints.

c) The prison ombudsman as an alternative solution

The above discussion demonstrates that whilst the demand for and the potential of the existing internal and external grievance channels is great, they fail to provide relief for all prisoner complaints.[297] They fall short in many different ways. Those charged with resolving complaints may not be independent, accessible, efficient, assertive, affordable and accountable enough. Those charged with discovering systemic problems may not receive enough information via complaints in addition to their own-motion initiatives to fully perform their task or may be

---

292   Morris/Henham (1998), p. 348
293   Taugher (1972), p. 177
294   Dünkel (1996a), p. 33; Dünkel/van Zyl Smit (1991), p. 727; Lesting/Feest (1987), p. 390; Lesting (1993), p. 49; Feest/Lesting (2009), p. 675; Walter (2012), p. 3
295   Selke (1992), pp. 92f and (1993), pp. 29 and 104
296   Cromwell (1974), p. 55; Anderson (1981), p. 255 and (1983), p. 139
297   Likewise: Taugher (1972), p. 177; Moore (1968b), p. 100

so rarely on site, as for example in the case of international organizations, that they cannot provide a constant monitoring.

But there is another option for meeting this demand: the prison ombudsman. The purpose of this section is not to determine the suitability of the institution to the demand, but to describe in general terms the construction of this office that has in the recent past been proposed and introduced as an alternative solution. The hope of its inventors and legal creators alike was that if a prison ombudsinstitution is set up correctly in matters of independence, funding etc., it may compensate for the deficiencies of the other grievance mechanisms.[298] Prison ombudsmen do not replace administrative decision-makers; instead, they constitute an addition to existing grievance channels and function as a measure of last resort.[299] Fitzharris sums this up saying that "[t]he attraction of the correctional Ombudsman idea lies in the fact that this mechanism has strengths precisely in those areas where existing grievance procedures are weak".[300]

In accordance with the double function of ombudsmen, prison ombudsmen are charged with discovering systemic problems in addition to resolving complaints. As independent agencies they are designed to resolve complaints efficiently, speedily and free of charge. The knowledge gained from this complaint resolution as well as own-motion investigations is put towards achieving systemic change. This requires them to be assertive about their recommendations and prove accountable by means of reporting.

The remainder of this section will describe the prison ombudsman as one kind of specialty ombudsinstitution. The analysis will extend to the legal basis, remit, investigations and expectations. This information will be complemented by a short account of the prison ombudsmen currently in existence.

2. Legal basis

The prison ombudsman is an institution embedded in the public sector. This seems unlikely to change even with the current discussion around private prisons and the first realizations thereof. This can be explained by the fact that the control of legality and supervision remains with the state in either case. Accord-

---

298 Münchbach (1973), p. 84; Haller (1965), p. 287
299 Kempf (1976), p. 12; Fulmer (1981), p. 306; Hansen (1972), pp. 172ff; Hertogh (1998), p. 77. The Annual Report/*Tätigkeitsbericht* of the Justizvollzugsbeauftragten des Landes Nordrhein-Westfalen, p. 203, notes that a fifth of all prisoners addressing the ombudsman also complain via other channels.
300 Fitzharris (1973), p. 52

ingly, the remit of the Prisons and Probation Ombudsman for England and Wales extends to private prisons.[301]

Prison ombudsmen occur in both possible public sector ombudsman sub-groups: in the form of legislative and executive ombudsmen. The Canadian Correctional Investigator for example, in 1992 received a statutory footing in the Corrections and Release Act – making it a legislative ombudsman. Fitzharris emphasizes that "[w]hile such placement does not guarantee impartiality, the structural independence thus provided is critical both to the concept and to potential complainants".[302] In contrast, the Kentucky Corrections Ombudsman is based on the Kentucky Revised Statute 196.035, 197.020 & 197.023 promulgated through Corrections Policy and Procedure 14.6, which makes it an executive ombudsinstitution.

As explained previously in section B I. 6. b), a pure administrative framework cannot equal a legislative basis in ensuring an ombudsman's independence. An executive prison ombudsman "is always vulnerable to political interference triggered by inquiries into sensitive areas of prison administration".[303] As the Canadian Secretary of State wrote in 1981, "[i]t is not so much whether there is actual direction by the minister, but how the office is perceived by the inmates. If the office appears to be part of the Ministry it loses credibility and the task becomes more difficult".[304] This is only partially true. Perception is by definition fragile and subjective and much effort is necessary for an executive ombudsman to keep his independence. Yet, whenever only the appearance of independence remains, the purpose of the ombudsman to resolve prisoners' complaints and achieve systemic change effectively becomes a matter of administrative goodwill. Actual supervision by the ministry can render the executive prison ombudsman useless. Nevertheless, like all executive ombudsmen, prison ombudsmen have played and are playing a crucial role in today's penal system by "un-covering problems that may not have come to the authorities' attention through other channels".[305]

3. Remit

An ombudsman's remit is described in a legal document similar in content – to the framework document and the Terms of Reference of the Prisons and Proba-

---

301   Seneviratne (2010), p. 3
302   Fitzharris (1973), p. 43
303   Morris/Henham (1998), p. 377
304   Canadian Department of the Secretary of State, Human Rights Directorate, p. 12
305   May (1975), p. 59

tion Ombudsman for England and Wales.[306] The remit generally extends to the consideration of both the merits and the procedure of the matter underlying the complaint. Frequently, the element of complaint investigation is complemented by own-motion power. The remit may be locally restricted to those detained in national or federal prisons or also apply to jails and other detention facilities such as immigration facilities.

While some prison ombudsmen may accept third-party complaints, frequently some restrictions apply for the subject matters and eligibility of complaints, with time limits a common example.[307] The ombudsman's remit may stipulate specific exceptions, such as ministerial policy decisions or health care, or additions, such as supervision of probation services.

Since the prison ombudsman is designed to be a means of last resort there is a significant overlap of its remit with those of other internal and external grievance channels. This is rather intentional and in line with the remit of general ombudsinstitutions. Fitzharris notes that "[…] it has been urged that the ideal Ombudsman model can function only where a reasonably effective primary complaint-handling mechanism (i.e., internal grievance procedure) already exists".[308]

4. Investigations

The practice of ombudsmen has already been discussed in general terms in section B I. 3. and 4. Since prison ombudsmen largely conform to this conceptual framework, only a limited amount of further elucidation appears necessary where the tool of investigation is concerned.

Two techniques of monitoring prison administration may be deduced from the ombudsman's double function of resolving individual complaints and supervising the administration: These are reactive and proactive investigation. Reactive investigation is used upon receipt of an individual complaint and may include a visit to the complainant and/or the administrator and/or the premises in

---

306 See http://www.ppo.gov.uk/terms-of-reference.html and http://www.Prisons and Probation Ombudsman for England and Wales.gov.uk/docs/ppo-framework-document1.pdf (last accessed June 6th, 2012)

307 E.g. for the Prisons and Probation Ombudsman for England and Wales it is left to his discretion, see p. 4 http://www.ppo.gov.uk/terms-of-reference.html (last accessed June 6th, 2012); for further information on the historical development of the Prisons and Probation Ombudsman for England and Wales' remit please see Henham (2000), p. 292 and Seneviratne (2001), pp. 93

308 Fitzharris (1973), p. 53

question. An investigation is proactive when the prison ombudsman acts on own-motion.

Prison ombudsinstitutions should make use of both methods. A solely reactive approach to prison ombudsman work may fall short in recognizing and rectifying systemic problems. An exclusively proactive approach, which considers individual grievances only as an indicator for systemic problems, would constitute a neglect of the prison ombudsman's primary function as a complaint-handler.[309] The use of either method has an impact on both the quantity and quality of cases received.

a) Reactive

In the case of a reactive investigation the prison ombudsman's focus lies on the handling of an individual complaint. Complaints may be made in person whenever the ombudsman visits the prison. As Anderson points out, "there is an intrinsic inequity and inefficiency in sporadic visits, especially given the shortness of prison terms. Only those inmates that happen to be incarcerated on visitation day [...] have the opportunity for a personal meeting with the Ombudsman. This is unfair to others and represents a distortion of focus".[310] Consequently, it is necessary that the ombudsman also receives complaints made by phone or mail. While all three communication channels depend on the complainants' knowledge of the existence of a prison ombudsman, the latter two contain further pitfalls. Not all prisoners have access to phones and even if they do, their access may be restricted to certain hours. Complaints can only be made via mail by literate prisoners or those well integrated enough to induce a fellow prisoner into putting their complaint into writing. It therefore appears that all three communication channels should be made available at the same time.[311]

Once the prison ombudsman has received an individual complaint and judged it eligible, he or she will investigates it by acquiring evidence for example through documents, site visits and interviews with the complainant, fellow prisoners and involved administrators. Once the investigation is complete the prison ombudsman makes a recommendation which will be brought to the notice of the complainant and the administration. In the annual report, the investigation will be listed in the statistics and may be discussed in detail if considered suitable as an example. In severe cases the prison ombudsman may write and table a special report.

---

309   Anderson (1978), p. 244
310   Anderson (1978), p. 244
311   Fulmer (1981), p. 308 mentions the impact the different communication channels have on the number of cases received.

The goal of reactive investigation is to provide individual grievance relief. The expectation in this case is that assuring the inmate that he/she will be treated according to the principles of legality and fair play will encourage similar behaviour.[312] This is why a prison ombudsman should never allow a complaint or inquiry to go unanswered even if the complaint appears trivial, frivolous or too stale to justify an investigation.[313] Although a prison ombudsman needs the discretion not to accept such complaints in order to remain functional, by showing the courtesy of a short reply the prison ombudsman has the chance to demonstrate society's concern for the inmate and encourage the re-socialization process by acknowledging the inmate's human dignity.

In the case of unjustified complaints, the reactive investigation also serves the secondary purpose of protecting the penal administrators from unfounded charges. A tertiary aim is to reduce the penal system's isolation from the public view by providing publicity.

b) Proactive

Whilst handling individual complaints, it is not always easy to keep in view the whole picture as the ombudsman will be rather focused on what has been complained about in the specific case.[314] To uncover potential maladministration, reactive investigation is therefore complemented by proactive investigation. Proactive investigations are own-motion investigations with a systemic approach.[315] They are usually elicited either as a self-contained project after a sideline discovery made whilst conducting a reactive investigation, or as a byproduct of either a conjoined investigation or a site visit. The latter are sometimes also called inspections with the exception of the UK, where formal inspections are left to the separate Prison Inspectorate. Despite the existence of this institution however the Prisons and Probation Ombudsman for England and Wales may nevertheless conduct announced as well as unannounced site visits – a feature common to all prison ombudsmen.

Site visits may be spurred by own-motion investigations but may also trigger them. It is likely that an increase in the number of inspections would entail a further increase in the number of own motion investigations.[316] Not surprisingly, these *sua sponte* matters have a higher chance to result in the ombudsman critiquing the administration.

---

312   Taugher (1972), p. 184
313   Tibbles (1971), pp. 434 and 437
314   c.f. André (2009), p. 4
315   c.f. Buck et al. (2011a), p. 133
316   Here and in the follwing: Anderson (1978), p. 216

Site visits serve manifold purposes. They provide the prison ombudsman with practical background and offer insight into the working procedures and perspective of the public authorities.[317] This is accompanied by a deepened knowledge of the premises as well as an opportunity to meet the officials on-site and learn about their working conditions. All of this is necessary to uphold the respect from the administrative personnel. This respect as well as the necessary independence may be threatened by falling into the other extreme: an excessive familiarity with staff.[318] A useful balance must be struck.

There are four potential kinds of inspections: formal, informal, announced and unannounced. The advantage of announced inspections is that all authorities will be present on the premises, all necessary documentation is readied and the administration may have actually already investigated itself and thus pre-emptively rectified its own behaviour.[319] André, one of the current Swedish Parliamentary Ombudsman, describes this phenomenon:

> "The preventive effects of inspections are beyond questioning. The mere knowledge that every authority may at any time be inspected helps to keep the officials alert. Usually, an authority after having been informed that an inspection is going to take place, is very anxious to look through its routines, to change what has to be changed, to hurry up the handling of old cases etc. This kind or pre-inspection action could lead to necessary changes. It does not really matter that it is often very apparent to the Ombudsman, upon arrival at the authority, that this cleanup has already taken place. On the contrary, it is highly satisfying to end an inspection by concluding that our mission, at least in some respects, has already been fulfilled by the authority itself – and it is of course in the interest of every authority to give as little cause for criticism as possible".[320]

Unannounced visits allow for a more realistic impression of every-day-life and potentially create less of a disruption. Formal inspections that require thorough preparation allow for precise inquiries and in-depth investigation. Informal, spur of the moment inspections may uncover maladministration of the beaten path and therefore adequately supplement the other forms of inspections. Anderson declared back in 1978 that "Ombudsmen could accomplish substantially more in prisons at little extra cost – by substituting (or [...] adding) [...] frequent, informal visits to prison in place of the present infrequent, formal visits."[321] Due to

---

317   Here and in the following: André (2009), pp. 4
318   Anderson (1983), p. 142
319   André (2009), pp. 5
320   André (2009), p. 5
321   Anderson (1978), p. 243; Prof. Walter, the North Rhine-Westphalian prison ombudsman favors formal announced visits and disagrees with Anderson's assessment that in Western democracies unannounced visits may uncover further maladministration, c.f.

their different lines of attack neither mode of inspection should be neglected. Overall, it appears that over the last few years systemic investigations have become an increasingly important part of prison ombudsman work.[322]

5. Expectations

The positive and negative expectations facing ombudsmen in general have been discussed in chapter B. I. 5. This section is therefore limited to those positive and negative expectations specific to prison ombudsmen.

a) Positive

The positive expectations facing a prison ombudsman are (in approximate order of increasing systemic impact):

- support of the re-socialization process
- reduction of court costs and inmate litigation
- riot prevention and control
- accountability of prison administration
- expedition of grievance procedures
- modernization of penology

The sheer extent of these expectations may seem daunting and is only feasible due to a considerable overlap, which allows the ombudsinstitution to impact multiple expectations with a single measure.

It is expected that the ombudsman is not only concerned with the physical handling of complaints, but aims to make a wider psychological contribution by reducing the tensions and anxieties which characterize prison life. By serving as a grievance channel the ombudsinstitution should aid the resocialization process for the greater good of society and inmates alike. If the inmates accept the ombudsinstitution as an independent agent within the sealed-off prison world, the ombudsman may come to symbolize "the use of reason and moral persuasion rather than force. This is very civilized – and civilizing!"[323]

At the same time, this is not only expected to speed up the grievance mechanisms and constitute a significant contribution to the development of fair stand-

---

pp. 4f, 21 of the interview conducted on April 25th, 2012 with the Justizvollzugsbeauftragter des Landes Nordrhein-Westfalen, Prof. Michael Walter.

322   Buck et al. (2011a), p. 135; Kaminski (2012), p. 288. This trend is also evident in the adaptations made to the North Rhine-Westphalian prison ombudsman's remit, c.f. D II. 2. b) bb)

323   Anderson (1975b), p. 7 and (1983), p. 143

ards and fair procedures within prisons but also to reduce inmate litigation and consequently court costs.[324] The ombudsman's function of safety valve is hoped to operate as an effective method of riot prevention and control. As an independent agent the ombudsman will not only be able to hold the prison administration accountable but also acquit it in case of unjustified accusation.[325] It is expected that the high moral standing of the ombudsman will lend weight to special and annual reports and encourage the modernization process of the penal system.

All this runs together to describe the prison ombudsman's humanitarian mission as a quest to acknowledge the human dignity of prisoners, who continue to define themselves by their demand and right to be treated as human beings.[326]

b) Negative

The negative expectations facing ombudsmen that were discussed in section B I. 5. also apply to prison ombudsmen. Tibbles sums them up saying:

> "The Ombudsman is not a reformer, he does not shape legislative policy, he is not a super-administrator, and he does not function as a trial court. Where the Ombudsman has worked effectively, it has been within a system where people generally trust the government. If governmental authorities, including prison administrators have no intention of improving governmental administration, or if they are thoroughly corrupt, the Ombudsman will not be able to lead a sweeping reform movement".[327]

Additionally, there are also some negative expectations specific to prison ombudsmen. These pertain to the remit, the legal basis, and the manner of grievance handling.

The remit of prison ombudsmen frequently excludes jails and cells used for police custody. In 1983 Anderson stated that "[j]ails have been excluded [...] on the assumption that conditions are so bad that an ombudsman could not function".[328] Even if this were true, it only constitutes more instead of less of a need for the supervision by a prison ombudsman. Another line of critique pertaining to the remit of prison ombudsmen holds that not all aspects of prison life are touched upon equally. While there certainly is cause for critique concerning the racial and social basis in the correctional process and the lack of adequate health care, rehabilitation and education programs, Tibbles aims it at the wrong ad-

---

324 Anderson (1983), p. 143
325 Jacobs (2004), p. 301
326 Matheson (1982), p. 267
327 Tibbles (1971), p. 439
328 Anderson (1983), p. 143

dressee:[329] it is the government which needs to produce the needed relief. The prison ombudsman may only be charged with continuously alerting them to these deficits.

The legal basis of the prison ombudsman gives rise to negative expectations whenever it falls short of being either a law or part of the constitution, thus making the prison ombudsmen executive ombudsinstitutions.[330] This exposes prison ombudsmen to the problems facing executive ombudsmen in general, which were already mentioned in section B I. 6. b) Due to the prison ombudsmen being specialty ombudsmen, there exists a specific group of stakeholders. Unlike other stakeholder groups, prisoners may be more strongly inclined to distrust any institutions and mechanisms that maybe associated with the administration, however remotely. This problem was already acknowledged in Canada in 1981.[331] The Canadian government concluded that the only solution to this problem was to place their Correctional Ombudsman on a statutory legal basis.[332]

The manner of grievance handling that is fundamental to the work of prison ombudsmen has also given rise to negative expectations. The most basic question is whether a prison ombudsman can function efficiently in states with very large prison populations comprised of several tens of thousands of prisoners.[333] There are three different approaches to attack the problem of size:

- having more than one ombudsman or adding staff;
- decentralization;
- filtering by encouraging the inmates to first apply to internal grievance-channels.

All of the above have hence been put to use. There are many prison ombudsinstitutions which are either run by more than one ombudsman or have an increasingly large staff. Countries using some form of federalism, such as the US or Germany, have decentralized prison ombudsmen – only some of their states have introduced prison ombudsmen. In the UK there is a common prison ombudsman for England and Wales and another one for Northern Ireland.

The process of filtering by encouraging the inmates to first apply to internal grievance-channels is universally used. Containing a matter within prescribed decisional channels takes advantage of whatever administrative organization

---

329   Tibbles (1971), p. 440
330   c.f. Anderson (1983), p. 142
331   See supranote 303
332   Another critique concerning the legal basis c.f. Anderson (1983), p. 142 – that prison ombudsmen should only be removable from their office for cause – has hence become common practice.
333   Here and in the following: Anderson (1983), p. 142

may have been established to consider specified categories of cases and may thus generally be considered a sound move.[334] While this procedure encourages the inmates in socially acceptable complaint-behaviour and aligns well with the idea of the Ombudsman as a measure of last resort, it has to be used with care.[335] Especially the latter point should not lead to a misguided rigid insistence on the formalities in cases which are unsuitable for internal grievance-channels or require speedy crisis intervention for this more likely aggravates than dissipates inmate tension.[336] For prisoners, a referral to the internal grievance mechanisms may quickly feel like red tape. Therefore, prison ombudsmen should take care to not only direct the constituent to the appropriate addressee and outline the steps that will either lead to the prisoner's satisfaction or allow the ombudsman to take up the grievance, but also to explain the reasons for declining to intervene before other channels. Otherwise the prison ombudsman may fall into the trap pointed out in the negative expectations of becoming just another step in the grievance-mechanisms to be followed.

There are two further negative expectations concerning the handling of grievances. One is that the prison ombudsman may find himself subdued by isolation or pressure and side with either the prisoners or the staff. In either case the loss of independence will cost the ombudsinstitution its ability to effectively resolve the complaints.[337] The other negative expectation is that the present inspection system "stimulates over-attention to paperwork at the expense of other activities. Since the Ombudsman is chiefly interested in documentary materials, both when he is making an inspection and when he is investigating a complaint, exactitude in record keeping and amplitude of writings may at times be indulged in not to protect the persons to whom records and writings pertain, but to protect the record-keepers and writers".[338] This demands from the prison ombudsman foremost an active understanding of the problem and the ability to balance the need and demand for records with an understanding of the development of situations specific to prisons. While this paragraph has named many pitfalls and given voice to a plethora of negative expectations, it may be appropriate to recall that just "because the Prison Ombudsman cannot do it all, is no reason not to let him do what he can".[339]

---

334   Gellhorn (1966b), p. 429
335   Fulmer (1981), p. 306
336   Matheson (1982), p. 273
337   Barton (1983), p. 150
338   Gellhorn (1966b), p. 223
339   Tibbles (1971), p. 440

6. Existence

This section that has looked prison ombudsmen from many different aspects and angles shall be rounded off with a brief overview of the prison ombudsmen in existence. The following Table 1[340] is a compilation of the prison ombudsinstitutions in existence today. The rather limited number of seven prison ombudsmen listed in this table is due to four reasons:

- the exclusion of all general ombudsmen without a special mandate some of which nevertheless perform significant prison work;
- the exclusion of all abolished institutions (e.g. the offices in New South Wales (Australia), Scotland (UK), Pennsylvania (US), Connecticut (US), Kansas (US), Minnesota (US), Oregon (US))
- the exclusion of offices either failing to meet the requirements of the definition of public sector ombudsmen set out in chapter B. I. (such as the offices in California (US) and Texas (US)) or
- whose type and level of activity is unclear or whose funding is withheld (Georgia (US), Missouri (US), Nebraska (US) and New Jersey (US)).

Thus, the table elucidates why in 2004 Jacobs had cause to opine that "[u]nfortunately, the prison ombudsman concept is not widely known and has not been met with enthusiasm for its importance".[341]

Currently, there are prison ombudsmen on two continents (Europe and North America) and in four countries (Canada, UK, US and Germany). Due to the exclusion of general ombudsmen working in prison, this should not be taken to mean that ombudsman work in prison has not reached global dimensions.[342]

---

340   For the table the newest available data – either from 2009/2010 or 2010/2011 has been used.

341   Jacobs (2004), p. 300

342   c.f. the rather impressive prison work of the general ombudsmen in New Zealand, the Caribbean and Scandinavia

Table 1: Overview of prison ombudsmen in existence

Name	Year	Country	Staff	Annual Budget (in T €)	Complaints received	Visits to prisons (p. a.)
Canadian Correctional Investigator	1973; statutory footing 1992	Canada	30	2,808	5,483	57 prisons, 1-4 visits each
Indiana Department of Corrections Ombudsman Bureau	1973-1981; 2003	US, Indiana		98	859	26 prisons, 17 visits made in 2009
Kentucky Corrections Ombudsman	1975	US, Michigan	4	256	786	15 prisons, each visited at least once
Michigan Legislative Corrections Ombudsman	1982	US, Kentucky	2	69		
Prisons and Probation Ombudsman for England and Wales	1994	UK, England and Wales	113.7 (50.2 investigating complaints)	6,388	4,466 (pertaining to the Prison Service)	138 prisons, visited according to necessity for investigations
The Prisoner Ombudsman for Northern Ireland	2005	UK, Northern Ireland	11	777	493	3 prisons, all frequently visited
Justizvollzugs-beauftragter des Landes Nord-rhein-Westfalen	2007; extension of remit 2010	Germany, North Rhine-Westphalia	4 (1 exclusively investigating complaints)	250	476	37 prisons, 40 visits – at least one each

The introduction of the most long-standing prison ombudsman took place in Canada in 1973. However, this was not the first prison ombudsman to be introduced. This title is held by the Pennsylvania Office introduced in 1971, which existed for three weeks only.[343] The table shows a proliferation rate for those offices that were sustained of about two per decade. Please note that under these circumstances knowledge transfer in between legal systems could have been possible even where the two offices introduced in 1973 are concerned as the Canadian Correctional Investigator was placed on a Statutory footing in 1992 and the Indiana Department of Corrections Ombudsman Bureau has been reinstated 22 years after its abolishment. Whether knowledge transfer between legal systems is possible will be discussed in section III. of this chapter. The question of its occurrence in case of prison ombudsinstitutions is deliberated in chapter D.

Please note that staff numbers and annual budgets roughly correspond with the number of complaints and prison visits.

III. Learning processes in between legal systems

The two previous sections of this chapter provided a closer look at how the ombudsman concept developed and how the diversification, including the invention of prison ombudsmen, ensued. What has so far only been implied is that this development was based on learning processes occurring between different legal systems.

1. The possibility of knowledge transfer

A precondition for this is that learning and knowledge transfer from one legal system to another is possible. Although Aristotle advised his "fellow citizens of the rationality of engaging in lesson-drawing from positive and negative experiences in the development of great city states" in his *Nicomachean Ethics* as early as 315BC and academicians nowadays proclaim a general upsurge due to globalization factors increasingly pressuring politicians to favour evidence-based, risk adverse decision-making which highlights knowledge transfer as the more "rational choice" compared to innovation, the possibility of its existence has not met with unanimous acceptance.[344]

---

343 Fitzharris (1973), p. 4
344 Evans (2009b), pp. 237f; for the globalization argument see also Mamadouh et al. (2002), p. 7

There are two conflicting views: While one accepts the occurrence of learning processes and the interchange of knowledge, the other insists that learning from foreign legal systems is impossible. The universalistic view sees law as a culturally autonomous system ultimately similar in form and content across all cultures. Under this assumption, law in all jurisdictions constitutes different "species of the same genus", subject to the same questions and criteria. A culturally neutral analysis without reference to local substance is considered possible. Legal dissimilarities between different jurisdictions can be classified as variations of the same theme. Consequently, universalists set out by looking for similarities and are generally accepting of the idea of constructive learning processes occurring between different legal systems.

The opposing view understands law as a part of culture – an articulation of the common identity of a particular society. In this case, it becomes essential to get to know another legal culture and understand its "local knowledge". A neutral analysis becomes impossible as a "different structure of meaning" through which legal discourse may be understood has to be established. Subscribers to this cultural view therefore search for differences between legal systems and believe the occurrence of inter-legal-systems-learning-processes to be unfeasible or so difficult that they are nearly impossible.

Since the views are irreconcilable, it has to be resolved which view proves more relevant in the context of this particular study.

a) Negated

According to the cultural view, the process of learning from foreign legal institutions is unfeasible or nearly impossible. To establish how the culturalist arrives at this conviction, a description of what it involves and how it works seems necessary.

Culturalism advocates "politics of understanding [… that] call for the voice of the other and, specifically, for the voice of the other-in-law to be allowed to be heard over the chatter seeking to silence it".[345] The voice of other is made accessible during the process of comparison by interpreters prepared to intervene for another legal culture.[346] This process of comparison involves two internal stages. One in which the interpretivist interpreter amplifies the appreciation for different structures of meaning and a second step preparing the process of externalization by determining how to convey as a cultural intermediary the acquired understanding in the unfitting terminology of the interpreter's primary legal language. In the context of this study, a culturalist would point out the dif-

---

345   Legrand (2003), p. 250
346   Here and in the following: Legrand (1995), p. 262

ficulty for a German scholar with his/her background in the German *Beauftrag-ten*-culture to fully grasp the ombudsman concept as well as the secondary diffi-culty of conveying any gained knowledge to fellow German scholars. Although this is considered to be the only possible approach to understand the "other", it is fraught with the conditions and presuppositions, the so called *Vorverständnis*, of the interpretivist.[347] The resulting legal perspective or *Vorstellung* can never be one from "within", of the community's inner perspective. Any attempt at it is doomed to fail. There is no such thing as a neutral perspective or objectivity in comparison.

> "As a foreigner, one's first knowledge of another legal system is always meditated in the sense that one necessarily views others within the meanings constructed in one's own language and legal language. Such mediation can never be effaced, for it always remains one's initial point of contact with another system: the fact that one approached the foreign system in a mediated way can never be undone or eradicated, no matter how long one eventually lives within the system. [...] Gadamer calls [this] 'the impenetrability of the otherness of the other.'"[348]

Consequently, critical distance even to the interpreter's own observations is nec-essary because "one cannot 'be' the other" and "the gap between that which is being said and that about which that which is being is being said simply cannot vanish".[349] From this, Legrand, who nowadays seems to be to culturalism what Zweigert/Kötz are to functionalism, concludes that "differentiation must be cen-tral to any comparative study".[350] Taken to the extreme, this attitude would pre-clude any sensible comparison as no true understanding of or insight into anoth-er legal culture may ever be gained.

When applied to the question of learning processes about legal institutions occurring in between legal systems, this culturalist view considers it impossible to understand or adequately learn anything about any legal institution – such as the ombudsman – outside of one's own legal system. Since one's own *Vorverständnis* may never be overcome, the comparativist interpreter may only work at carefully modifying his/her own *Vorstellung* of a specific institution in the secure knowledge that it will never reach that of an educated insider. Since one cannot transfer what one cannot understand, learning about legal institutions from another legal system is doomed from the outset. The extreme consequence of this idea would be the idea that wherever and whenever a new legal institu-tion is created it owes its existence either to the creative powers of those persons acting at that precise moment of time or the same persons' misunderstandings

---

347   Here and in the following: Legrand (2003), p. 251
348   Legrand (1995), p. 266; Gadamer (1989), p. 27
349   Legrand (2003), p. 251
350   Legrand (2003), p. 251; Zweigert/Kötz (1998)

due to deficient learning from other legal systems, which when thoroughly considered are in turn simply creative products of the same persons.

This consistent culturalist view has at once attracted appreciation and criticism for representing a neo-romantic turn.[351] While acknowledging the need for critical voices like Legrand, Whitman recalls that the Romantic tradition is not only famous for authentic sensitivity and occasional profundity but also for "generating moments of colossal silliness and of distasteful moral relativism" and warns that too much love for difference and "fascination with sheer 'otherness' will deteriorate into a kind of thumb-twiddling reverie". He points out that Legrand significantly differs from Gadamer whose goal in "understanding" is not simply knowledge of a thing, proposition or form of action but also its application. Although the process of application involves the inarticulate and difficult to communicate *Vorverständnis*, this does not mean that it is entirely impossible to convey.[352] Contrariwise, Gadamer's rejection of the Ditheyan[353] claim that all understanding must be "total" understanding tried to make the hermeneutic problem tractable. Following this Gadamerian approach, Whitman argues that "it is not meaningless to speak of 'understanding' legal practices even if we have not fully plumbed all of the *Vorverständnis*, all of the underlying sensibilities, that inform and motivate them" for "what we aim to 'understand' is not total *culture* – an impossibility. What we aim to understand is human action – a much less daunting undertaking."

If one were to follow the Gadamerian approach as favoured by Whitman, constructive learning processes about foreign legal institutions would become a possibility under the pre-condition that the comparativist interpreter tries to achieve as complete an understanding as possible. But how far would the interpreter need to take this process? If his understanding is not total, how could he even measure how far he/she has overcome the own *Vorverständnis* and approached the *Vorstellung* of the insider of the legal system hosting the institution? Although neither Gadamer nor Whitman negate the possible occurrence of constructive learning processes, they do not provide us with any methodology to judge or define an adequate example thereof. Consequently, their culturalist views, which are moderate compared to Legrand, do not present us with a viable working approach towards establishing whether learning processes about specific institutions from foreign legal systems do indeed occur.

---

351   Here and in the following: Whitman (2003), p. 314
352   Here and in the following: Whitman (2003), p. 325
353   Gadamer (1990), pp. 222-4

b) Accepted

As previously described, the culturalist view is opposed by the universalistic view, which sees law as a culturally autonomous system ultimately similar in form and content across all cultures. While not unanimous, the universalistic view holds that generally a constructive process of learning may occur in between legal systems, based on the assumption of the similarity of all legal systems.[354] Its followers acknowledge the significance of the idea imported or the legal features reproduced across time and space is determined by the local user and may lead to the sacrifice of autochthonous elements.[355] However, this is only the case because "legal systems *do* permit transcultural discussion and transcultural change".[356]

This opinion is shared by those advocating a moderate version of universalism. They hold that where learning processes are concerned, the culturalist and the universalist view are not entirely mutually exclusive. Some[357] even believe that there remains some methodological middle-ground. According to them, the last decade has "seen some reconciliation [...] and an agreement might be in sight that propositions of either similarity or difference should be abandoned in favour of an approach which allows for both similarity and difference"[358], while seeking both "explanation as well as understanding"[359] without preference. Cotterrell agrees that "there is no point in simply defending, in generalized, abstract terms, either the promotion of legal harmonization or protection of legal difference in distinctive legal cultures".[360]

This approaches the position of the moderate culturalists established in the previous section, namely that an understanding of human action is possible even with an incomplete grasp of all underlying *Vorverständnisse*. If law as a form of human action and legal institutions as the products of human action can be understood for example by means of transcultural discussion, it can also be imitated based on the learning processes that have occurred.[361] Law is more than simply purpose-oriented human action as it stakes a claim for normative justification by being the right action to take. Consequently, imitation and inter-legal-

---

354   For the extensive debate on functionalism see Zweigert/Kötz (1998), Bell (2006), Michaels (2006), Dannemann (2006)

355   Here and in the following: Graziadei (2006), p. 469f

356   Whitman (2003), p. 341

357   Cotterell (2000), p. 39; Whitman (2003), pp. 329, 336; Örücü (2002), p. 9; Zedner (1995), p. 519

358   Dannemann (2006), p. 391

359   Nelken (1997), p. 478

360   Cotterell (2000), p. 53

361   Here and in the following: Whitman (2003), p. 343

system-learning-processes are encouraged. Universalists acknowledge the possibility of the development of legal institutions such as the ombudsman by means of knowledge transfer in between different legal cultures.

The details of this noted approximation of the culturalist and universalist views do not have to be discerned here. For, in any case, the universalist view in all its forms embraces the idea of inter-legal-system-learning processes and offers a methodology to describe these learning processes. This suits this study's aim to demonstrate constructive learning progress using concrete examples of the implementation practice of prison ombudsmen. As Merryman states, it "is perfectly acceptable for a scholar to attempt to deal with a manageable piece of reality rather than take on everything".[362]

Following this position, this study considers the occurrence of learning processes in between legal system to be possible. This study will therefore go on to examine the methodology proposed by the universalists for its suitability to describe learning processes in between legal systems and its applicability to prison ombudsmen.

2. The perspectives

The study of the occurrence of learning processes in between nation states or legal systems is not limited to a specific academic field. In the past decades, it has increasingly become a focus of interest – especially when amalgamated with a comparative approach – for political and social scientists, as well as those interested in law and international relations. Its multi-disciplinary character has previously been acknowledged both as strength as well as weakness.[363] The latter becomes evident upon consideration of the lack of terminological, theoretical and methodological unity. Evans and Davies observe that "despite complementary research agendas, these disciplines have continued to speak past each other". Marsh and Sharman acknowledge both this obstacle to the extension of knowledge and the call for a process of standardization and especially terminological unification but opine that "this will not be easy and, to date, there have been few, if any, attempts to combine the various literatures into an integrated approach".[364]

Thus, some discussion of terminology seems unavoidable. The terminology includes everything from lesson drawing[365], policy convergence[366], policy diffu-

---

362   Legrand (1999), p. 40
363   Here and in the following: Evans/Davies (1999), p. 361
364   Marsh/Sharman (2009), p. 269
365   Rose (1993), p. ix

sion[367], policy coordination[368], policy transfer[369], policy mimesis[370], policy emulation[371], policy band wagoning[372], institutional isomorphism[373], institutional
transfer[374], institutional transplantation[375], legal transplant[376] or transplantation[377], legal reception[378], legal mixing[379] or cross-fertilization[380]. The design of
the different terms, on the one hand, shows their local heritage. De Jong et al.
summarize the latter saying:

> "Exporters and importers of legal frameworks are often members of the group of
> civil law systems where government and administration are often approached from a
> legal angle and where policy change is supposed to be initiated through transfor-
> mation of the legal framework. Exporters and importers of lessons, ideologies and
> ideas, often have Common Law systems where legal and judicial change is seen as
> the tailpiece of policy change instead of its key part".[381]

This is reflected in the terminology through a preference for either "policy transfer" or "legal transfer". On the other hand, the design of the terms shows their
respective affiliation with a specific discipline where they have been created to
depict the influence of different concepts such as the emphasis on agency or
structure, pattern-finding or process-tracing, coercive or voluntary transfer. Although the terms are not identical, "the difference in nomenclature [is] not overly
significant"[382] once it is recognized that the literatures using them are complementary.[383] Consequently, ideas developed within single disciplines may – upon
careful consideration – be applied to other, related disciplines and their problems. We are therefore left with seven objects that can potentially become the
objective of learning processes in between legal systems: "policy, goals, struc-

---

366   Coleman (1994), p. 274
367   Majone (1991), p. 79
368   Haas (1992), p. 3
369   Radaelli (2000), p. 25
370   Massey (2009), p. 383
371   Dolowitz/Marsh (1996), p. 344
372   Ikenberry (1990), p. 88
373   DiMaggio/Powell (1991), p. 73
374   Jacoby (2000), p. xi
375   De Jong (1999), p. 213
376   Watson (1974)
377   Mamadouh et al. (2002), p. 4
378   Graziadei (2006), p. 443
379   Örücü et al. (1996)
380   Graziadei (2006), p. 444
381   De Jong et al. (2002), p. 291
382   Dolowitz/Marsh (1996), p. 344
383   Marsh/Sharman (2009), pp. 269, 271

ture and content; policy instruments or administrative techniques; institutions; ideology; ideas, attitudes and concepts; and negative lessons".[384]

This study focuses on prison ombudsmen as institutions, which in the language of Evans constitutes a "second order change to the policy instruments themselves such as the development of new institutions and delivery systems".[385] This study's perspective on this change belongs to the realm of comparative law – specifically comparative administrative law since it asks about the institution as defined by rules and regulations and charged with a supervisory control function.[386] The focus on learning about specific legal institutions or problems is also a characteristic for microcomparison.[387] Its opposite, macrocomparison, aims at the comparison of the spirit and style of different legal systems as whole. The dividing line between micro- and macrocomparison will be approached during the course of this study when two examples will be given whose descriptions will include country surveys of the host penal systems. However, this mention of the examples' embedment within their legal systems is employed solely to achieve a greater understanding of the individual institution's systemic context. No complete description or comparison of penal systems is intended. Instead, the study relies on those efforts previously undertaken by others.[388] Consequently, this study may overall be allocated within the frame of microcomparison.

3. The two step process

Even within the limited field of microcomparison, no affirmed terminology for learning processes has yet been established – a fact that may be due to the large bandwidth of possible forms of learning processes as well as to the rapid growth of the field.[389] Whilst it was possible to simply acknowledge the terminological diversity where different disciplinary perspectives were concerned, some selection has to be made from the micro-comparative vocabulary available to establish coherence within this study.

The comparative law literature describes inter-legal-system-learning processes with such terms as "circulation of legal models" – favoured mostly out-

---

384 Dolowitz/Marsh (1996), pp. 349f
385 Evans (2009a), p. 247
386 Pollitt (2011), p. 115 explicitly considers ombudsmen a proper subject of comparative administrative law.
387 c.f. Zweigert/Kötz (1998), pp. 4f
388 c.f. Lazarus (2004) in English and Koeppel (1999) in German.
389 Here and in the following: Graziadei (2006), p. 443

side the common law world –, "transfer" or "reception" of law or with more generic terms such as "inspiration". Two of the most commonly used terms are "legal transplant" and "cross-fertilization". The former possibly has met with the most widespread use[390] and describes situations in which entire legal structures are transplanted from one legal system to another. While this is the most direct and visible form of an occurring learning process, the term "is based on a metaphor that was chosen *faute de mieux*" and is "ill-adapted to capturing the gradual diffusion of the law or the continuous nature of the process that sometimes leads to legal change through the appropriation of foreign ideas".[391] Leyland prefers the term "cross-fertilization" for the public law domain as "a more useful approach to considering the formulation and development of law" through "an absorption of influences".[392]

However, both terms are not ideal. This becomes apparent when they are compared to the also suggested term "reception", which places the focus not on the "donor" legal systems but on the "recipient" legal system. While "legal transplant" with its resemblance to medical technical terms seems to suggest a process involving a careful learning process at the time when a foreign legal system or a foreign legal institution such as an ombudsman is considered, it does not say anything about how the learned material is received within in the host system. Maybe an example borrowed from the world of medicine will elucidate this point.[393] Here, the transplant is extracted in a careful process during which the medical personnel takes note of the properties of the donor and examines the quality of the product before readying it for emergency transport. How the organ transplant will be handled during the transport across the border and how it will be integrated into the recipient by the foreign doctors, they can neither know nor influence. This may be done perfectly or the organ may be spoiled during the transport or wasted later due to a failure to attach it to the recipient or its incompatibility with the recipient's organism.

The term "cross-fertilization" is just as imprecise. It suggests a less conscious, less structured process of learning from a different legal system, but gives no indication about the reception process. Although this term draws on agricultural terminology (maybe the random flight of pollen across a field), a medicinal example is used to ensure the comparability with the first example. Cross-fertilization may be compared to a sloppy organ-extraction which in the

---

390   C.f. Menski (2006), p. 50; Michaels (2006), p. 341; Nelken (2003), p. 20; Plessis (2006), p. 487; Schlesinger et al. (1998), p. 17; Whitman (2003), p. 336
391   Graziadei (2006), p. 443
392   Leyland (2002), p. 217
393   Watson (1974), p. 27 already made use of medical comparisons for elucidation purposes.

best case does not improve the donor's health and in the worst case is extracted without taking care of ligaments, blood vessels etc. necessary for reattachment to the recipient. That it will be reattached is implied by the terminology, to whom, how and with what care is not indicated. However, that the recipient is "fertile soil", readily prepared to receive the donation is just as important. Reapplied to the question of learning processes this means that the implementation is originated and guided by local actors whose choice "about what to do with the imported model can include options that would leave the authors of the original model baffled, surprised, or disappointed", frequently producing not only a pluralism but outright hybridization of ideas – not all of which may prove to be functional.[394] Where ombudsmen are concerned, such a disappointment has first been proclaimed by Rowat and has since been repeatedly reiterated by others.[395]

Consequently, the "fit" or nature of the legal structure to be transferred does not solely determine the success of the transplant. Further factors to be considered are the character of the transfer process including "accessibility of information concerning the proposed change, the disclosure of its potential impact on the interested parties, and the degree and kind of the actors' involvement in the project"[396] as well as the adaptation of the legal product and the preparation of the receiving legal system.

To emphasize the point: While a learning process does not require the student to have a personified teacher and can be handled by means of self-education, it does always involve the taking of knowledge from one place and transferring it to another. A learning process necessarily consists of two acts. The same is true in our organ donation example: step 1 is taking the organ from the donor, step 2 placing it into the recipient. The example, however, is not perfect. An organ donation can theoretically be handled by a single doctor taking the organ from one person and placing it in another while the same is not true where inter-legal-system-learning is concerned. The first phase of the learning process, the acquisition phase, can theoretically be handled by a sole actor learning about another legal system or institution and resolving to push for its implementation without the knowledge of the "donor" state. Of course, in praxis the involvement of multiple agents such as epistemic communities[397], pressure groups, global finance and supra-national institutions is the more likely scenario. In any case, the implementation phase of inter-legal-system-learning can never be solitary, but involves multiple agents such as administrators, politicians etc.

394   Graziadei (2006), p. 458, 462, 465
395   Rowat (1985), p. 182; Seneviratne (1994), pp. 13f; Gottehrer et al. (2000), p. 357; Abedin (2011), p. 10
396   Graziadei (2006), p. 459, 461
397   For a definition see Stone (2000), p. 58

that may influence how the knowledge acquired in the learning process is handled. The reception must therefore always be considered.

Consequently, the terms "legal transplant", "cross-fertilization" and "reception" are not synonyms – as Graziadei notes they are used in the literature[398] – for they refer to distinct steps of the learning process. While the former two imply a two-step process, their focus is more on the acquisition phase; the latter "reception" solely refers to the implementation phase. However, both phases are of equal importance. Neither can be ignored without rendering the other useless.[399]

The medical example also shows that "legal transplant" and "cross-fertilization" are not synonymous. Here the difference is gradual and lies in the different amount of consciousness and care involved in the process. Consequently, the learning process occurring in between legal systems can be represented as follows:

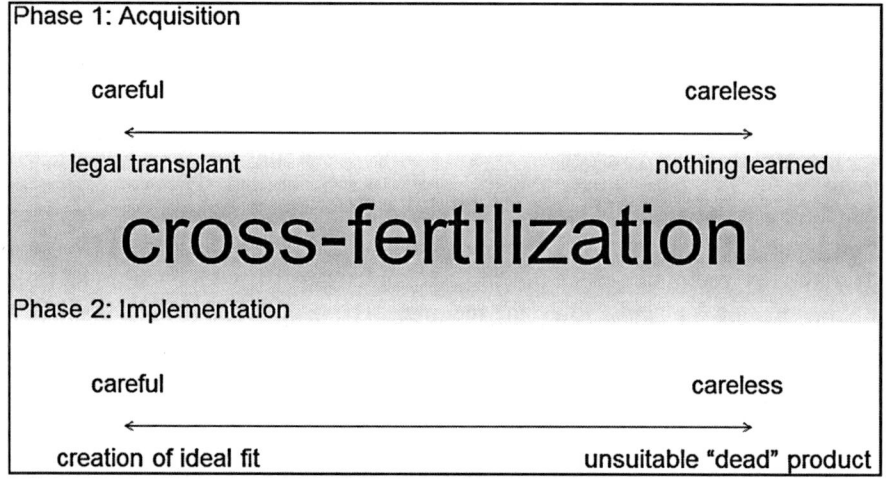

Figure 4: Learning processes between legal systems

---

398   Graziadei (2006), p. 443
399   Mossberger/Wolman (2003), p. 430, suggest a three step process of awareness, assessment and application. However, some learning processes skip the assessment stage making indiscriminate use of the learned knowledge. Even where it is carried out, it appears to be not so much its own step but an improved version of awareness, which graphically would look like **Fehler! Verweisquelle konnte nicht gefunden werden.** below.

From either point on the line symbolizing the bandwidth of possibilities in Phase 1 it is equally possible to move to any point on the line symbolizing the bandwidth of possibilities in Phase 2. This means that it is possible to perfectly accomplish the acquisition of knowledge in learning phase 1 creating an ideal legal transplant, fit it carefully into the host legal system in phase 2 and render it a highly useful working product. But the ideal transplant of phase 1 may also be mutilated in the implementation process or be simply incompatible with the host legal system causing the end product to either be discarded entirely or implemented as a mere carcass, which never takes up work or produces any result. This is exemplified in Figure 5.

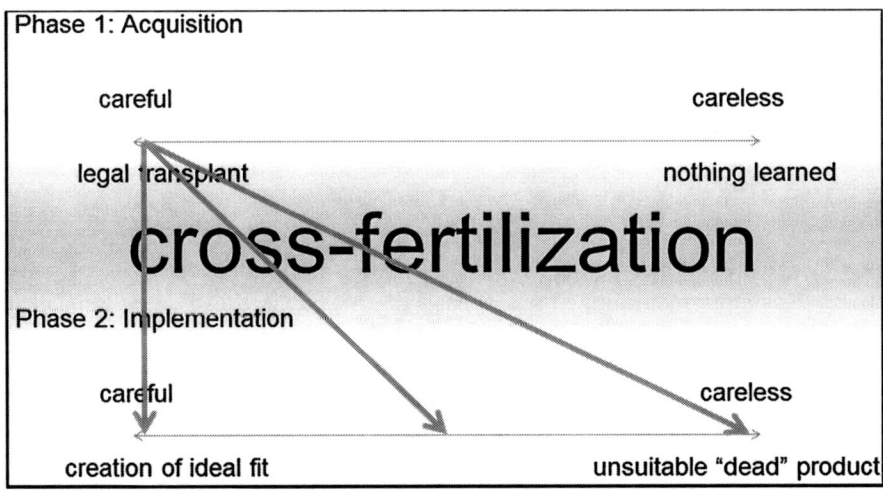

Figure 5: Possible outcomes of careful acquisition phase

The opposite is also possible. An idea originating in a foreign legal system may seep across the border – in theory, the knowledge can be so limited, for example to only a name, that absolutely nothing is learned. But wherever the merest knowledge of a diffuse concept is gained – even if no one makes an effort to study it properly – phase 1 is accomplished with a product of cross-fertilization. This again may be carelessly implemented leaving an unsuitable "dead" product or it may be carefully fitted into the host legal system.

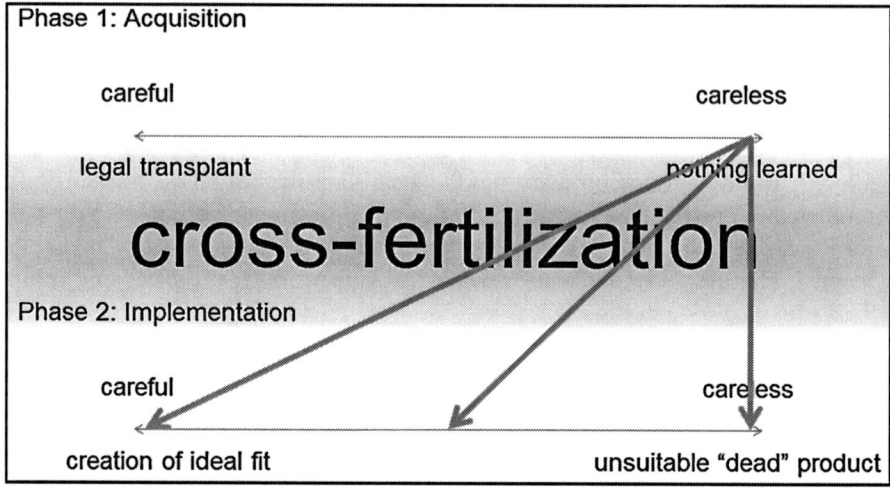

Figure 6: Possible outcomes of careless acquisition phase

The greater the knowledge gathered and the care taken during each phase, the closer the product will resemble the creation of an ideal fitting legal transplant. It is important to note the emphasis on the "ideal fitting" legal transplant. As a legal transplant alone in this case meaning greatest possible awareness of the learned object, is not enough as demonstrated by the second and third arrow in Figure 6. This is due to the width of options during the process of inter-legal-system- learning spanning: copying, emulation, hybridization, synthesis and inspiration[400]. Despite the "analytically separate and distinct" presentation, considering this to be a neat division would be rather contrived.[401] Nevertheless, each has its own *raison d' être* whose suitability to the host countries current situation and needs has to be established individually.

4. The driving factors

Knowing that learning processes do indeed occur in between legal systems raises the question about the source, catalyst or driving factors for their occurrence. Maybe a word of caution is necessary here: While "[i]nstitutional isomorphic processes can be expected to proceed in the absence of evidence that it increases internal organizational efficiency" and it is a truism that "[s]imilarity can make it easier for organizations to transact with other organizations, to attract career-

---

400   Dolowitz/Marsh (1996), p. 351
401   Marsh/Sharman (2009), p. 272

minded staff, to be acknowledged as legitimate and reputable, and to fit into administrative categories that define eligibility for public and private grants and contracts", this by no means equates to "conformist organizations do[ing] what they do more efficiently than [...] their more deviant peers".[402] This does not detract from the appeal of the question why such learning processes come about – in fact it is the opposite. Aligned with the qualitative approach of this study, this question treats knowledge transfer as a non-dichotomous, dependent variable in an attempt to explain why and to what degree learning occurs.[403]

The heterogeneity of local learning and experimentation processes frequently leaves their sources or motivational starting points cloaked in ambiguity.[404] Factors causing legal change can be as varied as migration of populations, political decisions, religious, moral or philosophical influences, technological change or any combination thereof. Comparative studies generally impact political decisions less than internationally unifying factors in the form of international treaties and conventions. According to Graziadei, the three factors most commonly at the root of legal change today are the "imposition of law through violence in one form or another; change produced by the desire to follow prestigious models; and reform for the purpose of improving economic performance".

Today, one such prestigious model driving inter-legal-system-learning-process is the ombudsman concept. Where legal learning processes are driven by prestigious models, it does not require in-depth knowledge of the lending legal system. This does not mean that there is none. Yet, most countries implementing an ombudsman were not aware that they were choosing between the traditional Scandinavian and the more modern Danish version. This consideration of loosely defined models or process of learning from different models provides "domestic actors more leeway to make combinations that fit their desires and circumstances".[405] Plausible evidence has been accumulating that "considering only one definite model makes the transplantation process less easy".

Our two step learning process model established above also suggests this outcome. This becomes apparent when a modified version of our previous example is applied. Let the donated product not be an organ but blood. This is usually taken from a blood bank and not specifically extracted for this recipient. This does not mean that there is no donor. It just constitutes a simplification

---

402   DiMaggio/Powell (1991), p. 73
403   c.f.,Marsh/Sharman (2009), p. 278. While no less legitimate, the treatment as an independent variable which uses the process of policy transfer to explain why a particular policy was adopted has been previously been declared less interesting - c.f. Dolowitz/Marsh (1996), p. 354.
404   Here and in the following: Graziadei (2006), p. 455f, 473
405   Here and in the following: De Jong et al. (2002), p. 288

where all usual requirements of care as to the donor's health, the extraction process etc. as well as the process of acquisition are on the one hand more standardized and on the other hand more flexible and speedy compared with a limitation to a single donor.

Graziadei's comparative law perspective on the driving factors for the occurrence of inter-legal-system-learning process can be further enriched by drawing on concepts developed in the adjacent disciplines mentioned above (chapter B III. 2.). There, the question of what catalysts are instigating learning process has been broken down into three parts: the matter of agents, voluntariness and timing.

The literature on policy transfer identifies at least eight main categories of transfer agents: "politicians; bureaucrats; policy entrepreneurs including think-tanks; knowledge institutions (KIs), academicians and other experts; pressure groups; global finance institutions; international organizations; and supra-national institutions".[406] The applicability of their double impact on the spread of the ombudsman idea in general through advocacy of lessons and their "nationwide and international network contacts that are a source of ideas for new programs"[407]has already been acknowledged by Dolowitz and Marsh[408] to be demonstrated by Rowat's study of ombudsmen, in which the latter argues that "[t]here is no doubt that the ombudsmen themselves have been very influential in bringing about further spread of the institution, particularly Professor Hurwitz in Denmark [...] and Sir Guy Powles of New Zealand".[409]

The question of agency is irrevocably connected with the next driving factor of inter-legal-system-learning – that of voluntariness. While unintentional convergence due to common outside pressures such as harmonizing macroeconomic forces is possible, there frequently is an element of intentionality involved in learning processes, which raises the question about the level of voluntariness or coercion involved.[410] Some agents such as global finance institutions (like the International Monetary Fund) and supra-national institutions (like the European Union[411]) tend to use coercion to achieve desired policy action.[412] Other agents such as domestic politicians and epistemic communities are precluded from using coercion and instead rely on voluntary processes for which the primary sug-

---

406   Evans (2009a), p. 244
407   Rose (1993), p. 56 and Dolowitz/Marsh (1996), p. 345
408   Dolowitz/Marsh (1996), p. 345
409   Rowat (1973), p. 119
410   Here and in the following: Evans (2009a), p. 244
411   c.f. Radaelli (2000), p. 26, whose particular focus is on the influence of the Commission
412   c.f. Dolowitz/Marsh (1996), p. 344

gested catalyst is "some form of dissatisfaction model or problem with the status quo".[413] For their desired policy change they use lessons "in a number of ways and for a variety of reasons. Both supporters and opponents of various policies uses lessons selectively to gain advantage in the struggle to get their ideas accepted." To that end policy lessons are frequently "put forward as politically neutral truths" whilst clandestinely being waged as "political weapons".

Evans and Davies developed a model identifying twelve stages of voluntary transfer.[414] Its graphic representation in Figure 7 has been expanded to distinguish the two phases (acquisition and implementation) of cross-fertilization processes established above. Please note that the passage from acquisition to implementation phase is a gradual one and could also be argued to occur as early as between categories three and four or as late as between categories nine and ten.

Process of transfer						
	1 Recognition	2 Search	3 Contact	4 Emergence of Information Feeder Network	5 Cognition & Reception	6 Emergence of Transfer Network
Acquisition Phase	- discourse pull - dissatisfaction - cyclical events - conflict - legitimation	- regime - international - transnational - national - regional - local				
	→	→	→	→	→	→
Implementation Phase	7 Elite & Cognitive Mobilization	8 Interaction	9 Evaluation	10 Decision Enters Policy Stream	11 Process	12 Outcome
	→	→	→	→	→	

Figure 7: The chain of events during a transfer process

The capacity of an issue to pass through all twelve stages of voluntary transfer is often contingent on the type of agent involved as well as the third driving factor for the occurrence of knowledge transfer in between legal systems, which is the timing of environmental factors asfor example changes in economic conditions or government.[415] Considering the bandwidth of cross-fertilization demonstrated above, it is not surprising that "the process of voluntary transfer can break off at any point past search and still result in a form of transfer (for example, the drawing of a lesson, symbolic or perceptual transfer)". Timing works as a trigger for the recognition described in stage 1 of Figure 8 and as

---

413   Here and in the following: Dolowitz/Marsh (1996), p. 346
414   Evans/Davies (1999), p. 377, Figure 2
415   Here and in the following: Evans/Davies (1999), p. 376

such is always a key driving factor. Evans and Davies list discourse pull, dissatisfaction, cyclical events, conflict and legitimation as factors for onset of a voluntary learning process. De Jong et al.[416] try to describe the same timing factor as "[s]pecial periods of regime transformation characterized by a sense of emergency and urgency (e.g. system upheaval, nation building or national financial performance crisis) [that] create policy windows and critical junctures that facilitate the transplantation process". At the same time, they acknowledge that "what makes for historical uniqueness, acute performance crisis or national system upheaval is relatively hard to define". Consequently, an allowance has to be made for a gradation between different levels of crisis. The lower the level the more likely it is that attempts are "protracted and not extremely influential [... meet] with generally mediocre enthusiasm [... proceed] slowly [...] simply fail [...] or were overall helpful but not very pervasive".[417] Nevertheless, there seems to be a consensus "that system upheaval or severe performance crisis at the national level are a comparatively fertile breeding ground for pervasive change".[418]

The role of timing and the kind of agents involved in the knowledge transfer and implementation processes of prison ombudsmen will be examined in chapter D.

---

416 Here and in the following: De Jong et al. (2002), p. 291
417 Here and in the following: De Jong et al. (2002), p. 292 (includes empirical evidence through comprehensive case study)
418 Certainly between Evans/Davies (1999) and De Jong et al. (2002); of the same opinion: Marsh/Sharman (2009), p. 272

C Methodology

This chapter deals with the selection and execution of the methods applied in this study.

I. Method selection

This chapter introduces grounded theory as the method underlying this entire research process. Additionally, it explains the application of qualitative instead of quantitative methods, describes the sources employed and the processes followed in this research study. It also explains the selection of the two studied examples which is necessary to demonstrate this study's findings. This section will conclude with a description of the possible influence of the researcher on the results.

1. Grounded theory

Grounded theory building was chosen over all other methods because of the project's focus on prison ombudsmen as a rarely explored phenomenon for which extant theory did not appear to be appropriate. This was done in the hope that a grounded theory building approach was more likely to generate novel and accurate insights into the phenomenon under study.

This researcher recognises that the design of this study may on first sight appear incongruent with the chosen methodology. While grounded theory is nowadays a well-established method, it is still infrequently used. Hence, this researcher opted for a classic mode of presentation in an effort to increase the usability of this study. The incongruence of methodology and design is strictly limited to the presentation of the results. The research itself was conducted in rigorous accord with the rules of grounded theory.

Grounded theory as a method was developed by Anselm Strauss and Barney Glaser during a joined research project in a process which they described in their only common methodological publication *The Discovery of Grounded Theory: Strategies for Qualitative Research* in 1967.[419] They begin their book stating that

> "Most writing on sociological methods has been concerned with how accurate facts can be obtained and how theory can thereby be more rigorously tested. In this book

---

419   For details on the history of their cooperation see Boychuck Duchscher/Morgan (2004), p. 606

we address ourselves to the equally important enterprise of *how the discovery of theory from data – systematically obtained and analyzed in social research – can be furthered.* We believe that the discovery of theory from the data – which we call *grounded theory* – is a major task confronting sociology today, for, as we shall try to show, such a theory fits empirical situations, and is understandable to sociologists and layman alike. Most important, it works – provides us with relevant predictions, explanations, interpretations and applications".[420]

Even in its conciseness this quote already reveals why "grounded theory is often heralded as revolutionary"[421]: It breaks with the traditional research logic of developing a theory and then systematically seeking out evidence to verify it by completely reversing it – "researchers using grounded theory set out to gather data and then systematically develop a theory directly derived from the data". The sequential proceeding in which planning, data collection and theory building constitute separate work stages is exchanged for a constant interplay between action (data collection) and reflection (data analysis via coding procedures and theory building) that starts as soon as the very first item of data is collected.[422] In face of their preliminary character, any results both direct the further process of data collection and analysis as well as assist the continuous specification of the research question accompanied by the incessant generation and development of hypotheses. The ensuing discovery of a theory grounded in data renounces the traditional idea of scientific theories as static models of the studied reality.

The diverse background of Glaser and Strauss – from the University of Chicago and Columbia University respectively – "combined the depth and richness of qualitative interpretive traditions with the logic, rigor and systematic analysis inherent in quantitative research".[423]

The success of the their grounded theory sometimes hides the fact that the common ground established between Glaser and Strauss during their "ironic conjunction of careers" remained rather small – in fact limited to their pointed critique of a positivistic-functionalistic social research oriented around the criteria of "objective" sciences.[424] This becomes evident in their further – exclusively separate – publications. Glaser's insistence on the centrality of "constant comparison" for the procedure exposes his understanding of grounded theory to be

---

420　Glaser/Strauss (1967), p. 1
421　Here and in the following: Walker/Myrick (2006), pp. 547f
422　Here and in the following: Mey/Mruck (2007b), p. 12
423　Walker/Myrick (2006), p. 548
424　Glaser/Strauss (1967), p. vii; Strübing (2007), p. 161

informed by the rather critical-rationalist oriented Columbia School.[425] As one of the leading representatives of a pragmatic reformulated interactionism in the style of the Chicago School, Strauss – who never answered Glaser's critique directly – may accept this as identifying the procedural focus but would insist that this fails to describe the methodological centre of grounded theory.

While both original authors still adhere to the same basic research process and procedures, their difference in background and opinion has formed two different versions of grounded theory – a fact that has unfortunately not manifested itself in a diversification of terminology.[426] While this similarity of "language and process make[s] any discussion of differences confusing", it explains why grounded theory is the "most frequently discussed, debated and disputed" of the qualitative research methods. Here, the effort to establish a coherent research design dictates a discussion of the commonalities and conflicts of grounded theory as a style of research and its methodological procedures.[427] While Glaser's critique improved the visibility of the controversial aspects– it not only facilitated the choice between the two variants but also necessitated its explication.[428]

The main conflicts identified in the literature center on the handling of theory, theoretical sensitivity and the matter of verification.[429]

The conflict about verification asks whether theory's claim is limited to the development of theory from empirical data or extends to its simultaneous verification.[430] Strauss suggests the triad of induction, deduction and verification, which he understands as a plausibility review of the functionality of the empiri-

---

425 Glaser (1992), p. 7 and (1998), pp. 21f. Glaser's approach has since been referred to as both "classical" and fundamentalistic" – c.f. Glaser/Holton (2007), p. 48; Mey/Mruck (2007b), p. 18. Here and in the following: Strübing (2007), pp. 160f

426 Strübing (2007), p. 159; Mey/Mruck (2007b), p. 22; here and in the following: Walker/Myrick (2006), pp. 550, 547

427 Mey/Mruck (2007b), pp. 19, 17; the differences have induced some to speak of grounded theory methodologies in plural – c.f. Mey/Mruck (2007c), p. 43 and, alluding to the non-canonical quality of grounded theory, Strübing (2007), p. 159 there fn 2 – with further references

428 Strübing (2007), p. 172

429 Mey/Mruck (2007b), pp. 22, 32, Strübing (2007), pp. 161-169; more detail oriented observations like those by Walker/Myrick (2006), p. 556 focusing on the timing of processes ("Glaser's method is to fracture and select in substantive coding, than relate and integrate in theoretical coding. Strauss's method is fracture in open coding, relate and integrate in axial coding, and then select and integrate in selective coding. Consequently, it is difficult to directly compare theoretical versus selective coding.") are likewise correct but more helpful during method application than during method selection.

430 here and in the following: Strübing (2007), p. 167

cally developed theories. Glaser rejects the idea of verification as a necessary part of theory building.[431]

The debate about the handling of theory and theoretical sensitivity centers on the relation between data and theory. Kelle notes that even the earliest version of grounded theory in the *Discovery*-book contained two different perceptions:

> "on the one hand the idea is stressed that theoretical concepts 'emerge' from the data if the researcher approaches the field with no preconceived theories or hypotheses, on the other hand the researcher is advised to use his or her previous theoretical knowledge to identify theoretical relevant phenomena in the data".[432]

Glaser and Strauss note this tension early on declaring that "Of course, the researcher does not approach reality as a *tabula rasa*. He must have a perspective that will help him see relevant data and abstract significant categories from his scrutiny of the data".[433] Their methodological advice concerning this data scrutiny is limited to the remark that "sources of theoretical sensitivity build up in the sociologist an armamentarium of categories and hypotheses on substantive and formal levels".[434] What the sources of theoretical sensitivity are, how the researcher acquires such an armamentarium and how a researcher may use it to "avoid drowning in the data" remains unclear.[435] Kelle summarizes this problem saying that

> "[i]f one takes into account the frequent warnings not to force theoretical concepts on the data one gets the impression that a grounded theorist is advised to introduce suitable theoretical concepts *ad hoc* drawing on implicit theoretical knowledge but should abstain from approaching the empirical data with *ex ante* formulated hypotheses".

Glaser and Strauss clearly failed to integrate the two concepts. Glaser later went on to defend the emergence idea – a process he tries to explain saying that "once the GT researcher lets the meaning emerge and sees the pattern, he/she will feel 'sure' that this is what is going on".[436]

In *Basics of Qualitative Research* Strauss and Corbin explicate their approach to coding. At its center stands a "coding paradigm" that guides the researcher in the systematical examination of the data for causal conditions, phe-

---

431   Glaser (1978), p. 93
432   Kelle (2005), sec. 48
433   Glaser/Strauss (1967), p. 3
434   Glaser/Strauss (1967), p. 46
435   here and in the following: c.f. Kelle (2005), sec. 7-9
436   Glaser (1992), pp. 45ff; Glaser/Holton (2007), p. 58 (et passim); here and in the following: Glaser (2007), p. 2 (et passim)

nomena, context, intervening conditions, action strategies and consequences.[437] Glaser vehemently rejected this approach to handling theory saying "I request that you pull this book. It distorts and misconceives grounded theory, while engaging gross neglect of 90% of its important ideas".[438] Strübing identifies this position as inconsequent – pointing out Glaser's own "theoretical coding families".[439] While claiming that the latter facilitate emergence, Glaser holds that they should be prerequisite knowledge of any researcher. In truth, they constitute a generalized approach to translate incident-based codes into theoretical concepts.

Especially astonishing is Glaser's explanation that researchers may frequently be too limited in their conceptual focus and that his list of eighteen "coding families" should broaden their theoretical horizon. This clearly constitutes case-unrelated previous knowledge and clashes with Glaser's rejection of Strauss's "coding paradigm" on grounds of it imposing a – possibly unsuitable – theoretical structure on the data.

As an account of the full breadth of the discussion of the methodological conflict would require too much detail at this point and has been provided in existing research on this subject, the researcher hopes to have at least given an impression of the inconsistencies in Glaser's argument.[440] The greater openness and sophistication of Strauss's approach warranted the application of his methodological variant in this study.

2. Qualitative instead of quantitative research

So far no explanation was given as to why this study was based solely on qualitative research methods instead of favouring quantitative research or a mixed approach. This can be explained by the fact that prison ombudsmen have not been widely studied making this study to a large degree a first endeavour to provide insights into this field.

Qualitative methods can be applied "earlier" in the scientific research praxis than quantitative methods.[441] In fact, qualitative methods must always precede quantitative methods, but do not necessarily have to be followed-up by such.

---

437   Kelle (2005), sec. 49
438   Glaser (1992), p. 2
439   here and in the following: Strübing (2007), pp. 161, 165; Glaser (1978), pp. 72f ; Glaser (1992). pp. 45ff
440   c.f. Strübing (2007); Kelle (2005); Mey/Mruck (2007b); Walker/Myrick (2006); Boychuck Duchscher/Morgan (2004)
441   Here and in the following: Garz/Kraimer (1991), p. 17; Kleining (1982), p. 226

Wherever qualitative research explains a research objective, quantitative research is no help; wherever qualitative research fails to provide an explanation, quantitative research cannot balance this deficit. Qualitative analyses may therefore manage without quantification and act as a stand-alone. The opposite is not the case. Additionally, to the quality of this study as an early-stage-endeavour, there are only very few prison ombudsmen currently existing world-wide – as was shown in the table included in section B II. 6. A third factor was the particular aim of this study, which was to gain in-depth background details on the proliferation and implementation etc. of prison ombudsmen. The advancement of basic knowledge is one of the typical purposes of qualitative studies.[442] Consequently, all factors speak in favour of a qualitative approach.

This can be re-confirmed via a comparison of this study against the four general characteristics of qualitative research, which are:

- The conviction that a social construction of reality is intended.
- The conviction that an understanding approach toward reality is inevitable.
- The conviction that a case study research followed by the possibility of categorization is central.
- The conviction that the researcher has to directly emerge himself/herself into the praxis (the idea of "going native").[443]

This researcher set out to build a theory on prison ombudsmen based on the social construction of reality in the knowledge that a thorough and comprehensive approach would be required. The case study research was expected to yield and has yielded possibilities for categorization which can serve as a framework for future research and discussion. This was achieved through a combination of detailed analysis of existing research and the conduction of interviews with established practitioners. To this end, the researcher thoroughly emerged herself into both literature and empiricism.

3. Research materials and sources

This leads us directly to the next point, that of the selection of the appropriate sources and research materials. In this study this was achieved by means of a comprehensive study of the available literature combined with interviews conducted with experts of the field.

---

442   c.f. Strauss/Corbin (1990), p. 21
443   Garz/Kraimer (1991), p. 13 (own translation)

a) Literature

Any analysis of literature is always a secondary source analysis. This umbrella term comprises any "information compiled by others including public, government-sponsored, research publications or reports or analyses made by private organizations".[444] Whenever secondary source analysis is employed, it is important to note that public or private data are usually collected "for other purposes by different agencies, and such information may not necessarily coincide with the immediate interests of investigators". This already contains two of the three characteristics of secondary source materials – notably that they are ready made and have been "collected independent of an investigator's research purposes". The third is the secondary sources' lack of limitation in time and space meaning that "investigators who use such sources did not have to be present when and where these data were gathered".[445]

All of these characteristics are linked to certain advantages and disadvantages, but only those relevant to this study shall be named here. The major advantage of secondary source materials realized in this study are the considerable savings of time and money rendered by the analysis of ready-made data, which is easily accessible to the public and the possibility of the triangulation of these secondary sources with information obtained through the conducted interviews.[446] Especially, the savings of time and money are significant to this study as travelling to the individual home countries of the prison ombudsmen to conduct research through observation, interviews etc. can thereby be avoided. The possibility of triangulating the secondary source data with the interviews is an additional benefit that will be realized in chapter E. The disadvantages of secondary source materials pertaining to this study are that the data have been collected for other purposes only incidentally related to the researcher's goals and interests and that missing data in available secondary sources cannot be reconstructed. The incompleteness of data is and has been an on-going problem for this study as it has been discovered that records of prison ombudsmen are for the most part very incomplete. Wherever records have been kept, they have been compiled for the use of politicians or administrators, sometimes apparently neglecting information relevant to scientific research on purpose to hide inconvenient truths.

Overall, "the use of secondary sources in criminological research is widespread" with the "strengths of using secondary sources far outweigh[ing] any

---

444   Here and in the following: Champion (2009), p. 297
445   Champion (2009), p. 309
446   For a complete list of all advantages and disadvantages c.f. Champion (2009), p. 320

limitations or disadvantages".[447] This is especially true where secondary source materials are used to supplement primary data collection methods - such as the interviews used here – as it provides an inexpensive mechanism for reinforcing internal and external validity. External validation affects a study's generalizability to other settings and elements, or as Champion puts it: "A close correspondence between what is generally known about a given topic as revealed by data in secondary source materials and the information disclosed by a given study attests to the study's generalizability."

Now that the general advantages of using secondary source analysis have been established, it may be worthwhile to take a closer look at the literature itself as there are two different kinds of literature: technical and nontechnical literature. The latter includes such sources as biographies, diaries, documents, manuscripts, records, reports, catalogues, and other materials which can either be drawn upon in their quality "as primary data or to supplement interviews and field observations in grounded theory studies".[448] This study primarily uses nontechnical literature in form of government documents, records and reports as primary data in the chapters B and D with some additional use of government records and newspaper articles as supplementary data to the interviews again in chapter D.[449] This is a common usage of nontechnical data in grounded theory studies as "much can be learned about an organization, its structure, and how it functions (that may not immediately be visible in observations or interviews) by studying its reports, correspondence or memos".[450] Compared with technical literature, nontechnical literature can be used for all of the same purposes, but "[s]ince it is often difficult to authenticate and determine the veracity of some documents, biographies, and such, it is very important to cross-check these against other sources of data if possible". This is ensured in this study through the possibility of cross-referencing the nontechnical data against the interviews presented in chapter D.

Technical literature comprises "[r]eports of research studies, and theoretical or philosophical papers characteristic of professional and disciplinary writing. These can serve as background materials against which one compares findings from actual data gathered in grounded theory studies".[451] This study makes extensive use of research reports, theoretical papers and disciplinary writing to establish the current state of research in the field – c.f. chapter B – and will again employ technical literature in chapter E to act as a basis of comparison for the

---

447 Here and in the following: Champion (2009), p. 321
448 Strauss/Corbin (1990), p. 48
449 For the usefulness of government records c.f. Champion (2009), p. 296
450 Here and in the following: Corbin/Strauss (1990), p. 55
451 Strauss/Corbin (1990), p. 48

primary data acquired though the conducted interviews presented in the same chapter. Besides the more obvious uses of technical literature in grounded theory studies as secondary data and supplementation, it also has many lesser uses including the stimulation of "theoretical sensitivity by providing concepts and relationships that are checked out against actual data", delivery of interpretative approaches based on "[k]nowledge of philosophical writings and existing theories", generation of questions to be posed in interviews, direction for theoretical sampling.[452] All of these lesser uses were also employed throughout this study.

b) Experts

Besides the literature analysis, this study uses the knowledge of experts as an additional source for research.[453] Every person may function as a potential expert – even if this status were limited to knowledge about one's own life. This status may also extend to other areas such as one's work, social and political engagements, research etc. It depends on the research interest whether a person has value to a study as a potential expert. In a way, it is the researcher who awards the expert status limited to a specific research question.[454] "A person is addressed as an expert, who in some way or other bears responsibility for the development, implementation or control of a problem solution or – who holds a privileged mode of access to information, persons or decision processes".

4. Data collection

When it comes to the choice of a research method, a careful selection from among an abundance of possibilities (observation, questionnaires, interviews, qualitative content analysis etc.) has to be made. The selection itself is based on the aim of the study as well as the accessibility of the sources by means of the preferred method. Frequently, a combination of methods will prove the most insightful, as the comparison and amalgamation of the outcomes may help to create a bigger picture. For this reason, this study combines the extensive use of qualitative content analysis with expert interviews, thus establishing a basis for triangulation.

---

452   Strauss/Corbin (1990), pp. 50-52
453   Please note that the question about how this expert knowledge is obtained will be resolved in the next section, while this section exclusively deals with the matter of defining experts as a form of research material.
454   Here and in the following: Meuser/Nagel (1991), p. 443 (own translation)

a) Qualitative content analysis

Why content analysis? Methods of content analysis which, based on manifest contents, allow an intuitive guess at latent connections may be found in all cultures.[455] Content analysis as an empirical method of data collection has become so widespread, that empirical social research without content analysis has become inconceivable. The last decades have seen a fierce debate between devotees of quantitative and qualitative content analysis. Due to the selectivity of quantitative methods, some content available within a specific text or communication may be ignored. Qualitative methods, in turn, are criticized for their lack of traceability, their subjectivity and arbitrariness. While this seems to suggest an antithesis, there really is none. The application of any method of content analysis is determined by the cognitive interest and as such they should be viewed as complementing rather than mutually excluding each other.

Content analysis is defined as "a method to investigate social reality, during which characteristics of a manifest text are used to conjecture characteristics of non-manifest contexts. [...] Here, social reality is used as an all-inclusive term for social structures of all kinds (social action of communicants as well as aggregated forms such as moral and normative concepts, organized as well as institutionalized action)".[456] Or, as Champion puts it: "Content analysis is the systematic qualitative and quantitative description of some form of communication. Thus, the contents of communications of different kinds are examined for the purpose of discovering patterns and meanings".[457] A concise definition specific to qualitative methods is currently non-existent. They can call no theory or paradigm their own; the same is true for their methods.

How should the qualitative content analysis be carried out? There is no single standard procedure that is routinely employed. Instead there exists a whole plethora of approaches from different scientific disciplines which are selected depending on the study's cognitive interest.[458] A strict separation of data collection and analysis is frequently impossible. Qualitative methods are not aimed at testing hypotheses and reasoning based on statistical properties, but rather at discovering and unlocking the significant content. Once a precise research question has been formulated, the structuring of the analytical material is of central importance. There are four criteria which can be used to characterize the procedural approach for any qualitative approach: being forthright, communicative, naturalistic and interpretative.

---

455   Here and in the following: Atteslander (2008), pp. 181-8, here 185
456   Merten (1996), pp. 15f, 59 (own translation)
457   Champion (2009), p. 321
458   Here and in the following: Atteslander (2008), pp. 197f

Being open or forthright concerns the theoretical concept as well as the behaviour towards the research topic and the research situation. "Theoretical concepts and hypotheses are not formulated based on scientific or everyday previous knowledge, but are developed through controlled understanding of the 'other' of the examined everyday concepts of the subjects".[459] The communicative aspect concerns the expectation that the social reality emerges through interaction and communication which has to be reflected in the research design either through the direct contact of the researcher and the researched subject or via appropriate records. The demand for being naturalistic aims at preserving the principle of constructive and fact-based analysis throughout the research process. The interpretation only concerns the analytical phase during which the collected data is not used to falsify pre-formulated hypotheses but rather to generate working hypotheses using the collected data in combination with interpretative methods.

b) Partially-structured, explorative, guided interviews

This study uses partially-structured, explorative, guided interviews in addition to qualitative content analysis. Why this combination? While qualitative content analysis is a valuable tool for establishing what is already known about a subject, it is always limited to the available data. Missing links that would be interesting to explore cannot be supplanted, but are a "given". This does not mean that this data does not exist; it merely means that it has so far not been collected. This missing information valuable to the study can be gathered by means of observation, questionnaires or interviews. While, in this case, an observation of institutional performance may provide some information not available through content analysis, this would be a rather slow and potentially incomplete process. Questionnaires are frequently used where the intent is to gather extensive amounts of standardized data. However, the need for information left in the form of missing links is likely to be better served through interactive communication processes which allow for a flexible and reactive drill-down on further aspects of interest and thus a more tentative approach to the missing information. This is most easily achieved through an interview as one of the least-rigid research methods.

The following section on the interview as a research method of choice will explain the selection of the specific interview form. It will also discuss the definition, advantages and disadvantages of interviews and elaborate on the design process as well as the ex-post analysis of interviews. This is being done to avoid the most common critique against qualitative studies – namely the lack of writ-

---

459   Here and in the following: Lamnek (2005), pp. 199f

ten documentation detailing the theoretical and methodological reasons for the selection of its methods.[460]

aa) Definition, advantages, disadvantages

Interviews are "particularly useful for describing various dimensions of social reality".[461] They are designed to "provide insights into unexplored dimensions of a topic." Compared with other research methods, "interviews invite more in-depth probing and detailed description of people's feelings and attitudes". This is so, because an

> "interview implies communication between two or more persons. Verbal stimuli (questions) are used to produce a verbal reaction (answer): This occurs during specific situations and is shaped through reciprocal expectations. The answers relate to experienced and remembered social events, and constitute opinions and evaluations. The interview instruments do not capture complete social behavior, but only verbal behavior".[462]

The author of this study relies on an S→P→R-Model (stimulus→person→reaction) and consequently, understands the interview situation as a chain of reactions.

> "During the social situation interview the individual question is [...] understood as a stimulus working in a broad environment, of which only individual stimuli are perceived by the persons involved. [...] The interviewee notices the stimulus, evaluates it and prepares a response. Each of these steps is completely influenced by expectations and internalized norms".[463]

All possible and factual influences on the interview situation are therein treated not as interference factors but as conditions for the transfer of reaction. Consequently, the entire interview situation has to undergo careful systematic control.

Besides the verbal quality of interviews, there are other defining characteristics such as the fact that "information is recorded by investigators rather than respondents, [...which] underscores the greater accuracy of interviewing regarding information obtained", the transitory quality of the relationship between interviewers and interviewees with the participants usually being strangers and the "considerable flexibility in the interviewing format".[464]

Interviews have many advantages such as the speed with which desired information can be obtained, the flexibility of the questioning process whilst maintaining control of the interview context, the possibility to ensure that the re-

---

460   In place of many: Aufenanger (1991), p. 36 (specifically referring to interviews)
461   Here and in the following: Champion (2009), p. 268
462   Here and in the following: Atteslander (2008), p. 101 (own translation)
463   Atteslander (2008), pp. 105f
464   Here and in the following: Champion (2009), pp. 246ff, p. 268

spondents understand questions and interpret them correctly and the fact that information can be more readily checked for its validity on the basis of nonverbal clues from respondents.[465] There are also disadvantages to the enhanced situational control which lie for example in the fact that the interviewer holds greater direct influence over the course of the conversation which can introduce a distortional quality.[466] However, overall the advantages of the interview format outweigh the disadvantages where this study is concerned.

bb) Selection of specific interview form

Why an expert interview? As noted above, experts function as an additional source of information in this study. Expert insights are of particular importance in the context of this analysis because knowledge about the institutional history, structures and performance of ombudsmen is held by a group of a select few.[467] These can be academics, practitioners and politicians. This study's focus on the scarcely researched field of prison ombudsmen limits the potential experts to the latter two. Potential interviewees are therefore limited to those practitioners working as or with prison ombudsmen and those politicians involved in implementation processes of prison ombudsmen. For this study, interviews with both kinds of experts have been conducted.

Expert interviews are set apart from interviews conducted with other subjects by a restriction of the interest and the ensuing limitation of the analysis from the entire life of the interviewed person to only that information pertaining to their contextual relation with the subject matter, in this case prison ombudsmen.[468] Since this study uses expert interviews to provide the missing data identified during qualitative content analysis, their function is limited to that of an additional source of information. This is in so far important as the analysis of the expert interviews may be discontinued whenever their purpose of establishing missing links is complete. This is the case whenever the themes and hypotheses pertaining to the consecutive explorative steps are saturated with information. Thus, a mere partial analysis of the interviews as well as a break-off during the stage of empirical generalization is legitimate. The process is concluded with the formulation of statements about representative, unexpected as well evidentiary findings.

Why an explorative interview? While the quantitative analysis conducted in advance to the expert interviews provides some insights into missing links, it is not known whether precise information about these problems exists. Additional-

---

465   Champion (2009), p. 289
466   Atteslander (2008), p. 125
467   c.f. Atteslander (2008), p. 131
468   Meuser/Nagel (1991), pp. 442, 445, 447f

ly, in some cases the researcher can only guess at the exact shape of the missing data rendering a limitation to a specific set of questions less adequate compared to a more open structure in which the expert's knowledge may be used to formulate the question which is most likely to produce an answer which would elucidate the missing link in question. Expert interviews are frequently used to pursue explorative aims.[469]

Why then a partially-structured interview? While the explorative expert interview holds the advantages described above, the selection of a completely open interview format is inadvisable. This is due to the limitation of the researcher's interest to the study's subject, here the missing links in qualitative content analysis of the literature available on prison ombudsmen. Interviews are called partially-structured whenever they are conducted based on a catalogue of pre-prepared and readily formulated questions, whose sequence is flexible enough to take up themes appearing in the answers.[470] This does not mean that there is not some natural order to be found among at least some of these questions. The degree of the structuring allows conclusions to be made about the scientific objective: The lesser the amount of structuring, the more likely it is that the interview serves the purpose of realizing qualitative aspects.[471]

Why a guided interview? A characteristic of guided interviews is the generation of a pre-determined set of questions based on the researcher's educated guesses at the information hidden behind the missing links. These questions are then posed not necessarily according to the order ascribed to them during the generation process but according to the flux of the interview itself. This demands the flexibility and aptitude on the side of the researcher to quickly determine the right moment to pose a specific question.[472] The less cogently an enforceable structure is given to the interview beforehand, the more the interview will resemble a process of continuous, spontaneous operationalization. The consequence of this is that the interviewer has a greater amount of influence on the interview and the resulting quality of the data. Interviews conducted according to this method also produce results with a lesser degree of comparability resulting in increased difficulties during analysis. The interviewee also has to have a higher level of willingness to cooperate as, for example, guided interviews tend to require more time than standardized forms of questioning. However, they constitute a fair balance between the limited interest of the interviewer in the

---

469 Atteslander (2008), p. 129
470 Atteslander (2008), p. 125; for a brief history of the development of the semi-structured interview format and its connection to Piaget's clinical interviews see Aufenanger (1991), pp. 38f
471 Atteslander (2008), p. 134
472 Here and in the following: Atteslander (2008), p. 132

expert, which is restricted to the subject of the researcher's study, and the expert status of the interviewed counterpart.[473] The work involved in developing the materials for a guided interview forecloses the danger that the interviewer will turn out to be an incompetent interlocutor, thus reducing the expert's level of potential regret for having consented to the interview. An additional benefit of the guided interview is the avoidance of not-to-the-point-discussions while allowing the expert to illustrate his/her view unhindered.

Finally, the literature differentiates between soft, hard and neutral interviews.[474] The first demands a certain amount of passivity difficult to sustain during guided interviews whilst gaining answers to all questions interesting to the researcher. The second, with its interrogation-like approach, is inappropriate to expert interviews as it increases the danger of an untimely break-off of the interview. Consequently, only a neutral interview style is possible under the conditions of this study. However, a complete exclusion of all emotions from the relationship between interviewer and interviewee devalues the person as part of the reactive communication system. Where individuals are involved (here researcher and expert), a complete exclusion of emotion is unrealistic. Whenever the interviewer strives too much for neutrality, this may actually produce unintended, adverse reactions in the interviewee such as worry, fear or other emotional responses. Therefore, this study follows the alleviated approach towards neutrality favoured by E. und N. Macoby, who recommend that the interviewer be restrained and strive towards making a professional impression signaling a true interest in what is being said without revealing personal opinions on the subject matter.[475]

cc) Design

The crucial difference between every day and scientific interviews lies in the theory-guided control of the interview situation.[476] The scientific method is based on systematic focus and theory. The control of every single step of the process has two purposes. On the one hand, it is supposed to guarantee the scientific application of the interview as a research method while on the other hand it serves as a quality control mechanism measuring how much the resulting data has been influenced by the situational conditions – and these comprise all steps of the research activity – under which the interview has been conducted. How-

---

473 Here and in the following: Meuser/Nagel (1991), p. 448
474 Here and in the following: Atteslander (2008), p. 128
475 Maccoby/Maccoby (1974), p. 63
476 Here and in the following: Atteslander (2008), p. 103 (own translation)

ever, total situational control is impossible and the demand to eliminate all disruptive factors is absurd.[477]

In terms of the design process, it starts off with a concise definition of the problem, the selection of the experts, if necessary the gaining of access to organizations, the arrangement of interview appointments, the training of the interviewers, and finally also encompasses the design of the questions and the selection of appropriate conservation methods.[478]

When designing the interview questions it is important to avoid unnecessary generalization as this reduces the personal engagement of the interviewee and consequently generates less involved answers.[479] The asymmetrical motivation during interviews, the greater interest of the researcher in the answers compared to the interviewee in answering, demands that the interviewer strives to establish a common ground for the communication thus decreasing the risk of selective reactions and one-sided influences.[480]

Of equal importance is the formulation and deliverance of the questions itself. Here words unknown to the interviewee should be avoided just as much as purely hypothetical questions or the generation of an atmosphere of fear – all of which increases the artificiality of the responses.[481] Even in partially-structured, explorative, guided interviews, the order of questions is of importance.[482] At the beginning, there should be a warm-up phase leading up to the posing of the crucial questions to refresh the memory and establish rapport. Further on, probing may be used to "uncover areas of inquiry previously neglected by the researcher".[483]

The standard conservational format today is to tape-record the interview. The concern that this "totally eliminates the anonymity factor and jeopardizes the truthfulness or candour of respondents" is not much of an argument where small-scale studies with expert interviews are concerned. In this case, the interviewees have prior knowledge of the lack of anonymity, and are frequently quite used to speaking publicly or being recorded. This is especially true in the case of politicians as interview partner. Their truthfulness and candour can be somewhat preserved by the promise to only cite approved material. Respectively, the bene-

---

477 Atteslander (2008), p. 161
478 Champion (2009), p. 284; for advice on training, appropriate clothing and behavior of the researcher during the interview see Champion (2009), pp. 286f
479 Atteslander (2008), p. 112
480 Atteslander (2008), pp. 119ff
481 Atteslander (2008), p. 113
482 Here and in the following: Atteslander (2008), pp. 129f
483 Champion (2009), p. 288

fit of tape-recording, which lies in the possibility of generating a verbatim transcription, outweighs any other arguments.

dd) Analysis

The selection of partially-structured, explorative, guided expert interviews is not unproblematic as it constitutes a methodologically only sparsely explored terrain.[484] This pertains to a lesser extent to questions of field accessibility, interview design and the conduct during the interview itself and to a larger extent to matters of analysis. There, the question remains unanswered of how an understanding of the unfamiliar or the "other" is to be achieved in a methodologically controlled manner. The wide dissemination faces a notable lack of methodological reflection which can by no means be brushed aside with Radbruch's famous dictum that only sick sciences tend to self-reflect on research methodology.[485]

The process of analysis relies on the material acquired during the transcription of the tape-recordings. While usually the field notes and tape-recordings of interviews in small-scale studies should be transcribed fully, the opposite is true of the transcription of expert interviews.[486] As "theory should guide not only what you look for and where you go to find it in the field, but also what you look for in your data", there may be a time "especially near the end of your study when your analysis tells you that there is a whole in your theoretical formulations that needs closing and that further data collection is needed to close it". In this study, this may well be the case where all interviews, especially those conducted with practitioners, are concerned as these are originally intended to filling in the missing links from the qualitative content analysis. Generally, the transcription will be more extensive in cases of successfully conducted discourse.[487] The transcription of expert interviews may forgo complicated notational systems as pauses, nonverbal and para-verbal elements are not part of the interpretation.

Due to time constraints, the qualitative analysis of collected data is frequently performed without applying one of the few available interpretative methods such as the objective hermeneutics or the narrative data analysis.[488] While there

---

484   Here and in the following: c.f. Meuser/Nagel (1991), p. 441
485   Radbruch (1969), p. 253 „Wie Menschen, die sich durch Selbstbeobachtung quälen, so pflegen auch Wissenschaften, die sich mit ihrer eigenen Methodenlehre zu beschäftigen Anlaß haben, kranke Wissenschaften zu sein; der gesunde Mensch und die gesunde Wissenschaft pflegen nicht viel von sich selbst zu wissen."
486   Meuser/Nagel (1991), p. 455; here and in the following: Strauss/Corbin (1990), pp. 30f
487   Here and in the following: Meuser/Nagel (1991), pp. 455f
488   c.f. Aufenanger (1991), p. 35

are some manuals, for example for the interpretation of moral interviews[489], the hermeneutic-reconstructive method has to be applied where new objects and themes are tapped in interviews.[490] This is the case here. Of mere practical scientific and methodological interest is the question whether this method has to be applied as sequential analysis or using a shortcut model. Sequential analysis requires an interpretation of each sentence, while the shortcut model allows the interpretation of summarized responses. This corresponds with the requirement not to treat individual answers as isolated data, but primarily as indicating connections.[491] These may appear in form of thematic units of converging substance scattered across interview passages and constitute the particular interpretative focus where expert interviews are concerned.[492] Since the shortcut model reveals just as many central aspects during interpretation, assuming that the appropriate care has been applied during the process of summarizing the content, the latter will be used here for reasons of scientific economy.[493] The interpretation will therefore be conducted using the following steps: reading the entire interview, summarizing the content, interpreting the summary and compiling the structural hypotheses.[494] The latter gives cause for the reciprocal verification of interpretation and theoretical knowledge aimed at formulating statements about representative, commonly shared bodies of knowledge, structures of relevance and constructions of reality.[495]

c) Integration

In its quest to gather knowledge and provide new insights into the field of prison ombudsmen, this study makes use of more than one source and more than one method. The application of different methods and viewpoints to the same data in order to use the strengths of one method to even out the weakness of another is sometimes referred to as triangulation. Triangulation represents a research strategy nowadays mainly employed in qualitative empirical social research. While it has been contested that this ensures a higher validity of the research results, it supposedly at least affords a richer depiction of the empirical reality and may

---

489   c.f. Colby/Kohlberg (1987)
490   Here and in the following: Aufenanger (1991), pp. 46f
491   Atteslander (2008), p. 122
492   Meuser/Nagel (1991), p. 453
493   For details on the short-cut model and an extensive comparison and evaluation of the two approaches see Aufenanger (1991), pp. 54ff
494   Aufenanger (1991), p. 48
495   Meuser/Nagel (1991), pp. 452, 455

100

level systematic mistakes.[496] This is summarized in Richard Levin's famous quote: "[O]ur truth is the intersection of independent lies".[497]

Lately, it has been pointed out that the term triangulation has been employed to elide the interchangeable description of the use of multiple methods as "integrated", "combined" or "mixed" and that "this elision is problematic because it obscures an essential difference between the *outcome* of mixed methods (claims to triangulation) and the *process* by which different methods and datasets are brought into relation with each other".[498]

This study uses a mix of different qualitative data attained via content analysis of secondary sources and of expert interviews in order to reap the benefits of increased accuracy of the "research findings and the level of confidence in them" on the one hand and to generate "knowledge through a synthesis of the findings from different approaches" on the other hand.[499] The purpose of the use of multiple methods is here limited to increasing the "depth or breadth of data gained", which does not involve triangulation at all.[500]

Consequently, a different terminology has to be adopted. In this study, "integration" seems more appropriate than "combination" as the former "requires that different methods (or types of data) are given equal weight, and with respect to operationalization, that they are oriented toward a common goal or research question and are, therefore, necessarily independent while retaining their paradigmatic modalities".[501] This is the case here as the qualitative content analysis of the literature and the expert interviews do not only hold equal weight whilst being independent, but are both aimed at shared research questions in "pursuit of the goal of 'knowing more'".[502] While this inter-meshing could occur at the level of conceptualization, it is common for mixed-method projects to integrate at later stages. Here, the integration of methods and data takes place during the analysis and interpretation stage.

The use of mixed methods complicates the process of analysis as diverse sets of data have to be examined without losing the characteristics of each type of data.[503] While each set could be analysed "within the parameters of its own paradigm but addressing common analytical questions", this study employs the "following a thread" approach developed by Moran-Ellis et al. in which, based

---

496   Blaikie (1991), p. 115; Fielding/Fielding (1986), p. 33
497   In place of many: Fielding/Fielding (1986), p. 23
498   Moran-Ellis et al. (2006), p. 45 (emphasis in the original)
499   Moran-Ellis et al. (2006), p. 47
500   Moran-Ellis et al. (2006), p. 49
501   Moran-Ellis et al. (2006), p. 52
502   Here and in the following: Moran-Ellis et al. (2006), p. 51
503   Here and in the following: Moran-Ellis et al. (2006), p. 54

on the literature and the original research questions, an analytical question in one dataset is followed across the other data sets "to create a constellation of findings which can be used to generate a multi-faceted picture of the phenomenon".

This methodology based on an inductive approach – further "developed through a focused iterative process of data interrogation which aims to interweave the findings that emerge from each dataset" – is especially suitable to grounded theory studies as the one at hand.

5. Selection of two examples

Now that the research materials and methods for analysis have been established, two examples upon which this study's findings can be demonstrated have to be selected. The selection of the appropriate ombudsinstitutions has to take into consideration that the spectrum of comparison may at least potentially be enriched where the research subjects belong to different legal systems.

According to the International Ombudsman Institute, 945 ombudsinstitutions are currently active in 140 countries.[504] Many of these ombudsmen are in some manner mandated to work in prisons. Yet, this study focuses on prison ombudsmen only. The definitions, structures, work-methods etc. of ombudsmen in general and prison ombudsmen in particular were established in the previous chapter B. The overview table included in section II. 6. in particular may serve to fully comprehend the selection of the legal systems.

According to this table there are prison ombudsmen in Canada, Germany, the UK and the US. Seven confirmed prison ombudsinstitutions currently exist within these four countries: the Canadian Correctional Investigator, the Michigan Legislative Corrections Ombudsman, the Prisoner Ombudsman for Northern Ireland, the Indiana Ombudsman Bureau, the Kentucky Corrections Ombudsman, the Prisons and Probation Ombudsman for England and Wales and the Justizvollzugsbeauftragter des Landes Nordrhein-Westfalen.

Canada, the UK and US are part of the common law family while Germany represents the only country within the civil law family having implemented a prison ombudsman. Given this distinction, it is relevant to discuss the advantages and disadvantages of performing a comparison within a specific legal framework or across the two systems. The selection of legal systems, which are alike, allows for an easy process of description. However, it potentially leaves little room for a comparative analysis. [505] Therefore, the choice of countries

---

504   Ayeni (2009), p. 4
505   Here and in the following: Dannemann (2006), p. 409

should depend on the purpose of the enquiry and the methodological approach. Legrand holds that

> "if one compares strictly within one's own legal tradition, one may form the (unwarranted) view that certain epistemological assumptions are necessary or natural while they are simply characteristic of laws in a particular historico-socio-cultural configuration. If the benefits derived from the act of comparison are to be optimized, the observer needs to be confronted with the breadth of possibilities, something which is best achieved at the level of 'most-different-units design', that is, as it involves comparison across the civil-law and common-law traditions".[506]

This, of course, is firmly based within Legrand's viewpoint of culturalism which is based on the detection of differences. Nevertheless, the reasoning can be integrated into the comparative method favoured here, which combines the search for similarities and differences and asks for the applicatory aim. While some similarity is necessary to obtain comparability, for example limiting the choice of legal systems to those with prison ombudsmen, the research interest here would benefit from the confrontation with the greatest possible "breadth of possibilities". It should be attempted to cover the most general framework possible to achieve a comprehensive overview of different designs, approaches and practices. To this end, the comparison should include both systems belonging to the civil-law and belonging to the common-law legal traditions. This necessitates the inclusion of Germany as the only civil-law country having implemented a prison ombudsinstitution and leaves the comparative counterpart to be determined.

Considering the limited number of legal systems and prison ombudsmen, it may seem feasible and favourable to include all three remaining legal systems with their six prison ombudsmen. However, Zweigert/Kötz advise to apply sober self-restraint in research "not so much because it is hard to take account of everything as because experience shows that as soon as one tries to cover a wide range of legal systems the law of diminishing returns operates".[507] Their rationale for this approach is the frequent adoption of mature legal systems and the lack of "originality and balanced maturity in solving problems" demonstrated by affiliated legal systems. Considering that this study aims at proving inter-legal-system-learning-processes[508] it appears to be superficial to accept this as an argument against the study of all prison ombudsmen. Especially so since the Canadian and the US legal systems, which are in large part based on the British framework, have since developed with different degrees of independence.

---

506   Legrand (2003), p. 288
507   Here and in the following: Zweigert/Kötz (1998), p. 41
508   See chapter B III. for details

Gutteridge recommends to look for similarity in "the stage of legal, political and economic development" when selecting the legal systems under comparison, in order to avoid what he calls "illusory comparison".[509] Ancel suggests that comparing radically different legal systems might yield more significant results than comparing similar legal systems.[510] Upon closer consideration, these views may not be complete opposites. Civil and common law systems would satisfy Ancel's recommendation to compare radically different systems. Of the three countries governed by a common law system – Canada, the UK and the US – the UK is the most similar to Germany in legal, political and economic development. In particular, the legal similarity may be deduced from the common membership in the European Union. In addition, the prison populations of England and Wales (85,200) and North Rhine-Westphalia (13,551) when calculated per 100,000 inhabitants (159.46 and 75.97 respectively) allow for an interesting contrast. The resulting differences, for example in complaint levels, have potentially influenced the prison ombudsinstitutions in these countries providing a rich mining-ground for comparison.

On the institutional level, the Prisons and Probation Ombudsman for England and Wales and the Justizvollzugsbeauftragter des Landes Nordrhein-Westfalen are comparable in so far as they are both executive ombudsmen. Nevertheless, they are different with respect to other points such as staffing, funding and complaint numbers thereby allowing for observation of a wide range of structural designs and work practices. They were also introduced more than a decade apart allowing for the possible incorporation of new developments in design. The Prisons and Probation Ombudsman for England and Wales, introduced in 1994, with an institutional history of already more than 17 years will facilitate understanding for evolutionary institutional developments, while the Ombudsmann für den Justizvollzug Nordrhein-Westfalen, introduced as recently as 2007, allows to detect the struggles of an institution in the process of establishing itself. This study will make use of the entire timespan of data available on the existence of both institutions.

In addition to these arguments in favour of the selection of the UK and Germany and the Prisons and Probation Ombudsman for England and Wales and Justizvollzugsbeauftragter des Landes Nordrhein-Westfalen respectively, there are also further arguments relative to the feasibility of this study. The collection of data which involves visits to both institutions is easier if both research objects are within short traveling distance. Moreover, there is the expectation that frequent visits to the UK should work to heighten the sensitivity to and un-

---

509   Gutteridge (1946), pp. 8-9
510   Ancel (1971), p. 65; c.f. Dannemann (2006), p. 389

derstanding of the British legal *mentalité*. Indeed, it can pose a challenge for a lawyer trained in the civil law mind-set to establish an understanding of the common law. In Leyland's words, the foreign scholar has to face "the formidable obstacle of having to understand the common law mind before studying the cognitive framework of our law and vice-versa. Integration of foreign ideas and principles is made virtually impossible because only those who have the perception and understanding of the culture will approach or interpret a concept as a native would".[511] While this is clearly relevant to the process of comparison, the methodological approach to law as human action favoured here allows comparative undertakings even where no "total understanding" of the legal culture has been established.[512] This does not relieve the researcher from the task of forming an understanding – of the foreign legal culture, however incomplete. This has been undertaken here by attending classes on the British common law combined with self-study of the British penal system through academic literature.

Under these preconditions, the selection of the Prisons and Probation Ombudsman for England and Wales and Ombudsmann für den Justizvollzug Nordrhein-Westfalen as the objects of this comparison appears to be the best possible solution.

6. Influence of the researcher

A chapter on methodology is not complete without taking necessary note of the researcher's influence on the research process. In particular, special attention has to be paid to the problem of affecting the outcome of comparative research.

This influence can for example be introduced through the researcher conducting the study at hand, but may also result from the inclusion of second-hand knowledge within one's research which may open the study up to the influence of others. This is especially true for studies such as this, since it relies exclusively on qualitative content analysis of literature and second-hand knowledge conveyed though expert interviews. The researcher must be aware that this influence does not only equal the acceptance of "other investigators' careful observations, but also [of] a whole mass of careless and casual popular impressions and legends whose reliability we have generally no means of checking".[513]

Consequently, the researcher should be able to display some theoretical sensitivity indicating an "awareness of the subtleties of meaning", "the capacity to understand, and capability to separate the pertinent from that which isn't" – all

---

511   Leyland (2002), p. 220
512   c.f. chapter B III
513   Atteslander (2008), p. 117

of which is done "in conceptual rather than concrete terms".[514] This theoretical sensitivity is central to the grounded theory approach applied in this study and is derived from literature, which includes theoretical texts and applied research, the background of the researcher as well as the analytical process itself. Strauss/Corbin describe this occurrence saying that: "Insight and understanding about a phenomenon increase as you interact with your data. This comes from collecting and asking questions about the data, making comparisons, thinking about what you see, making hypotheses, developing small theoretical frameworks (miniframeworks) about concepts and their relationships."

There are also aspects specifically pertaining to the influence on qualitative research. Here, the main gateway is the interpretation process. While some hold that this should be minimized by only gathering the data and letting them speak for themselves without presenting an analysis, others favour an approach of accurate description "when doing their analysis and presenting their findings".[515] Considering that a complete presentation of all collected data is impossible and a reduction consequently unavoidable, the latter option seems more sensible. It requires an "accurate description of what is being studied, though not necessarily all of the data that have been studied". The materials selected for presentation are meant to illustrate the reality of the studied subject, "while the researcher's interpretations are meant to represent a more detached conceptualisation of that reality".

The influence of the researcher on comparative studies pertains to three interconnected points: First, the problem of being of one culture and/or in between cultures which can cause a lack of objectivity. Secondly, the matter of how one can possibly compensate for this in getting to know another legal culture and finally how much understanding can ever be attained.

The researcher does not exist in a vacuum - there is always a materially embedded, culturally situated pre-understanding to any approach to another legal system.[516] Consequently, any attempt to grasp a foreign legal culture necessarily occurs in the context of a biased perspective which allows only the descriptive reproduction and analysis of "those facets of the legal system that he can perceive from the outside".[517] This effectively eliminates the possibility to understand a legal system completely from within.[518]

---

514   Here and in the following: Strauss/Corbin (1990), pp. 41-44
515   Here and in the following: Strauss/Corbin (1990), pp. 21f
516   Legrand (2003), p. 225
517   Lasser (2003), p. 221
518   Curran (1998), p. 58

This bias means that a comparatist can never achieve objectivity.[519] Today, this may be considered a truism. In consequence, the comparatist in acknowledgement of the own situatedness "must recognize that her work represents an intervention and must, therefore, account for her motives."[520] However, this subjectivity, while inherent to comparison, does not make the process entirely arbitrary, since it refers to objective facts.[521] Indeed, the impact of the subjectivity may be reduced wherever the author of a comparative study acknowledges the underlying epistemological interests, motives and reasons and reflects upon them.[522] This author's interest in prison ombudsmen was sparked by a research topic covered in the context of the university-administered part of the law state exam in the elected core area of criminology and criminal justice. Notably, the question of the practicality of the introduction of a prison ombudsman in Germany was analysed at a time when no such office existed in Germany yet.

The comparatist's cultural starting point can rarely be justified.[523] Whether the resulting expectations are likely to assist in understanding the foreign legal culture is less relevant than the need to "understand the shape given to our ideas by such previous socialization". This author was socialized in the civil law world and in particular in the Germanic variation of the Roman legal family. The German legal system is one defined by its strong constitutional basis which grants equal rights to all human beings, be they German or foreigners, free men or prisoners.[524] This expectation defines the author's perception of prisoners as legal persons, as possessors of human rights in general and a right to resocialization in particular, which entails the right to have their grievances handled by an effective external grievance mechanism. This socialization unavoidably influences the expectations towards prison ombudsmen and the foreign legal system included in the comparison, here the British.

Comparison necessitates the effort to form some sort of grasp, however incomplete, of the foreign legal culture in order to understand foreign norms and legal texts, identify parallel rules or parts of the law. and to then be able to translate them into one's own legal language, which is especially problematic due to the "partially autonomous reality created by the norms, doctrine, and the concepts of a legal system that do not [...] find exact counterparts in another".[525] Here, the comfort derived "from seeking out the familiar in alien surroundings

---

519   John Merryman in Legrand (1999), p. 55; Legrand (2003), p. 288
520   Lasser (2003), p. 219
521   Here and in the following: Jansen (2006), p. 313, 315
522   Here and in the following: Jansen (2006), p. 313, 315; Lasser (2003), p. 219
523   Here and in the following: Nelken (2000), p. 15
524   c.f. Lazarus (2004), p. 23
525   Jansen (2006), p. 306f

and structuring the world in terms derived from our native culture", if left un-checked, may result in grasping "at the apparently alike and to leap at similarity in an overeager bid to make sense of the world".[526] This viewpoint regarding one legal system from the perspective of another reduces the independence and hence value of the output of any comparative effort. Consequently, the attempt to "develop an acute sensitivity to the peculiarities of the local" has to be made – although the aforementioned partiality makes complete objectivity and neutrality a challenging goal. As Zedner puts it more drastically: "We are necessarily the child of the one [legal culture] and, at best, the distant cousin of the other".

Therefore, the endeavor to establish some limited understanding of another legal culture is not without its pitfalls as any comparative engagement located at the "interstices of the relationship between observed and observer" poses a two-fold risk of alienation: "Not only is the comparatist estranged from the observed culture (for she can never be of that culture), but she also finds herself disaffect-ed from her own culture as she pursues the unsettling process in which the con-ventional and the uncomfortable are questioned, in which incongruity is invit-ed".[527] And yet, being a cosmopolitan comparatist is not necessarily easier as this only represents a different form of alienation.[528]

Considering all this, how does one go about getting to know a legal culture? Nelken identified three possible approaches for tackling this "epistemological and methodological problem of comparative research": the first approach is to rely mainly of foreign experts, which he calls being "virtually there"; the second approach involves going abroad to interview foreign officials, which he refers to as "researching there" and the third approach, appropriately named "living there", implies drawing on one's own experience of living and working in the country concerned.[529] All three approaches to varying degrees face the disad-vantage of relying on foreign expert knowledge, which creates the problem of knowing whom to approach and evaluating credibility – possibly across time and space – which may lead to the dismissal of the findings of these methods as anecdotal or influenced by stereotypes and oversimplification.[530] While this is inherent to all comparative research undertaken by single researchers, collabora-tive research projects are also fraught with problems such as running "up against differences in academic culture such as the lack of empirical research traditions in many countries" and therefore do not necessarily solve this dilemma.[531] Thus,

---

526 Here and in the following: Zedner (1995), p. 519
527 Legrand (1995), p. 262
528 Nelken (1995), p. 445
529 Nelken (2000), p. 23
530 c.f. Nelken, (2000) p. 25; Nelken (1995), p. 435f
531 Nelken (1995), p. 435f; Zweigert/Kötz (1998), p. 42

the author of this study feels legitimized in attempting the comparison through a combination of being "virtually there" and "researching there". The study is based on an extensive literature review combined with interviews with foreign officials, namely the staff of the Prisons and Probations Ombudsman for England and Wales, which falls into the category of "researching there".

This leaves the question of how much understanding is necessary and how far it can possibly be attained. Merryman criticized the casual comparison undertaken by individuals who propose "things for a legal system about which they know nothing" and emphasizes that "a little knowledge can be a dangerous thing".[532] Thus, he demands that the comparatist get to know not "just the doctrinal part, not just the rules, and so forth, but the way it works – the whole fabric" of a legal system. Nevertheless, he acknowledges the impossibility to achieve total understanding and discounts the all-or-nothing premise by confirming that a scholar should "attempt to deal with a manageable piece of reality rather than take on everything".[533] However, Merryman's elaborations are rather theoretical in nature and do not necessarily qualify how a 'manageable piece of reality' should be defined. Sztompka[534] differentiates between two alternatives: the purpose of "comparison in an extensive direction" is to widen the scope of applicability (of a concept) or the scope of the object itself and predicates an attempt to seek for commonalities and uniformities among variety. The consequence of such a strategy is that "we know more, but we know less in the sense of detail, correctness and specificity". The aim of "comparison in an intensive direction" involves a narrowing of "the scope of applicability, or the scope of objects, or the scope of predicates" resulting in "the opposite of the former approach. The gain in informational content (interpreting power) is paid with the loss of comprehensiveness (systematizing power). We know more, but about less". Nelken suggests combining these strategies wherever possible.[535] Which of these approaches is to be preferred again depends on the cognitive research interest. In order to include the greatest possible bandwidth of structures, the scope of objects in this study has been limited to one prison ombudsman each from a civil and common law system. The loss of detail in studying an institution of a foreign legal system which may never be completely understood is compensated by the increased informational content providing a broader interpretational foundation for the intended systematization.

---

532   Merryman in Legrand (1999), p. 29
533   Merryman in Legrand (1999), p. 40
534   Sztompka (1990), pp. 54ff
535   Nelken (1997), p. 478

Finally, one should note that the process of highlighting the researcher's natural bias and motives is likely to be incomplete. One the one hand, there will never be a point where all pre-conditions and motivations are accounted for and on the other hand, the comparatist may not even be aware of all of them. Nevertheless, it has been attempted here to acknowledge all those instances of researcher bias necessary to provide the reader with an insight into the conditions under which this study was undertaken in the hope that this might enable him to form a personal opinion of the evaluation's results and the researcher's influence on them.

II. Method execution

The following account of method execution rounds off the selection of methods and sources. It may be useful to state that the inductive nature of grounded theory is based on generating rather than testing hypotheses and as such "the results of grounded theory are not reports of acts but probability statements about the relationship between concepts, or an integrated set of conceptual hypotheses developed from empirical data."[536] This study will refrain from lengthy descriptions of procedures in favour of explicating a few central steps. For a complete and detailed description please refer to Strauss and Corbin's *Basics of Qualitative Research.*[537]

The coding procedures applied during this research effort followed the matrix provided by Mey and Mruck, which itself is based on Strauss (1987) and Strauss/Corbin (1990) but has been adapted using elucidations by Böhm (2000) and Kelle (1997).[538] The three involved coding phases are understood as fluid rather than precisely separable process stages. The phases represent different approaches to the data which the researcher may combine and between which the researcher may move rather freely.[539] Axial coding was understood here as a mere frame which researchers may apply depending on the subject matter and personal ability to abide ambiguity.[540] This researcher preferred to follow the leads emerging from the empirical material which through the cyclic process of

---

536 Thulesius/Grahn (2007), p. 49
537 Useful overviews in various lengths may be found Mey/Mruck (2007b); Boychuck Duchscher/Morgan (2004); Walker/Myrick (2006)
538 Mey/Mruck (2007b), p. 29 there: "overview 3"
539 Mey/Mruck (2007b), pp. 28-30; Flick, pp. 258f
540 Here and in the follwoing: Charmaz (2006), p. 61 who explicitly states: "Those who prefer simple, flexible guidelines – and can tolerate ambiguity – do not need to do axial coding. They can follow the leads that they define in their empirical materials."

collecting, coding, and comparing incidents in the data became manifest in the form of new concepts. These concepts were then compared with each other and to new incidents as more data were collected. This process was continued to the point of saturation where new data did no longer change the theory.

The literature used in this study has been gathered according to the rules of grounded theory in a process carefully guided by the research questions.[541] The gathered literature has then been examined using the strategies of qualitative content analysis set out above – the results of which will be presented in the next chapter.

The interviewees recruited for this study have been selected on grounds of their in-depth knowledge about the history, implementation and work life of prison ombudsmen. As these interviews were aimed at filling in missing links concerning the knowledge about prison ombudsmen discovered during the process of qualitative content analysis of the literature and were not intended for quantification, they have been limited to a very few experts only. For each interview, an individual field manual or questionnaire guide was developed tailored on the one hand to the individual expert's knowledge whilst on the other hand being limited to questions about missing links only. Consequently, a systematic collection of the experts' knowledge about prison ombudsmen was neither intended nor attempted. Reaching out to the experts was undertaken depending on the local custom either directly by the researcher or was facilitated by the researcher's doctoral advisor. All selected experts not only consented to being interviewed but also to having the interview tape-recorded. The full transcripts obtained from the tape-recordings have then in turn been examined by means of qualitative content analysis. It is important to note that two of these interviews (with Roswitha Müller-Piepenkötter, former North Rhine-Westphalian Minister of Justice, and Prof. Michael Walter, current North Rhine-Westphalian prison ombudsman) were conducted in German. Wherever this thesis directly quotes from these interviews, careful translation was attempted by the researcher. Nevertheless, these quotes should be understood to only give an impression of what has been said instead of a full literal, contextual and situational representation.

The results of the quantitative content analysis of the literature and the interview transcripts has then been integrated using the "following a thread" approach by Morran-Ellis et al.. This was found to be the most efficient way to integrate the interview data into the existing data acquired during the qualitative content analysis of the literature. There, an analytical question was posed and followed across the interview data to create a (more) complete picture of the prison ombudsman phenomenon. Although the same was attempted in the oppo-

---

541   c.f. above and chapter A

site direction, the design of the interviews to fill in "missing links" did not leave much room for the generation of new analytical approaches derived from interviews toward the original research questions from this vantage point. The integrated information gained through analysis and interpretation of the datasets is presented in the following chapter.

D Analysis

This chapter draws on the Prisons and Probation Ombudsman for England and Wales and the Ombudsmann für den Justizvollzug Nordrhein-Westfalen as two examples of prison ombudsmen. The analysis of these subjects is sub-divided into a country survey aimed at depicting the specific legal and factual environment of these institutions and an analysis of the process of the legal introduction thereof. The subsequent synthesis includes conclusions drawn from the discussion about the proliferation and implementation in general. In order to demonstrate the extendibility of the concept, the chapter also includes a brief overview of further ombudsinstitutions not studied here.

I. The Prisons and Probation Ombudsman for England and Wales

The Prisons and Probation Ombudsman for England and Wales as the longer standing institution will be described first. This is done in the hope of reducing the national bias of the researcher by allowing for a fresher, less biased perspective on "the other" in an attempt to approach a neutral position.

1. Country survey

This section sets out to describe the institutional setting of the Prisons and Probation Ombudsman for England and Wales within its home country. The information provided will outline the current state of research on the institution and offer a brief overview of the history of imprisonment in the UK as well as the British and Welsh inmate population and their characteristics. A short explanation of the legal basis of imprisonment and the current prison organisation will follow with special attention being paid to the external and internal grievance channels available. Please note that this country survey is strictly limited to the background information necessary for an understanding of this study's argument.[542]

---

542 For an in-depth discussion of the British and Welsh penal system, please turn to the appropriate literature such as Livingstone (2008). A useful comparison of the penal systems in the UK and Germany is available from Koeppel (1999) and Lazarus (2004).

a) Current state of research

Since a description of the Prisons and Probation Ombudsman for England and Wales and the Ombudsmann für den Justizvollzug Nordrhein-Westfalen cannot be complete without also describing the circumstances under which these offices were created and how they compare to other institutions of similar nature, it is not enough to limit the research to publications specific to these two institutions. Instead some supplementation with literature about prison ombudsman in general – in particular also research dating from before the introduction of the two institutions – seems useful to ensure a better historical understanding and provide background on the institutionalization process.

In this context it is interesting to highlight the various names used to describe specialist ombudsmen for prisons: penal, corrections, jail and prison ombudsman occur as well as appellations passing over the term "ombudsman" (or the translations thereof in the local tongue) altogether in favour of other terms.[543] Today, prison ombudsman seems to be established as the generic term with the term corrections ombudsman as a close second.[544]

The literature about prison ombudsmen can generally be divided into four categories.

Category 1: Those works which speak about the work done by and achievements of general ombudsmen in prisons.[545]

Category 2: The early writings of the 70s and 80s campaigning for the introduction of prison ombudsmen and those writings accompanying the first steps of the freshly introduced American prison ombudsmen.[546]

Category 3: Newer works (1990 to today) which still strive for the introduction of schemes to all parts of their countries – that is all provinces, states or *Länder* – despite their knowledge of some failed introductory attempts and abolished schemes.[547]

---

543   Kretschmer (2005), pp. 217ff
544   Alarcón (2007), p. 591
545   Anderson (1978 and 1981b); Douglas (1984); Fliflet (2009); Groves (2002); Matheson (1982)
546   Anderson (1975b, 1981a and 1983); Barton (1983); Birkinshaw (1985); Cromwell (1974); Fulmer (1981); Johnson (1988); May (1975); Taugher (1972); Tibbles (1971); Williams (1975); Williams (1984)
547   Alarcón (2007); Heskamp (2007-2008); Jacobs (2004); Kretschmer (2005); Ryan/Ward (1993); Selke (1992)

Category 4: Those writings that criticize the independence and evaluation of introduced schemes and the scarcity of empirical research on them.[548]

This literature provides the context and fundament for the writings dealing specifically with the Prisons and Probation Ombudsman for England and Wales and the Ombudsmann für den Justizvollzug Nordrhein-Westfalen. The latter mostly belongs to the third category with three exceptions, which in asides simply acknowledged introductory announcements[549] or merely interviewed the representative of the newly established office of Ombudsmann für den Justizvollzug Nordrhein-Westfalen.[550]

It is interesting to note that the literature available on the Prisons and Probation Ombudsman for England and Wales and the Ombudsmann für den Justizvollzug Nordrhein-Westfalen is of disparate quality and quantity. However, this may still be due to the length of their respective institutional existence.

In fact, research on the Prisons and Probation Ombudsman for England and Wales has been accumulated since 1994. Although there is no one book exclusively limited to the Prisons and Probation Ombudsman for England and Wales, quite a few works make mention of the institution in passing. Essays have been published discussing its introduction, merits and suitable alterations to, for example possible changes to its legal structure.

A paper presented at a seminar held by the Austrian Human Rights Institute in 1992 mentions the contemplation of a special prisons ombudsman to be introduced in the UK.[551] The books mentioning the Prisons and Probation Ombudsman for England and Wales itself are listed in the following. First, there is a book on public sector ombudsmen that mentions the announcement by the Home Office of an upcoming introduction of the Prisons Ombudsman (as it was called back then).[552] The first book to actively refer to the Prisons and Probations Ombudsman for England and Wales is a German comparative work on the control of penal systems.[553] The first English description of the Prisons and Probations Ombudsman for England and Wales' work appeared in 2002.[554] The most recent book speaks about the ombudsman enterprise in general limiting its mention to costs per case and exemplifying the "ad hocery" of ombudsman in-

---

548   Hyson (2009a); van Roosbroek/van de Walle (2008); Selke (1993)
549   Ryan/Ward (1993); Neubacher (2008)
550   Sanker (2007)
551   Yardley (1994)
552   Seneviratne (1994)
553   Koeppel (1999)
554   Seneviratne (2002)

troduction using the Prisons and Probations Ombudsman for England and Wales' title and independence.[555] Finally, there are also some handbooks etc. on administrative[556] and prison law[557] mentioning the Prisons and Probations Ombudsman for England and Wales.

An essay published by Ryan/Ward describes the academic interest in a prisoners' grievance man right before the time of introduction of the Prisons and Probations Ombudsman for England and Wales. In fact, a postscript mentions the Home Office's announcement of the introduction.[558] It is interesting to note that the first essay focusing on the Prisons and Probations Ombudsman for England and Wales is not a description of his work – which only appeared almost a full decade after its introduction – [559], but a critical review.[560] Since then the discussion has been heavily dominated by Seneviratne and has been centred on strategies for improving the effectiveness of the Prisons and Probation Ombudsman for England and Wales and the inclusion thereof into the remit of the commission for joining up the public sector ombudsmen.[561] The description of the Prisons and Probation Ombudsman for England and Wales' work by Rotthaus[562] is in so far a curiosity as it was published in German and serves as an explanatory note for his applauding the introductory announcement of a prison ombudsman by the Ministry of Justice of North Rhine-Westphalia. This essay at the same time serves as one of the very few essays available on the German institution.

b) Brief history of imprisonment in England and Wales

"Prisons, as places of confinement, have existed since time immemorial. Yet prisons as we know them today – places to which offenders are sent as punishment, there to be changed – are a product of the industrial age."[563] Before 1877 there were two separate prison systems: the local prison system and a much smaller number of prisons run by central government, which were governed by two entirely separate administrative authorities.[564] Until 1857, transportation to

---

555   Buck et al. (2011a), pp. 41, 198
556   In place of many: Leyland/Anthony (2009), p. 146f
557   In place of many Livingstone (2003), p. 46ff
558   Ryan/Ward (1993)
559   Seneviratne (2001); Shaw (2004), as the second officeholder, described his own work and the institutional history
560   Morris/Henham (1998)
561   Henham (2000); Owers (2006); Seneviratne (2010, 2000a)
562   Rotthaus (2008)
563   Morgan/Liebling (2007), p. 1104
564   For details to this section see, Livingstone (2003) et al., pp. 1-5

the colonies presented the primary mode of penal treatment. However, the 1779 Act which authorized "hard labour" as a punishment for offenders, who would normally have been deported, created a need for more prisons. This need was met with the erection of national penitentiaries starting in 1816 at Millbank. The 19th century saw a progressive reform movement[565] towards more centralization that culminated in the Prison Act 1877 which transferred exclusive authority over prisons and prisoners in England and Wales to the Home Secretary. At this point there were some 31,000 prisoners in the system.[566] The un-repealed portions of these acts and the rules made thereunder formed the legal basis for the administration of prisons until the enactment of the Prison Act of 1952, which still constitutes the primary source of legislative authority. From 1945 to 1985 the prison system in England and Wales increasingly experienced overcrowding, which reached 10-15% by the 1980s.[567] The accompanying prison disorder led to the report of the May Committee in 1978-1979. Its only lasting achievement - despite being considered a landmark among analysts of prison policy – was the introduction of the Prison Inspectorate.[568] In 1990, the most widespread and destructive prison disturbance of English history occurred with distinctive gradations in 20 prisons including Strangeways prison in Manchester.[569] These riots led to another prison policy landmark, the judicial inquiry spear-headed by Lord Justice Woolf, who made twelve recommendations including the introduction of an independent complaint adjudicator, changes to grievance procedures and the delegation of more responsibility to prison governors.[570] Some head-way has been made towards a rights-based culture, although none of the monitoring bodies have been granted real statutory power.[571]

The prison estate consists of two main types of institutions. The first type is made up by the local prisons and remand centres, which are charged on the one hand with the prisoner reception from and delivery to the courts and on the other with the assessment and allocation of those serving sentences.[572] The second are the prisons housing sentenced prisoners including the Youth Offender Institutions and the adult training prisons, which exist in the two operational forms of open and closed institutions.

---

565   C.f. Prison Act of 1823 (gaol reform), 1835 (inspectors to be appointed by Home Secretary), 1865 (regulations for government of prisons).

566   Bottoms (1987), p. 178

567   Morgan/Liebling (2007), pp. 1100f

568   Morgan/Liebling (2007), pp. 1103, 1115

569   Shaw (2004), p. 125, Woolf/Tumim (1991)

570   Woolf/Tumim (1991), pp. 19f, 26

571   Eady (2007), p. 273

572   Here and in the following: Morgan/Liebling (2007), p. 1117

c) Inmate population and characteristics

In England and Wales the lowest number of inmates (5,300), was recorded after the First World War in 1918.[573] During and after WWII the rate increased from 11,000 in 1938 to 32,500 in 1968 – even though the courts were using imprisonment proportionately less than before the war.[574] In 1985 it had reached 46,233.[575] In 2008, there were 83,392 persons incarcerated in England and Wales; Germany sees approximately two-thirds of the amount of inmates in the UK, at 89 per 100,000 inhabitants.[576] Though international comparisons are fraught with difficulty, it seems obvious that England and Wales rely on the use of imprisonment to a greater extent than the rest of Western Europe.[577] However, this does not imply a greater faith in the effectiveness of prisons. Instead, they are considered too cost-intensive, overcrowded and hard to manage where a positive regime can only be maintained with difficulty. In addition, they only meet their purpose to an unsatisfactory degree. With approximately 75% of all young offenders and over 50% of all adult offenders reconvicted within two years of their release, the value for re-socialization of prison seems severely limited. The public protection cited during election times appears rather insignificant considering that so small a portion (estimated at 0.3%) of those responsible for offences are caught, convicted, and imprisoned.

England and Wales currently only know two types of custodial sentences: imprisonment and detention in a young offender institution. Nevertheless, there are other reasons for imprisonment such as non-payment, non-compliance with court orders or remand for those prisoners pending trial and sentence.[578] As a result, the overwhelming majority of prisoners are in prison for a matter of days, weeks, or months rather than years.[579] This is why it is important to differentiate between prison "receptions" and the "average daily population" (ADP). The latter shows that with 47% of the ADP serving sentences of four or more years, long-term adult prisoners dominate prisons numerically as well as culturally.

---

573   Bottoms (1987), p. 178
574   Bottoms (1987), p. 181
575   Bottoms (1987), p. 179
576   Walmsley,   Prison   World   Population   List,   p.   5.   Available   from http://www.prisonpolicy.org/research/international_incarceration_comparisons/   (last accessed June 6th, 2012). Prison population rate per 100,000 inhabitants: 153.
577   With the exception of Luxembourg. Walmsley, Prison World Population List, p. 5. Available from
      http://www.prisonpolicy.org/research/international_incarceration_comparisons/ (last accessed June 6th, 2012). Here and in the following: Morgan/Liebling (2007), p. 1104
578   Morgan (1991), p. 162
579   Here and in the following: Morgan/Liebling (2007), p. 1118

Yet, the kind of crime that usually leads to convictions is largely committed by adolescents and young adults. Consequently, the average prisoner is a young, socially and economically disadvantaged male charged with repetitive property offences.[580] Prisoners in their twenties make up a large part of the prison population (20% of the sentenced receptions are younger than 21) and dominate life in most prisons.[581] Prison sentences, especially immediate prison sentences, are generally levied on recurrent offenders – two-thirds of which have more than three previous convictions.

Sentenced women prisoners differ from their male counterparts in many ways. They are usually older, serve shorter sentences, have fewer and less severe previous convictions and are less likely to reoffend. At the same time, they are more likely to be addicted to drugs, and to have experienced repeated emotional, sexual, and physical abuse.[582] The consequent difference in needs has been recognized by the Prison Inspectorate which concluded that the sharing of sites with men does not benefit women and that equality of provision for women should not mean the exact same provision as for men.[583]

Today, about a tenth of the prison population of England and Wales is Muslim; approximately the same amount is made up by ethnic minorities.[584] However, ethnic minorities signify 25% of all remands in custody, 18% of all sentenced receptions, and 25% of the ADP. These numbers are even more extreme when only female prisoners are considered. On the whole, foreign nationals make up 12% of the prison population – of which more than 75% are non-white, most of them black. If one excludes foreign nationals and children under 16 years, one will find that in England and Wales black residents are imprisoned at roughly eight times the rate of white residents – a differential greater than in the US.

The improvement of material comfort for prisoners (such as telephone usage and more frequent family visits) has not alleviated all pressures experienced by inmates, especially the psychological one. In addition, these improvements tend to be offset by, for example, the expanding length of sentences.[585] Sometimes, psychological pressures prove unbearable causing the suicide rate of 78 prisoners in 2005, which was still a substantial reduction from previous years. Interrelated with this problem is the fact that 10% of male and 20% of female prisoners have been mental hospital patients at some point prior to their imprisonment and that very high proportions of all prisoner groups – 78 per cent of male remands,

---

580   Morgan/Liebling (2007), p. 1118
581   Here and in the following: Morgan/Liebling (2007), p. 1122
582   Morgan/Liebling (2007), p. 1120
583   Morgan/Liebling (2007), p. 1121
584   Here and in the following: Morgan/Liebling (2007), pp. 1121f, 1125
585   Here and in the following: Morgan/Liebling (2007), pp. 1102f

64 per cent of sentenced males, and 50 per cent of sentenced females – are diagnosed with some form of personality disorder.

d) Legal basis of imprisonment

The legislative framework for prisons and imprisonment in England and Wales is the Prison Act of 1952. The statute comprises 55 sections, 41 of which are still valid.[586] Except for section 47(2) the Prison Act establishes no clear statutory rights for prisoners. Further sections stipulate the introduction and continuation of the Chief Inspector of Prisons, the Independent Monitoring Boards (in exchange for the former Boards of Visitors) and the statutory officers including the governor of prisons – all of which are instituted with original powers derived from the statute and not exercised on behalf of the Home Secretary.

The statute places the oversight in the hands of the Home Secretary, who is empowered by the rule-making power of section 47(1) to regulate all details of prison life. This section's broad powers are the legal basis for the Prison Rules[587], which do not constitute a piece of primary legislation.[588] Ungenerous in their provisions, rarely specific, and, if so, generally granting prison mangers extensive discretion as to whether and which facilities will be provided, the Prison Rules validate the operational reality and legal position *status quo ante*.[589] The fact that both the Prison Act and Rules are short and diffuse documents has been previously explained with the British government's excessive tendency for secrecy.[590]

Administrative guidance concerning the Prison Act of 1952 and the Prison Rules is rendered by an Instruction Unit based in the Secretariat at Prison Service headquarters in form of the Prison Service Orders (PSO) and Instructions, which are complemented by a series of Prison Service Standards. All three of these offer only non-statutory guidance to those managing the prison system and have no legal status. The Standing Orders are designed by Prison Department Headquarters to provide explanatory interpretation to the governors. The Standing Orders in turn are detailed by Circular Instructions that are frequently changed in about 100 issues per annum. Like any policy applied by the Prison

---

586 For details to this section see, Livingstone et al. (2003), pp. 5-15
587 The current version of which are the Prison Rules 1999, SI 1999/728, as amended by the Prison (Amendment) Rules 2000, SI 2000/1794, the Prison (Amendment) Rules 2002, SI 2002/2116, the Prison (Amendment Rules) SI 2005/896 and SI 2005/3437, the Prison (Amendment) Rules 2007, SI 2007/2954, the Prison (Amendment Rules) 2008, SI 2008/597. The Prison Rules currently comprise six parts.
588 C.f. Livingstone et al. (2003), p. 19
589 Morgan/Liebling (2007), p. 1109
590 Here and in the following: Morgan (1991), p. 172

Service, they are only lawful in so far as they comply with the Human Rights Act and the Prison Act and Rules.

Although there has lately been significant judicial activity in developing a prisoners' rights jurisprudence, prisoners' rights protection remains partial and equivocal.[591] Even after the introduction of the Human Rights Act in 1998, judges are disinclined to intervene in many areas of prison life. While the statutory regime furthers political control and accountability of prison administration, there is a strong disinclination in England and Wales to provide prisoners with legally enforceable entitlements. However, it is now common opinion that individual rules are justiciable in the sense that breaches may give rise to a public law remedy. Of this, the prisoners have made use on a case by case basis, to determine, for example, their residual position after Lord Wilberforce's dictum in *Raymond* v. *Honey* ([1983] 1 A.C. 1, 10): "A prisoner retains all those rights that are not taken away either express or by necessary implication".[592]

The convoluted nature, imprecision and arbitrariness of the legal basis for imprisonment in England and Wales has in the past given rise to criticism and been declared to impact the decision making regarding prisoners as well as the prison regimes themselves. "With no compelling codification impulse, no dominant rights rhetoric within prison policy-making, nor a Constitutional Court with the institutional and symbolic power to force a legislature to define prisoners' rights, England is without a statutory code of prisoners' rights and an overarching systemic conception of prison administration."[593]

e) Current prison organisation

Due to the differences existing between penal institutions, the current prison organization for England and Wales can only be recounted in a generalized manner. This section will include general information on the executional aim, the administrative structure, personnel structure, living conditions as well as on disciplinary and control measures.

The executional aim of the current penal system is encompassed in the *Statement of Purpose* posted at the entrance of every prison: "Her Majesty's Prison Service serves the public by keeping in custody those convicted by the courts. Our duty is to look after them with humanity and to help them lead law abiding and useful lives in custody and after release". According to this *Statement*, the executional aim is to achieve security whilst maintaining basic standards and attempting the lasting rehabilitation of the inmates.

---

591   Here and in the following: Lazarus (2004), p. 3
592   Morgan/Liebling (2007), p. 1109
593   Lazarus (2004), p. 128

The Prison Service is headed by a Director-General, who is assisted by a Deputy Director-General. The latter oversees the work of the Area Mangers, the Manger of Women's prisons and Young Offender Institutions and the Manger responsible for juveniles. Below the Directors-General are currently five Directorates: High Security, Personnel, Finance, Operations and Health. Some of the Directors as well as the Director-General and the Home Secretary are members of the Prison Service Strategy Board. This Board is intended to provide a forum to discuss the strategic direction of the Service and Prison Service plans and their performance. The Carter Report or Correctional Services Review of 2003 recommended the concept of offender management. The National Offender Management Service has overall responsibility for protecting the public and reducing re-offenses, and is ultimately responsible for issues and policy around prisons.[594] They coordinate such services as providing prisoners with one probation officer throughout their sentence and then on release.[595] Since 2004[596], Her Majesty's Prison Service is a part of the National Offender Management Service (NOMS), which since 2007 is located within the Ministry of Justice. HM Prison Service is responsible for the management of the 138 public-sector prisons.[597] The remaining 11 prisons in England and Wales are privately managed prisons, organized in a separate strand of NOMS currently coordinated through the Office of Contracted Prisons.

The personnel structure in prisons has been continuously improving. Currently, there are 48,000 full-time equivalent staff.[598] 30,000 of these are uniformed prison officers. This leads to an "overall prisoner to staff ratio of 1.4:1, and a prisoner to officer ratio of 2.82:1". After WWII, the prisoner to staff ratio still averaged around 7.5:1. Staffing, security and housing costs are the biggest factors adding up to the considerable sum of £26,412 per prisoner per annum.[599]

Prison conditions are influenced by such diverse subjects a good order and discipline, healthcare and the day-to-day life. The latter usually is subject to the personal preference of free citizens - possibly assisted by state agencies. Where prisoners are concerned, the structuring of the day, the provision of food, work, education and living space all depends on the provision by prison authorities. It is an impossible task to describe in a succinct manner the everyday life of a prison. It also falls outside the purpose of this study. Thus, only a limited over-

---

594   http://www.justice.gov.uk/about/noms (last accessed June 6th, 2012)
595   Livingstone et al. (2003), pp. 31f
596   C.f. Morgan/Liebling (2007), p. 1109 for an overview of the history of the prison service
597   http://www.justice.gov.uk/about/hmps (last accessed June 6th, 2012)
598   Here and in the following: Morgan/Liebling (2007), p. 1102
599   Morgan/Liebling (2007), p. 1101

view over prison conditions is offered here.[600] Since the late 90s, all prisoners have 24h access to toilet facilities, no prisoners are held three to a cell designed for one and the average prisoner had 23.7 hours of purposeful activity per week. However, overcrowding necessitates continued holding of two prisoners held to a cell designed for one.[601] Continued and rising overcrowding also threatens other improvements to conditions. The law has functioned only to a limited extent as a guarantor of living conditions. It influences living conditions in two ways: on the one hand through the policing of the application of particular rules and standards relating to, for example, exercise, food, heating and time out of cell and on the other hand by means of examining whether the conditions drop below the minimum standard of human rights concerning the protection from torture, inhuman or degrading treatment, or punishment. Courts usually assume a hands-off approach were the examination of living conditions in the first category are concerned and indicated that "only the most unpleasant conditions, those which pose an imminent threat to life or health, will be seen as falling below minimum human rights standards".[602] Today many significant rulings on prison conditions are made by the ECtHR ruling on Article 3 of the ECHR, which protects against torture and other forms of inhuman or degrading punishment. The UK has previously been found guilty of breaches of Article 3.[603] In its judgments, the Court regularly refers to the general standards for imprisonment outlined in the Second General Report of the ECPT (ECPT/Inf (92)3).

In prisons, good order and discipline is maintained through a combination of disciplinary and non-disciplinary powers. Without doubt, there is a need to maintain order in prisons to avoid the growth of a climate of fear – dominant for example in the US. Good order is upheld by discipline. This area traditionally produces the sharpest conflicts between prisoners and staff. The present system concerning disciplinary charges is laid down in the Discipline Manual (PSO 2000) and in the revised Prison Rules. According to rule 53(1), governors are instructed to lay a disciplinary charge within 48 hours of the discovery of an alleged offense. Criminal offences are to be reported to the police. If a governor decides not to refer to the police Prison Rule 53(A), this necessitates the decision of whether to handle the event personally or refer it to an independent adjudicator. The Discipline Manual demands a referral wherever the offence poses

---

600   For details on reception, induction, accommodation, recreation, searches, mandatory drug testing, food, clothing, work, education, facilities and privileges please see Livingstone et al. (2003), p. 216-46, for healthcare please consult its chapter 6.
601   On average 17.2% in 2000, c.f. Livingstone et al. (2003), p. 214
602   Livingstone et al. (2003), p. 215
603   For example in Price v UK (2002) 34 EHRR 53, Application 33394/96. For details see Livingstone et al. (2003), pp. 253f

"a most serious risk to the order and control of the establishment or to the safety of those in it" and would lead to the award of additional days if the prisoner is found guilty. The function of the independent adjudicator was introduced in the wake of the Ezeh and Connors v UK (2002) 35 EHRR 28, Applications 39665/98 and 40086/98 decision and in many ways is similar to the recommendation of a Prison Disciplinary Tribunal by the Prior's Committee.[604] Prison Rule 53(4) allows governors to segregate prisoners prior to adjudication to prevent a continuation of the conflict. The extensive use of this option has given rise to criticism.[605] Prison Rule 54(3) gives the right to legal representation wherever a case is referred to an independent adjudicator and the Discipline Manual indicates that prisoner appearing before a governor on disciplinary charge should be asked if they wish legal representation.

The list of disciplinary offense is currently comprised of 29 items and set out in Prison Rule 51. Besides general offences, it also contains those cases specific to the prison environment such as intentionally obstructing an officer in the execution of his duty, Prison Rule 51(6). Prison Rule 54(2) specifies that at any inquiry into a charge the prisoner has to be given a full opportunity of hearing what is alleged against him/her and a full opportunity to present his/her own case.[606] The punishments are set out in Prison Rule 55 and include caution, forfeiture of privileges, stoppage of earnings, cellular confinement etc. According to Rule 55A, an independent adjudicator may also award up to 42 additional days' imprisonment. In 2000, there was an average of 99 awards of additional days per 100 population, making additional days the most frequently awarded form of punishment.[607]

Under the heading of control (47(1) Prison Rules) fall all those powers available to prison authorities that are non-disciplinary and consequently do not depend upon proof of a disciplinary offence by the affected prisoner. Control measures therefore cannot be imposed as punishment. Nevertheless, they can achieve as drastic a change in the living conditions of prisoners as disciplinary measures while not being accompanied by equal procedural safeguards. Although control measures officially are included in the supervisory jurisdiction of the High Court, they constitute an area where in practice the existing legal framework awards governors and Area officials a nearly unencumbered discretion to regulate prisoners' lives. The Human Rights Act of 1998 has not had much impact where control measures are concerned. Rules 45, 46, 48 and 49 of

---

604   C.f. Livingstone et al. (2003), pp. 382, 385
605   C.f. Livingstone et al. (2003), p. 399
606   For procedure and evidence at disciplinary hearings please refer to Livingstone et al. (2003), p. 404-8, the appeals process is described on pp. 413-6
607   Livingstone et al. (2003), p. 409

the Prison Act set out four ways in which to deal with a prisoner constituting a threat to prison order:

- segregation within the same prison
- transfer to a different prison
- allocation to a Close Supervision Centre
- use of an approved method of restraint and/or confinement in a special cell in case of violence or disruptive behaviour.[608]

f) External and internal grievance channels

The prison law in England and Wales knows both internal and external grievance channels. In this section, only those that are in any way specific to England and Wales will be discussed in any detail. For those grievance-channels available to all European prisoners, please refer to section B II. 1.

The internal grievance channels available are the governor and the Independent Monitoring Board (IMB). They are statutory requirements, c.f. section 6 of the 1952 Act, and allow prisoners to bring their requests and complaints before the governor or the IMB either orally or in writing. Rule 11 (3) ensures confidentiality of written complaints.

The IMB, formerly Board of Visitors, is not required to be available every day. Although, rule 79 calls for frequent visits to the prison, this does not imply a prisoner's right to demand a confidential meeting at any time. A prisoner dissatisfied with only being able to speak with one member of the Board can reasonably ask to have access to the full Board at one of their regular meetings. The IMB is a body of unpaid, independent lay volunteers appointed by the Secretary of State to monitor the day-to-day life and ensure that proper standards of care and decency are maintained.[609] The boards have four functions:

- monitoring the fair treatment and welfare of prisoners in the everyday-life in their local prison and handling any complaints or requests they make
- monitoring the regimes, state, and administration of prison
- listening to the concerns of staff and
- reporting matters of concern to the Governor or Director and, if necessary, the Secretary of State.

The IMBs have no statutory power to change either individual administrative decisions or policy. A common feature of many structures similar to the IMB is the concern raised about their efficiency and independence. A review of the

---

608   For the critique of additional measures such as the removal of clothes etc. see Livingstone et al. (2003), p. 449

609   Here and in the following: Morgan/Liebling (2007), p. 1115

Boards of Visitors led to several changes: The change of title to IMB and the relocation to the same building as the Prison Ombudsman were intended to improve the perceived independence[610], whilst the publication of their reports was aimed at proving their efficiency. However, it is not clear that their credibility has improved in light of these changes.

Consequently, prisoners prefer another internal grievance channel, which represents the most commonly used method of complaint – an application to the governor.[611] Although rule 11 states that prisoners may complain every day to the governor, rule 81 allows the governor to delegate any of his powers. Accordingly, as long as a system is arranged for a staff member to be available to daily hear complaints and requests, a prisoner cannot insist to complain to the governor in person. Since the Rules specify no time limit for replies, they must be understood to comply with the European Prison Rule 42 (4) that prison authorities deal with complaints "promptly" and "without undue delay" unless they are obviously frivolous or groundless. Prisoners must adhere to the time limits set out for submitting complaints in PSO 2510 in order to ensure their eligibility.

Up until April 2nd, 2012, ordinary complaints were resolved in a three-tier process. The first tier involves a response by the prisoner's wing officer. If dissatisfied with this response, the prisoner may take the matter to a member of the management staff (second tier) and finally to the governor (third tier). All staff members involved are encouraged to confer with the prisoner about the problem in person and must give reasons for their decisions. If all routes fail to prove satisfactory from the prisoner's point of view, according to PSO 2510 staff must be able to inform the prisoner of further external avenues of complaint.[612] However, since this process has been considered unwieldy and slow, the removal of the third tier has been tested in a trial period of multiple months during which the Prisons and Probation Ombudsman for England and Wales was asked to monitor the complaint levels. When no increase was registered, the third tier was removed. In an interview the Assistant Ombudsman stated: "Unfortunately, that means that the governor of the prison doesn't get to see the complaints anymore. And that's a problem for us. Because when we get to see the complaint it has been answered by prison staff and we make a full recommendation which goes to the headquarters of prison service. A prison is being criticized when the governor hasn't even seen the complaint."[613] It is too early to say whether this drawback will lead to the reconsideration of the removed third tier. In any case,

---

610   C.f. Livingstone et al. (2003), p. 13
611   Fowles (1989), p. 19
612   C.f. Livingstone et al., (2003) p. 43
613   p. 4 of the interview conducted on April 2nd, 2012 with Assistant Ombudsman, Olivia Morrison-Lyons. Full transcript available through this study's author.

the accompanying improvement concerning the promptness of the grievance handling has to be welcomed and a concerted effort to retain this achievement should be made.

The external grievance channels available to prisoners in England and Wales are HM Chief Inspector of Prisons, the judiciary (either in form of civil actions or judicial review), the Home Office Controller of Contracted-Out Prisons and the Prisons and Probation Ombudsman for England and Wales as well as penal pressure groups.

HM Chief Inspector for Prisons (HMCIP) was recommended by the May Committee (1979: 92-6) and exists since 1981 outside the Prison Service, but inside the Home Office. HMCIP is charged with reporting to the Home Secretary "on the treatment of prisoners and conditions in prison" (Prison Act 1952, section 5A(3)), and does so by undertaking regular inspections of prisons, thematic reviews of aspects of policy and by occasionally investigating major incidents. HMCIP is not engaged in grievance handling and therefore does not constitute a proper external grievance channel. It is mentioned here because prisoners may approach and are heard by the Inspectorate's staff during their inspectorial visits and systemic investigations.

A proper external grievance mechanism is the judiciary. In all cases when a citizen could take civil action, a prisoner is also allowed to sue for damages, for example when the administration has not fulfilled all their obligations to exercise due care. Prisoners may also sue for a judicial re-examination of administrative decisions. Legal action has to be taken within three months from the point in time when the decision was made. First, they must apply to the divisional court. Appeals of decisions made there are directed to the Court of Appeal. In cases of extraordinary legal import another appeal directed at the House of Lords is possible. For a long time, it was an uncontested belief held by the British courts that an involvement in everyday prison life would undermine the governors' authority and lead to difficulties with the up-keeping of discipline.[614] Accordingly, they practised a hands-off approach. As Lord Justice Shaw stated in 1979, "in the scheme envisaged by the [Prison] Act and shaped by those Rules, the courts have no defined place and no direct or immediate function." (R v Board of Visitors of Hull Prison, ex p St Germain and others [1978] 1 QB (CA) 425, 454). Lately, English courts have defined their own role through the assertion and development of their inherent jurisdiction under public law. Their encroachment upon the executive terrain of prison administration has been a

---

614   Here and in the following: Koeppel (1999), p. 47

painstakingly slow process in which the courts have developed prisoners' legal rights under common law and given the Prison Rules some legal force.[615]

Another external grievance channel, which is obviously only available to prisoners in private prisons is the application to the Home Office Controller of Contracted-Out Prisons. One of these "is placed in each private prison to monitor performance under the contract and enforce compliance with the Prison Rules, adjudicate on disciplinary charges and investigate allegations against staff. While it is argued that private prisons are thus more accountable than public prisons, and deliver better and cheaper regimes through contractual incentives, scepticism remains."[616]

The Prison and Probation Ombudsman for England and Wales is another external grievance channel. Since it is one of the two subjects of this study and will be examined in detail in chapter D I., only its existence is mentioned here.

The status of penal pressure groups[617] as external grievance mechanism is somewhat hazy. While the prisoner may freely communicate with the groups, they cannot directly influence any administrative decision. However, they can make injustices and insufficiently provided administrative care public and in that way work towards a reconsideration of individual administrative acts. Obviously, this has no binding effect on the prison administration which may (or may not) react as it sees fit.

2. How was the Prisons and Probation Ombudsman for England and Wales implemented?

Drawing upon the institutional setting provided by means of the country survey above, this section will scrutinize the implementation of the Prisons and Probation Ombudsman for England and Wales. Implementation can be observed from two angles: the process and the outcome. This analysis will commence with the description of the process upon which the examination of factual evidence of the structural outcome will draw.

a) The process of implementation: History of the Prisons and Probation Ombudsman for England and Wales

The analysis of the implementation process will be carried out through a description of the institutional history, which is deliberately kept rather short – especially compared to the history of the Justizvollzugsbeauftragter des Landes

---

615   Lazarus (2004), p. 130
616   Lazarus (2004), p. 151
617   C.f. Morgan (1991), p. 163

Nordrhein-Westfalen – as much has already been written about the Prisons and Probation Ombudsman for England and Wales.[618] Nevertheless, a brief presentation is necessary to allow all readers to follow the argument used to reconstruct the Prisons and Probation Ombudsman for England and Wales' development as a product of cross-fertilization.

aa) Brief history of institution

In retrospect, the act of first having recommended a prison ombudsman for and within the UK cannot be attributed clearly. Fowles notes that "both John Prescott MP and Graham Zellick proposed it after the Hull prison riot. John Prescott proposed the establishment of a separate prison ombudsman in the report of his independent inquiry into the riot and its aftermath. Zellick made a similar proposal in an article in The Times shortly after the announcement of the Fowler inquiry into the Hull riot".[619] What is clear, however, is that "[t]he prison ombudsman scheme resulted from concerns, expressed through the 1980s, that the mechanisms for dealing with prisoners' grievances were inadequate".[620] These concerns were brought into sharp focus in 1990 by the severest prison disturbances in the history of England and Wales.[621] These led to the Woolf Report (Cm 1456, 1991). At the time there was a general feeling that swift action was necessary.[622] While the Association of the Members of the Boards of Visitors[623], the All-Party Penal Affairs Group and the British Section of the International Commission of Jurists (Justice) in its Report "Justice in Prison"[624] proposed a "Prisons Ombudsman", the Prison Service in its evidence to LJ Woolf argued that a trial phase for the new internal grievance mechanisms should determine the necessity of an external complaints channel. Woolf and Tumim recognized that a balance between security, control and justice was a necessary precondition for stability in the prison system.[625] Consequently, they rejected the Prison Service's demand for delaying the introduction of an external grievance channel stating that

---

618 Morris/Henham (1998); Seneviratne (2001, 2002 and 2010)
619 Zellick, Graham (1976), „Why Prisoners should have an ombudsman of their own", The Times October 4th and Prescott, John (1976), "Hull Prison Riot, August 31st to September 3rd, 1976. Submissions, observations and recommendations of Mr John Prescott MP, Hull East", Unpublished Report dated December 21st; both cited according to Fowles (1989), p. 32
620 Seneviratne (2002), p. 90
621 Meant are of course the riots in Strangeways Penitentiary and others.
622 Ryan/Ward (1993), p. 44
623 Ryan/Ward (1993), p. 43
624 Woolf/Tumim (1991), p. 414
625 For an in-depth analysis of the Woolf Report see Morris/Henham (1998), p. 347

"the presence of an independent element within the Grievance Procedure is more than just an 'optional extra'. The case for some form of independent person or body to consider grievances is incontrovertible. There is no possibility of the present system satisfactorily meeting this point even once it has bedded down. A system without an independent element is not a system which accords with proper standards of justice".[626]

Based on this reasoning and acknowledging the substantive inadequacies of existing procedures and practices to achieve justice as well as the ideological, organizational and financial crisis in the UK prison system, the report's authors Woolf and Tumim recommended the introduction of what they called an independent complaints adjudicator.[627] This recommendation significantly differs from the Prisons Ombudsman. At the time, the UK had no tradition of introducing ombudsmen, instead preferring commissioners and adjudicators. Commissioners such as the PCA usually featured a statutory footing, while the administrative appointment is a typical feature of the design of adjudicators.[628] Offices of the later type were already associated with a "speedy resolution of complaints and a commitment to improving standards of administrative practices". This was taken into consideration when the need for an independent element in the prison system was finally accepted by the Government in the White Paper *Custody, Care and Justice.*[629] The 1992 consultation paper[630] still proposed the introduction of an independent complaints adjudicator. Yet, following a process of consultation carried out in the same year, the name of the office was changed to Prisons Ombudsman.[631] Thus, when Kenneth Clarke, then Home Secretary, announced the introduction of the institution in 1993, it was called Prisons Ombudsman. This represented a change in name only as its status and remit – like that of an adjudicator – were not to be established in primary legislation. It was in this design that the office of the Prisons Ombudsman commenced work in 1994. Later, it has been said that this "has effectively deprived the office-holder of the political and substantive *locus standi* to engineer fundamental changes in prison administration".[632]

In the beginning, its status and terms of reference where to be found in the 1992 Prison Service Documents called *Proposal for Ministerial Considera-*

---

626   Woolf/Tumim (1991), p. 419
627   Woolf/Tumim (1991), pp. 20, 26
628   Here and in the following: Morris/Henham (1998), p. 351
629   Home Office (1991) at para. 8.7
630   Home Office, 1992
631   Shaw (2004), p. 126
632   Morris/Henham (1998), p. 351

tion.[633] The commencement of the ombudsman's work was not entirely smooth – especially considering the early relations between the ombudsman and the Prison Service. This led to the Home Secretary considerably narrowing the Prisons Ombudsman's remit and, with it, its independence. This situation continued until the Select Committee on the Parliamentary Ombudsman determined upon examining the Prisons Ombudsman's role and powers that the non-statutory framework was inadequate.[634] Accordingly, it recommended not only an extension of the remit to include administrative decisions of Ministers, but also unfettered access to relevant documents. Following discussion with the Prisons Ombudsman, the Labour Government elected in May 1997 agreed to new, more extensive terms of reference.

The 2000 Cabinet Office Review proposal for an integrated service of public sector ombudsmen in England did not include the Prisons and Probation Ombudsman for England and Wales in the new Commission arrangements, on the basis that it occupies a niche role, is not established by statute and is a proper part of the executive.[635] Whenever the Prisons and Probation Ombudsman for England and Wales is placed on a statutory footing, its relationship with the Commission will have to be readdressed.

In 2001, the Prisons and Probation Ombudsman for England and Wales additionally received jurisdiction over complaints pertaining to the probation system. Since 2004, the Prisons and Probation Ombudsman for England and Wales has also been charged with investigating deaths in custody. The remit was further extended in 2006 to include complaints made by those held in immigration detention. Since the latter three functions are not of interest to this study, they will not be further investigated here. The departmental re-organisation occurring in 2007 ensued in the transferal of the prisons and the probation service, including the Prisons and Probation Ombudsman for England and Wales, from the Home Office to the Ministry of Justice presided over by the Lord Chancellor who is also the Secretary of State for Justice.[636] After an extensive revision phase, the Cabinet Office in 2011 decided on the future of some government bodies including the Prisons and Probation Ombudsman for England and Wales, which together with HM Inspectorate of Prisons and the Independent Monitoring Boards was retained on grounds of transparency.[637]

---

633 Here and in the following in detail: Seneviratne 2001, pp. 93f
634 Seneviratne (2002), pp. 91f
635 Seneviratne (2000a), pp. 582, 587
636 Leyland/Anthony, (2009) p. 147
637 Fowles/Wilson (2011), p. 203

bb) The Prisons and Probation Ombudsman for England and Wales as a product of cross-fertilization

Now that a brief overview over the history of the Prisons and Probation Ombudsman for England and Wales has been provided, it will be analysed whether the Prisons and Probation Ombudsman for England and Wales is in fact a product of cross-fertilization. This would be the case if there was evidence of an inter-legal-system-learning-process which involves a knowledge transfer split into an acquisition phase used for information gathering and an implementation phase during which the acquired knowledge is implemented in the host country – here England and Wales.

When the Prisons Ombudsman was proposed, the ombudsman concept was already well-known within the United Kingdom.[638] It had already instituted the PCA in 1967, which had successfully operated for more than a decade when the idea of a prisons ombudsman first sprung up in the 1980s. Mossberger and Wolman point out that policy transfer as

"a form of decision making by analogy [… which uses] another entity's experience as a source of ideas and evidence […] presents a number of practical challenges. Differences in political systems and the policy environments are likely to be more pronounced in cross-national transfer than in cases in which subnational governments emulate the experience of others within the same national boundaries".[639]

The same is naturally true where policy models are emulated within nations. Thus, the question is whether the Prisons Ombudsman was an adaptation of an idea already manifested within Britain in the form of the PCA or whether it is based upon sources from abroad. The latter is a possibility since Canada (1973) as well as three US states (Indiana 1973, Michigan 1975, Kentucky 1982) had already established prison ombudsmen at the time.[640]

Evidence of knowledge gathering and with it the existence of an acquisition phase can frequently be affirmed through the existence of driving factors such as catalysts, agents and timing. The historic catalyst that may have originally set off a potential transfer process was the mounting dissatisfaction with the prison system in the 1980s. This dissatisfaction included the demand for a separate prisons ombudsman at least since shortly after the conflict inherent in the Hull prison riots and inspired a number of different agents to become involved in the discussion which created a discourse pull.[641] The literature on policy transfer

---

638   See section above
639   Mossberger/Wolman (2003), p. 428
640   For details see table in chapter B II. 6.
641   For the Hull riots see the section above; for dissatisfaction, conflict and discourse pull as catalysts for transfer processes see B III. 4. and there especially Figure 8

acknowledges eight categories of agents: "politicians; bureaucrats; policy entrepreneurs including think-tanks; knowledge institutions (KIs), academicians and other experts; pressure groups; global finance institutions; international organizations; and supra-national institutions".[642] The mounting dissatisfaction with the penal system producing the discourse pull was expressed by academicians, pressure groups and most prominently JUSTICE.[643] The latter, in unpremeditated conjunction with the prison experts and academicians Birkinshaw and Wener, involved itself in the cause for a prison ombudsman expressly weighing the usefulness of extending the PCA model or introducing an entirely new body.[644] Due to

- the PCA's mode of operation,
- absence of own-motion powers,
- limitation to investigations of procedural injustice,
- lack of any perceivable impact on the penal system,

combined with the expectation of

- no savings to be gained from a combination of the two institutions,
- the creation of an unmanageable workload,
- as well as a conflict of roles,

all three attest to "no hesitation in preferring" "an independent investigator" "with a more assertive role in questioning policy and regulation" whose "role would go beyond the model of the ombudsman as presently perceived in this country" and conclude that "[t]herefore we recommend the establishment of another Parliamentary Commissioner, a Prisons Ombudsman".

These agents were joined in their discourse pull creating quest for an independent prison ombudsman by quite a few more that also acted as transfer agents pertaining to the effort of providing potential sources from abroad.[645] The 1977 JUSTICE Report "Our fettered Ombudsman" is the first to mention the Canadian Correctional Investigator as potential model.[646] The idea was quickly adopted by the 1979 May Committee Report, which notes that "there may be

---

642   Evans (2009a), p. 244

643   For a description of the historic development and details on the involved academicians see Henham (2000),, p. 291

644   Here and in the following all three: Birkinshaw (1981), p. 154; Wener (1983), p. 19 and JUSTICE (1983), p. 40

645   Douglas (1984); Williams (1984), p. 91 "… there is now sufficient evidence from other jurisdictions to justify looking seriously at the case for a prison ombudsman in this country …"

646   JUSTICE (1977), p. 23

useful lessons to be learned from experience there although time has not allowed us to pursue the matter to a conclusion".[647] This first step of the policy transfer process produced what Mossberger/Wolman call "awareness" – the diffusion of policy ideas "through professional organizations, broader networks of specialists (policy communities or epistemic communities), the efforts of policy entrepreneurs, the media, and chance contacts".[648] While this may be true for the 1977 JUSTICE report and the May Committee, the academicians pursued a more research extensive and institutionally inclusive approach towards information gathering for knowledge transfer. Birkinshaw in 1981 examined both American and Canadian prison ombudsmen "to see whether any useful ideas or suggestions can be elicited" expressly noting that "no wholesale transplantation is suggested" – a recommendation that appears particularly wise in light of the modern view on cross-fertilization and policy transfer.[649] Wener included the experience of both the Swedish, Danish and New Zealand general ombudsmen's activities in prison and those of the Canadian specialty prison ombudsman in his 1983 report, which singled out the Canadian Correctional Investigator as a best practice example.[650] At least, the 1983 JUSTICE report "Justice in Prison" – inspired by the May Committee Report's positive mention of the Canadian Correctional Investigator – which purposefully set out to collect "some information about the Canadian experience" must be considered an active search for information.[651] It may therefore be safely concluded that Prisons Ombudsman idea in its British manifestation drew upon sources from abroad, particularly from the Canadian experience.

But as Evans notes, "[t]he proof of policy transfer lies in its implementation. In other words, it is not possible to identify the content of a transfer and by implication whether transfer has occurred without adopting an implementation perspective".[652] It can be seen from the 1987 and 1989 Home Office Reports[653] as

---

647 Committee of Inquiry into the United Kingdom Prison Services "May Committee Report", p. 94
648 Mossberger/Wolman (2003), p. 430
649 Birkinshaw (1981), pp. 149, 153; c.f. chapter B III. – in place of many De Jong et al. (2002), p. 288, who recommend following loosely defined models during transfer processes, and Mossberger/Wolman (2003), p. 431, who recommend assessment of the similarity of problems and goals.
650 Wener (1983), pp. 18f and 17; a similar study is also available from Douglas (1984)
651 JUSTICE (1983), p. 42 and appendix
652 Evans (2009a), p. 246; Mossberger/Wolman (2003), p. 431 also recognize this demanding „[a]pplication. The final criterion is whether information about the policy in another country is actually used in the decision process. The criterion does not require the 'borrowing' country adopt the policy in whole; the policy may be adopted with modifications or even rejected."

well as the Home Office evidence to the May Committee that the dissatisfaction and its accompanying discourse pull were unable to achieve the critical level necessary to move from the acquisition phase of cross-fertilization to the implementation stage. In fact, in its evidence to the May Committee the Home Office cited "constitutional problems of reconciling the power to override decisions made by the Prison Service with the notion of ministerial responsibility" in conjunction with the fact that these powers alone would set a prisons ombudsman apart from the PCA as the reason why they "would not wish to exclude the possibility of establishing a new prison ombudsman, but could not take the view that a sufficient case for one had yet been made".[654] Mossberger and Wolman describe this phenomenon as "plant[ed] ideas that lie dormant until policy makers recognize them as potential solutions to a particular problem and then begin to engage in prospective evaluation".[655]

The jump start for this phase occurred again in form of a conflict, namely the April 1990 prison riots in Strangeways Penitentiary and others, which have been "the longest and most devastating riot in British penal history" and were described as "unprecedentedly serious" and "25 days of [...] siege" with "various forms of disruption occur[...ing] in more than 30 establishments".[656] As this incident is much closer in time to the introduction of the prison ombudsman, it must be considered the more immediate reason for implementation.[657] In its aftermath, the original agents were joined by politicians (the All-Party Penal Affairs Group) and pressure groups (the Association of the Members of the Boards of Visitors and the Prison Reform Trust) in their demand for a prisons ombudsman.[658] Their evidence led Woolf and Tumim to recommend an independent grievance channel in their 1991 official report on the prison disturbances of April 1990, which they – in accordance with the British tradition of introducing "adjudicators" whenever bodies lacking a statutory footing were created[659] – called "Complaints Adjudicator".[660] The Home Office accepted the recommen-

---

653   Home Office (1987); Home Office (1989)
654   Fowles (1989), p. 33; Home Office Evidence to the May Committee (1979), p. 241; repeated in May Committee Report (1979), pp. 93-4
655   Mossberger/Wolman (2003), p. 430
656   Morgan (1991), p. 715; Player (1992), p. 137
657   In agreement Henham (2000), p. 290
658   It is interesting to note that at the time Stephen Shaw, a later Prisons and Probation Ombudsman for England and Wales incumbent, was director of the Prison Reform Trust charity. Here and in the following: Woolf/Tumim (1991), pp. 415, 419ff
659   See section above at F I. 2. a) aa) for details
660   For details on the tensions inherent to the Inquiry – "speed, a broad-ranging investigation and an open and extensive consultation style" – and the resulting broad-brush approach see Morgan (1991), pp. 715ff and Morgan (1992), p. 232

dation as well as the title[661], but changed the latter following a process of consultation in what appears to be a last minute decision that resulted in January 1993 in the outgoing Home Secretary Kenneth Clarke's announcement of the planned introduction of a "Prisons Ombudsman".[662]

Some authors fail to see or at least remark on any difference between the Complaints Adjudicator and the Prisons Ombudsman. Others on the one hand acknowledge it as "welcome news that Woolf's proposals have not been watered down by Home Office", whilst at the same time critiquing that the announced institution was "a significantly watered-down version of the Prisons Ombudsman that the penal lobby had hoped for".[663] The first incumbent, Sir Peter Woodhead, explains the change in name saying that "the title 'Prisons Ombudsman' is [...] is generally understood as indicating justice, openness and fairness. Furthermore, the title 'Adjudicator' suggests executive powers which I do not possess in a definitive sense".[664]

This quote emphasizing the positive connotation of the term "prisons ombudsman" in combination with Shaw's evidence on the consultation processes inside the Home Office proves that the final selection of the name for the implementation of the already accepted idea of an independent grievance channel was influenced by knowledge transferred during the acquisition phase. This knowledge verifiably reached Home Office via an unbroken chain: 1990 Prison Riots eliciting the evidence given in 1990 by transfer agents (the All-Party Penal Affairs Group, the Association of the Members of the Boards of Visitors and the Prison Reform Trust) to LJ Woolf, whose official report, tabled in 1991 (*Prison Disturbances April 1990: Report of an Inquiry*) was accepted in the 1991 Government White Paper *Custody, Care and Justice*.[665] The acceptance was carried over into the 1992 consultation paper *An Independent Complaints Adjudicator for Prisons: A Consultation Paper*[666] which finally produced the announcement of a Prisons Ombudsman by Home Secretary Kenneth Clarke in 1993.

---

661 Again: see section above at F I. 2. a) aa) for details; Home Office (1991), at para. 8.7; Home Office (1992)

662 Shaw (2004), p. 126; Ryan/Ward (1993), p. 48; Livingstone et al. (2003), p. 51

663 Ryan/Ward (1993), p. 49

664 C.f. section above at F I. 2. a) aa) for details: change in name only because status and remit – like that of an adjudicator – were not to be established in primary legislation; quote taken from the Board of Visitors Newsletter, Autumn 1994 cited after http://www.british-prisons.co.uk/index.php?option=com_content&view=article&id=46&itemid=59&lang=en (last accessed June 6th, 2012)

665 Home Office (1991) at para. 8.7

666 Home Office (1992)

Consequently, it can be noted here that during a long, multi-layered acquisition phase a knowledge transfer occurred which directly impacted on the implementation phase. Thus, the Prisons and Probation Ombudsman for England and Wales is the product of a cross-fertilization process. Graphically this cross-fertilization process with its extended acquisition phase may look like this:

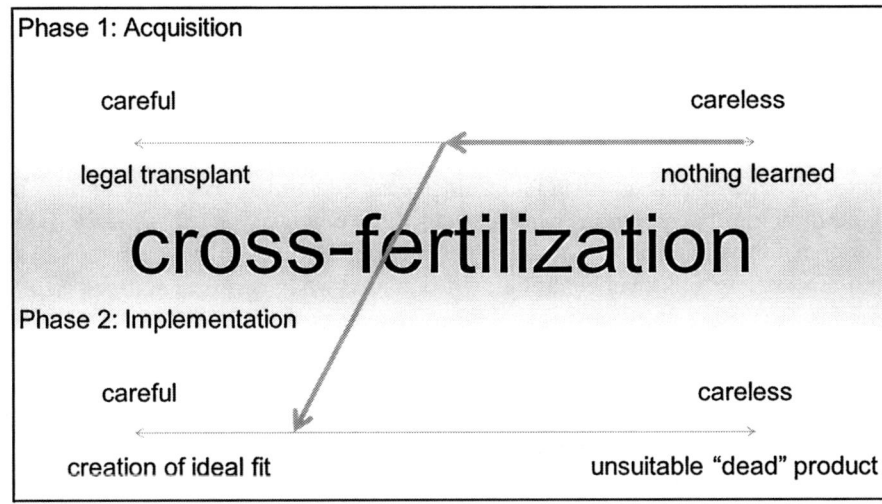

Figure 8: The Prisons and Probation Ombudsman for England and Wales as a product of cross-fertilization

When this particular historic process is compared to the current academic knowledge on the success of policy transfer or cross-fertilization processes, three points appear particularly interesting:

- The acquisition phase appears particularly long. (1980-1994)
- The knowledge gained during the transfer process remained rather diffuse. (During the implementation phase, Home Office seems to have relied on the Woolf Report, whose favourable evidence in turn was exclusively based on knowledge provided by transfer agents.)
- No distinct model for the Prisons and Probation Ombudsman for England and Wales can be singled out. (While the acquisition phase includes quite a few reports on the Canadian Correctional Investigator, the implementation phase distinctly lacks any evidence of it being considered as a model.)

The length of the acquisition phase with its many common indicators of the onset of a transfer process (conflict in form of the Hull Prison Riot, general dissatisfaction with the penal system producing a discourse pull and again conflict in form of the 1990 prison riots) confirms the importance of the driving factors mentioned above: catalysts, agents and timing.

The Hull Riot as well as the dissatisfaction and discourse pull failed to reach the British public and politicians. This confirms De Jong et al.'s proposition that windows of opportunity for policy transfer open only at times of special periods of regime transformation, which are characterised by a sense of urgency. In addition, it shows that the accompanying system upheaval must cross a certain threshold before transfer effectively occurs.[667] The protracted acquisition phase stretching from the Hull Riot to the end of the 1980s simply failed to reach the level of a national crisis in the area of penal affairs. Additionally, the transfer agents (academicians and JUSTICE) neglected to approach or even gain the favour of domestic champions who consequently "passively resist[ed] the wished-for transformation" of the penal system, which "points to the importance of building strong and loyal coalition's for one's reform enterprise, across all government tiers".[668]

Both shortcomings were overcome due to the occurrence of the riots in Strangeways and other penitentiaries in April 1990 which presented a penal system crisis large enough to alert the All Party Penal Affairs Group to the need for action. The latter, together with the Association of the Board of Visitors and the Prison Reform Trust as an influential pressure group, formed a strong coalition of transfer agents. Their joined influence channelled through the Woolf Report carried weight with Home Office as a domestic actor. This historic evidence for timing as a driving factor was minted by De Jong et al. into the advice to reformers to prepare "for oncoming windows of opportunity and save their energies to act at such moments".[669]

De Jong et al. demonstrate the diffuse quality of the knowledge gained during the Prisons and Probation Ombudsman for England and Wales' acquisition phase to be following a "bricolage" approach to knowledge transfer, which they have found to be more successful than attempts of directly Xeroxing a specific model.[670] Consequently, they would consider the fact that no distinct model for the Prisons and Probation Ombudsman for England and Wales was considered an asset as "[l]oosely defined models, or even lesson drawing from different models at the same time, provide domestic actors more leeway to make combinations that fit their desires and circumstances". In other words, the generic

---

667   De Jong et al (2002), pp. 291f
668   C.f. De Jong et al. (2002), p. 287
669   De Jong et al. (2002), p. 292
670   Here and in the following: De Jong et al. (2002), pp. 287f

character of the transplant, here the prison ombudsman idea, facilitated the transplantation process.[671]

With this transfer of a mere idea instead of a specific legal framework, the British importers conformed to De Jong et al.'s diagnosis that in "Common Law systems [...] legal and judicial change is seen as the tailpiece of policy change instead of its key part".[672] This transfer of an idea without prior in-depth examination of the legal frameworks of similar institutions also may be used to explain the failure to introduce the Prisons Ombudsman with a statutory footing, which the Canadian Correctional Investigator received in 1992 and the Michigan Legislative Ombudsman had since 1975. It thereby also highlights the necessity of the three adaptations later made to the remit of the Prisons Ombudsman.[673]

This analysis of the historic course of events pertaining to the implementation of the Prisons and Probation Ombudsman for England and Wales demonstrates its compatibility with the current academic knowledge on transfer processes and as such affirms the classification of the Prisons and Probation Ombudsman for England and Wales as a product of cross-fertilization.

b) The outcome of implementation: Structures of the Prisons and Probation Ombudsman for England and Wales

The examination of the institutional structures will comprise the institution's legal basis and categorization and its role and remit. The latter is supplemented by a description of the theoretical execution and an examination of the praxis.

aa) Legal basis and categorization

The office of Prisons Ombudsman was created in accordance with the Home Secretary's general powers relating to prisons and prisoners according to section 1 of the Prison Act 1952.[674] The Prisons and Probation Ombudsman for England and Wales is wholly independent of the National Offender Management Service (including HM Prison Service and Probation Services in England and Wales), the UK Border Agency and the Youth Justice Board. Today, the Prisons and Probation Ombudsman for England and Wales officeholder is appointed by the Minister of Justice following an open competition – led by the Parliamentary Select Committee.[675] The committee's recommendations are non-binding but

---

671   De Jong et al. (2002), p. 290
672   De Jong et al. (2002), p. 291
673   See section above at F I. 2. a) aa) for details
674   Livingstone et. al. (2003), p. 51
675   Here and in the following: Terms of Reference Document, June 2009 available from http://www.ppo.gov.uk/terms-of-reference.html (last accessed June 6th, 2012), p. 1;

will be considered before deciding whether the appointment process will be continued. The Prisons Ombudsman is sponsored by the Ministry of Justice and reports to the Secretary of State, who is accountable to Parliament for "matters relating to the discharge of the Ombudsman's remit and for laying the Ombudsman's annual report before Parliament".[676]

The Prisons and Probation Ombudsman for England and Wales is independent of the Ministry of Justice (MoJ) in discharging his/her remit as set out in the Terms of Reference – including the decision of the appropriate means of conducting investigations, assessing evidence, reaching conclusions and communicating the outcomes of investigations.[677]

The Prisons and Probation Ombudsman for England and Wales has no statutory basis. The Ombudsman's responsibilities and roles are set out in the framework document between the MoJ and the Prisons and Probation Ombudsman for England and Wales as well as the Terms of Reference document, which are set by the Secretary of State after consultation with the officeholder.[678]

This has led to the declaration that prison ombudsmen "occupy an unusual place" where independence is concerned.[679] Specifically, this lack of statutory footing as well as the fact that the Prisons and Probation Ombudsman for England and Wales is subject to the overall jurisdiction of the Parliamentary Ombudsman has consequences for the perceived independence of the institution and causes its continued exclusion from the status of full-voting-member in the BIOA.[680]

A commitment to place the office on a more permanent legal basis has been made in the Framework Document:

"The Ombudsman is an administrative appointment but the Government is committed to putting the Ombudsman on a statutory basis at the first suitable legislative opportunity. A review of previous draft legislation to put the Ombudsman on a statutory basis is in progress. The Ombudsman's future aspiration is for his office to have

---

Framework Document between the Ministry of Justice and the Prisons and Probation Ombudsman. Available from http://www.ppo.gov.uk/docs/ppo-framework-document1.pdf (last accessed June 6th, 2012), p. 4

676 Framework Document, p. 5 - c.f. fn. 675
677 Framework Document, p. 2 - c.f. fn.675
678 Framework Document, p. 5 - c.f. fn. 675
679 Buck et al. (2011a), p. 233
680 Seneviratne (2001), p. 95. Another impediment to the status is that the Prisons and Probation Ombudsman for England and Wales, like other independent adjudicators, falls under the jurisdiction of the PHSO; Seneviratne (2002), p. 93; Seneviratne (2000b), p. 15

greater administrative independence from the MoJ although there is no agreement to this effect with the Government or the MoJ".[681]

Although the current officeholder does not believe that gaining statutory footing will make a "jot of practical difference" to the work of the office, it will improve upon the perceived independence. "This will reduce the vulnerability of the office to political interference, and promote confidence in the impartiality of the system".[682] However, to date this commitment has not been fulfilled in legislation, although multiple bills were introduced throughout the last years. The first attempt at establishing a statutory footing was made in January 2005 with the inclusion of proposals about the Prisons and Probation Ombudsman for England and Wales in the Management of Offenders and Sentencing Bill, which did not come to fruition due to the calling of the general election in May 2005. When the bill was taken up after the election, it did not include the part on the Prisons and Probation Ombudsman for England and Wales.[683] The next attempt was made in 2007 in Part 4 of the Criminal Justice and Immigration Bill. Part 4 intended the establishment of a Commissioner for Offender Management and Prisons that would have performed "the functions currently performed by the Prisons and Probation Ombudsman for England and Wales". This would have been in line with the UK tradition described in the section above to favor commissioners and adjudicators over ombudsmen. Commissioners – as opposed to adjudicators – generally feature a statutory basis established by primary legislation.

The Bill cleared all stages of the House of Commons, but was criticized there as well as during the first reading in the House of Lords for the arrangements on the institutions independence. [684] This concern was shared by the Prisons and Probation Ombudsman for England and Wales and academics alike and focused on such facts as the determination of both budget and remit by the Secretary of State, who was also to be empowered to give directions about how to conduct investigations. This was considered to defeat the major objective of providing a statutory footing – that of aligning perceived and factual independence. This critique resulted in the government excluding Part 4 from the second reading in the House of Lords.

Although so far both attempts to establish a statutory footing have failed, the idea is still on the Prisons and Probation Ombudsman for England and Wales'

---

681   Framework Document, p. 4 - c.f. fn. 675
682   Seneviratne (2002), p. 94
683   Here and in the following: Seneviratne (2010), p. 15
684   Here and in the following: for further detailed critique of Part 4 of the Criminal Justice and Immigration Bill see Seneviratne (2010), pp. 37-44

agenda. With the publication of the 2011-12 Business Plan, the then Acting Prisons and Probations Ombudsman, Jane Webb, used the opportunity to restate the institutional claim, saying:

> "The office remains a non statutory body in spite of a commitment from the Government over many years to put the office on a statutory footing. We will continue to press for the introduction of legislation in this Parliament to bring this about. Given that a key part of our role is to ensure that the state complies with its human rights obligations, it is difficult to justify non statutory status".[685]

Due to the described statutory footing, the Prisons and Probation Ombudsman for England and Wales has to be categorizes as an executive specialty ombudsman.

bb) Role and remit

The Ombudsman's published statement of purpose reads as follows:

> "Within one united office, to deliver two services that contribute to just and humane penal and immigration detention systems: To provide prisoners, those under community supervision, and those in immigration detention with an accessible, independent and effective means to resolve their complaints. To provide bereaved relatives, the Prison Service, the Probation Service, the Border and Immigration Agency, and the public at large, with timely, high-quality investigations of deaths in prison custody and other deaths in remit".[686]

The part of the Prisons and Probation Ombudsman for England and Wales' role relevant to this study is the provision of prisoners "with an independent and effective avenue of complaint which is fair and even-handed, has the confidence of prisoners and the Prison Service, and contributes towards a just prison system".[687] The Prisons and Probation Ombudsman for England and Wales investigates complaints submitted by individual prisoners who have failed to obtain satisfaction through the grievance system internal to the Prison or Probation Service and who are eligible in all other respects. By providing independent oversight over procedural issues and substantive decisions alike, the Prisons and Probation Ombudsman for England and Wales assists in "ensuring that justice is done, and is also seen to be done".[688] This is always done in accordance with its Terms of Reference.

---

685 Prisons and Probation Ombudsman for England and Wales, Business Plan 2011-12 available from ppo.gov.uk (last accessed June 6th, 2012) p. 7
686 Framework Document, p. 3 - c.f. fn. 675
687 Annual Report 1999-2000, p. 3
688 Seneviratne (2001), p.100

Replies including an explanation of recommendations given are made in writing to all those whose complaints have been investigated.[689] The Prisons and Probation Ombudsman for England and Wales is allowed to issue a formal report where necessary. Special reports may be tabled in parliament though the Secretary of State.[690] Besides this, the Prisons and Probation Ombudsman for England and Wales publishes annual reports, publicizes the office and disseminates general lessons learned from investigations – for example through his newsletter called "On the Case".

The remit of the Prisons and Probation Ombudsman for England and Wales is described in the terms of references document, which extends the ombudsman's powers of investigation to all decisions relating to individual prisoners taken by Prison Service staff, people acting as agents of the Prison Service, people working in prisons but not employed by the Prison Service (such as educational staff) and members of the IMB. The ombudsman also has unfettered access to Prison Service documents for the purpose of investigation within his terms of reference.

The Prisons and Probation Ombudsman for England and Wales is "neither advocate for the complainant nor apologist for the Prison Service".[691] Unlike the Parliamentary and Health Service Ombudsman (PHSO), the Prisons and Probation Ombudsman for England and Wales is not restricted to procedural issues or "matters of maladministration, but may consider the merits of decisions, including all disciplinary findings and punishments save those imposed by District Judges, and the remit of the office-holder covers both state-run and contracted-out prisons".[692] The consideration of the merits of a decision goes beyond what can be achieved via an application for judicial review as the courts may only consider the merits of a particular decision in wholly exceptional circumstances.[693] The Prisons and Probation Ombudsman for England and Wales, however, may "seek out the cause of injustice at the systemic level in the way that a court of law could never do".[694] Unlike the courts, the Prisons and Probation Ombudsman for England and Wales cannot overturn an administrative decision in case of the validity of a complaint. Explicitly excluded from the Prisons and Probation Ombudsman for England and Wales' remit are matters involving the clinical judgment of doctors as well as all policy decisions irrespective of their

---

689   Here and in the following: Framework Document, p. 3 - c.f. fn. 675
690   Terms of Reference Document, p. 2 – c.f. fn. 675
691   Morris/Henham (1998), p. 363
692   Morgan/Liebling (2007), p. 1116
693   Here and in the following: Livingstone et al. (2003), p. 52
694   Morris/Henham (1998), p. 363

effect on the individual prisoner.[695] Policy decision are considered to be all those personally taken by a Minister and the official advice to Ministers upon which such decisions are made; the merits of decisions taken by Ministers unless especially approved for consideration by the Minister; matters outside the responsibility of the Prison Service; matters currently pending in criminal proceedings or civil litigation; and the decisions of outside bodies such as the Crown Prosecution Service, the Parole Board and its secretariat, the police and the judiciary. Also excluded are the personal exercise by Ministers of their function in the setting and review of tariff and the release of mandatory and life sentence prisoners. However, this part of the Terms of Reference has been dealt with in the ECtHR decision Stafford v UK (2002) 35 EHHR 32 and may be considered no longer applicable.[696] After consulting with the Prisons and Probation Ombudsman for England and Wales, the Secretary of State may commission the ombudsman to undertake special investigations outside the formal remit, as per section 2.1. of the framework document. Unlike many other European ombudsinstitutions, but like all other UK institutions, the Prisons and Probation Ombudsman for England and Wales may not take up cases upon own-motion initiative.[697] However, this does not impact the quality control function, which allows the officeholder to exploit opportunities presented by his casework "to exhort improvements in standards of prison administration for the enduring benefit of all prisoners rather than simply the individual complainant who is sufficiently knowledgeable, determined and articulate to pursue his grievance all the way to the Ombudsman".[698]

The Prisons and Probation Ombudsman for England and Wales' powers are limited to the making of a recommendation to either the Director-General of the Prison Service or the Chair of the Area Board, depending on the context. The Prisons and Probation Ombudsman for England and Wales can take recourse to remedies in two forms. The officeholder may issue an individualized recommendation such as damages and/or apologies or publish generalized recommendations which are aimed at improving policy consistency or change procedures or practices.[699] When a complaint highlights a general problem, it is not necessary for that specific complaint to be upheld in order to make a generalized recommendation. On the other hand, a complaint may be upheld without any recommendation having been made. The latter case may "arise where the com-

---

695   The PHSO may consider these when the treatment for the prisoner was provided by the NHS.
696   Livingstone et al. (2003), pp. 52, 562
697   Buck et al. (2011a), p. 126
698   Morris/Henham (1998), p. 364
699   Here and in the following: Seneviratne (2010), pp. 9f

plaints are about delays or lack of facilities, where the relevant service is deemed to be doing all it can to address the issue".

Finally, the framework document gives the Prisons and Probation Ombudsman for England and Wales extensive powers to publish his actions in independent interaction with the media.

cc) Execution

The execution of the work of the Prisons and Probation Ombudsman for England and Wales consists of four main parts of which complaints management naturally is the largest. Additionally, the Prisons and Probation Ombudsman for England and Wales also handles its own business and corporate planning framework, risk management, and performance monitoring and reporting.[700]

Complaints can be made about many diverse subject matters, but historically complaints concerning prison discipline and adjudications make up the largest category, which "is not surprising, given the consequences in terms of lost remission for breaking prison rules, particularly where prisoners feel that they have not had a fair hearing".[701]

The Prisons and Probation Ombudsman for England and Wales' work is significantly driven by demand.[702] This means that the workload – largely made up of incoming complaints – is determined by processes internal to the Prison Service. Consequently, the Prisons and Probation Ombudsman for England and Wales can influence complaint influx by improving the internal grievance process for example of the National Offender Management Service. This goes hand in hand with ensuring that complainants use the available internal procedures first and that internal investigations are handled thoroughly. If successful, this may improve the complaint turn-over times of the ombudsinstitution itself.

Although the Prisons and Probation Ombudsman for England and Wales has the right to conduct unannounced visits, Assistant Ombudsman Morrison-Lyons says: "We don't tend to do that"[703] and adds: "It's obvious we are coming when somebody has died", but emphasizes that the usual procedure is that "If we have complaints, we make an arrangement to arrive there." Consequently, most complaints reach the Prisons and Probation Ombudsman for England and Wales by mail. Morrison-Lyons explains: "Technically, if they know how to write and

---

700   For details on these please see Framework Document, p. 9 - c.f. fn. 675
701   Seneviratne (2002), p. 94
702   Here and in the following: Prisons and Probation Ombudsman for England and Wales, Business Plan 2011-12, p. 4 – c.f. fn. 675
703   here and in the following: p. 13 of the interview conducted on April 2nd, 2012 with Assistant Ombudsman, Olivia Morrison-Lyons. Full transcript available through this study's author.

read, yes, they have to make a written complaint. But if they have a disability or there is something wrong with them we can take the complaint over the telephone or technically in person."[704] Although this is the general rule, Morrison-Lyons confirms that none of the complaints in 2010-11 were made in person and complaints over the phone reach the Prisons and Probation Ombudsman for England and Wales only occasionally.

The complaint handling process itself commences by determining the complaint's eligibility. Complaints are eligible whenever they are made by a prisoner and have cleared all stages of the internal grievance process without the prisoner obtaining satisfaction. An internal channel is considered to be cleared either upon administrative response or lack of a reply for six weeks.[705] The fact that complaints to the Prisons and Probation Ombudsman for England and Wales are only eligible upon completion of the three internal grievance stages places the ombudsman at the apex of the complaints system. Eligibility also depends on a time element as the complaint has to be made within three calendar months after reception of a substantive reply from the Prison Service.[706] The ombudsoffice itself tries to determine the eligibility of a complaint within ten working days of receipt.[707] Complaints from third parties such as relatives or organizations on behalf of prisoners may be accepted upon the Prisons and Probation Ombudsman for England and Wales' discretion where the individual concerned is either dead or unable to act on their own behalf.

According to the new Terms of Reference, the Prisons and Probation Ombudsman for England and Wales is the arbiter of eligibility and thus has its own jurisdiction.[708] The ombudsman may request all documents necessary for the determination of eligibility from the Prison Service or the NPS area board[709] and has "the right to interview prisoners and staff as well as involved third parties".[710] While the ombudsman can investigate all eligible complaints, the officeholder may decide "not to accept a complaint otherwise eligible for investi-

---

704   here and in the following: p. 4 of the interview conducted on April 2nd, 2012 with Assistant Ombudsman, Olivia Morrison-Lyons. Full transcript available through this study's author.

705   Here and in the following: Seneviratne (2001), p. 96

706   For details an exception of this rule see Terms of Reference Document, p. 8 – c.f. fn. 675

707   Prisons and Probation Ombudsman for England and Wales, Business Plan 2011-12, p. 7 – c.f. fn. 685

708   Here and in the following: Livingstone et al. (2003), p. 47

709   Here and in the following: Terms of Reference Document, p. 4 – c.f. fn. 675; Livingstone et al. (2003), pp. 47, 52

710   Seneviratne (2001), pp. 96f

gation, or not to continue any investigation, where it is considered that no worthwhile outcome can be achieved or the complaint raises no substantial issue".[711] In this case or whenever a complaint "is considered ineligible, the Ombudsman will inform the complainant and explain the reasons, normally in writing". The matters subject to the Prisons and Probation Ombudsman for England and Wales' investigation are set out in numbers 12.-14. of the Terms of Reference Document with some exclusions listed in 3. and 35.[712] During the investigation, the Prisons and Probation Ombudsman for England and Wales makes a point of assessing whether the "professional expertise of prison ... staff has been exercised reasonably – and [if so does] not readily substitute [his] opinion for that of a prison or probation officer if their decision has been reasoned and is proportionate. [...] it is not [his] role to impose [his] judgment over that of someone else unless they have acted irrationally or in ignorance of relevant facts".[713] Wherever possible, the Prisons and Probation Ombudsman for England and Wales tries to resolve complaints in an informal, restorative manner. This is part of the reason why "around one-third of the cases he takes up result in an outcome in some way favorable to the prisoner".[714] The ombudsman aims to give a substantive reply to the complainant within 12 weeks from accepting the complaint as eligible or – if a substantive reply is not possible in that time period – to provide a progress report.[715] Unfortunately, delays occur on a regular basis with the 12 week target reached only in about 75% of cases.[716]

Before completing an investigation, the ombudsman provides copies of the report to the Director-General, who will check it for factual accuracy. The report will also be distributed to all identifiable staff members, who are given the opportunity for representation.[717] The finalized report of a completed investigation is supplied to the complainant and the Prison Service. Whenever the Prisons and Probation Ombudsman for England and Wales issues a formal report and recommendations, his findings and recommendations are widely accepted by the Director General in the case of public-sector prisons or the Office for Contracted

---

711   Here and in the following: Terms of Reference Document, p. 3 – c.f. fn. 675
712   Terms of Reference Document, pp. 4-6, 12f – c.f. fn. 675
713   Shaw (2004), p. 128
714   Morgan/Liebling (2007), p. 1117
715   Livingstone et al. (2003), p. 51; Prisons and Probation Ombudsman for England and Wales, Business Plan 2011-12, p. 7 – c.f. fn. 685
716   Seneviratne (2001), pp. 96f
717   Here and in the following: Seneviratne (2001), pp. 96f; Terms of Reference Document, pp. 13 – c.f. fn. 675

Prisons in the case of private-sector prisons.[718] According to the Terms of Reference, the relevant authority has to "provide the Ombudsman with a response indicating the steps to be taken by that authority within set timeframes to deal with the Ombudsman's recommendations. Where that response has not been included in the Ombudsman's report, the Ombudsman may, after consulting the authority as to its suitability, append it to the report at any stage."[719]

As in all public institutions, complaints will occasionally be made about the conduct of staff. For this eventuality, the ombudsinstitution operates an internal complaints procedure which will also resolve all complaints made directly to the Ministry of Justice.

The Prisons and Probation Ombudsman for England and Wales may appoint the staff necessary to discharge his/her functions according to the officeholder's own discretion.[720] However, the ombudsinstitution is bound by budgetary restraints. All staff members appointed by the Ombudsman are civil servants, employed by the Ministry of Justice, and are subject to the Ministry of Justice's terms and conditions.[721] As of 2011, the office "comprises two operational teams: one responsible for complaints investigations and the other responsible for fatal incident investigations. Each team is headed by a Deputy Ombudsman. A third Deputy Ombudsman runs the team that provides corporate services to the office. In March 2011, the office had a complement of 113.7 staff (full time equivalents)".[722] Relevant to this study are the ombudsman and its secretary and the complaints investigations section with 48.2 staff members, which are split into five investigation teams. The teams are headed by an Assistant Ombudsman, one of which also oversees the team assessing the eligibility of complaints.

The budget of the ombudsman is mainly made up of staff (about 80%), travel, subsistence and costs for the electronic case management system.[723] The budget allocation for 2011-12 is £5.35 million, which represents a 7.5 per cent reduction compared to 2010-11. This reduction is part of those cuts made across the Ministry of Justice and its sponsored organizations. Not included in the

---

718 For details see Livingstone et al. (2003), p. 51; Morgan/Liebling (2007), p. 1117 and above section D I. 3. d)

719 Terms of Reference Document, p. 14 – c.f. fn. 675

720 Here and in the following: Terms of Reference Document, p. 11 – c.f. fn. 675

721 For details on the recruitment process, see here and in the following: Terms of Reference Document, p. 12 – c.f. fn. 675

722 Here and in the following: Prisons and Probation Ombudsman for England and Wales, Business Plan 2011-12, p. 11 – c.f. fn. 685

723 Here and in the following: Prisons and Probation Ombudsman for England and Wales, Business Plan 2011-12, p. 8 – c.f. fn. 685

budget are the Ombudsman's main premises in London and a small facility in Manchester, which are directly provided by the Ministry of Justice.

The Prisons and Probation Ombudsman for England and Wales' case load relevant to this study is limited to complaints cases. From January 1st to the 31st of December 2010, the Prisons and Probation Ombudsman for England and Wales received 4,466 complaints about prisons.[724] Only 2,271 of these were deemed eligible for investigation. Among the most common reasons for lack of eligibility are a failure to complete all stages of the internal complaints process, origination of the complaint from a third party or an exceeding of time limits or the remit of the Prisons and Probation Ombudsman for England and Wales. 2,242 investigations into prison matters were completed in 2010. A slightly dated, but "well-researched cost per case figure for a completed assessment (£134) and for a completed investigation (£1,189)" is included in the Prisons and Probation Ombudsman for England and Wales' Annual Report for 2003-4.[725] A figure of the complaints cases over the last three years may be taken from the Annual Report for 2010-11:[726]

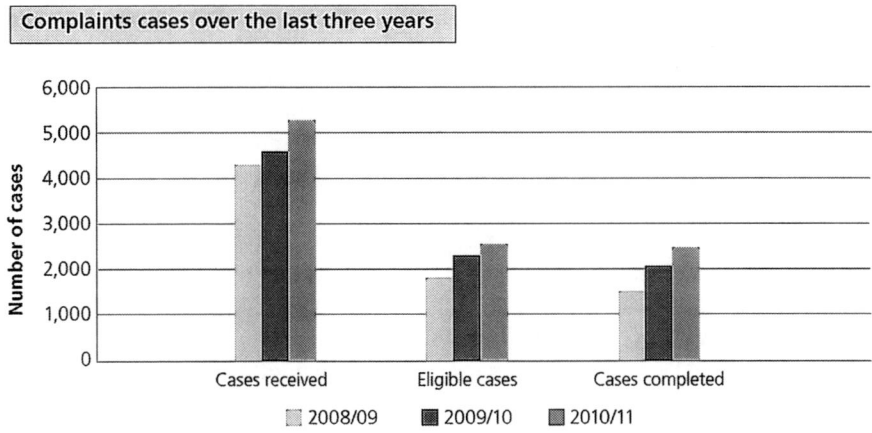

Figure 9: Prisons and Probation Ombudsman complaint cases over the last three years

---

724   Here and in the following: Annual Figures for Complaints Jan-Dec 2010 available from http://www.ppo.gov.uk/annual-reports.html (last accessed June 6th, 2012)

725   C.f. Buck et al. (2011a), p. 41

726   Prisons and Probations Ombudsman for England and Wales, Annual Report 2010-11, p. 49 available from http://www.ppo.gov.uk/annual-reports.html (last accessed June 6th, 2012)

The casework also has a strong management component as at any one time there are "nearly 500 on-going cases to manage [...] where the investigation has been completed but the inquest is awaited."[727] Additionally, the complexity of cases has been increasing causing a growing trend for the involvement of lawyers. Besides the casework, the workload of the Prisons and Probation Ombudsman for England and Wales' staff also includes training courses for prison staff, presentations to prisoners, maintaining an up to date homepage as well as the Prisons Ombudsman's case digest "On the Case".

The latter part of the workload is aimed at lowering the threshold for prisoner to gain access to the Prisons and Probation Ombudsman for England and Wales' services. Although this access is confidential, shall not be impeded by prison authorities and is free of cost,[728] not all prisoners make use of or even know of the Prisons and Probation Ombudsman for England and Wales as a complaint service. The severest impediments to prisoners accessing the services are their lack of knowledge of the institution and of how to complain and the increasingly common reading and writing difficulties.[729] Also, the "complexity of the process and time taken for complaints to be dealt with [by the Prisons and Probation Ombudsman for England and Wales is] difficult to understand" for the prisoners. Accordingly, number two of the strategic objectives of the office is to "be more accessible to all who have contact with our services".[730] The statement of values also takes this access problem into account and states that the Prisons and Probation Ombudsman for England and Wales "will provide a service that meets the needs of the people who use our services and their expectations. We will promote awareness and understanding of the services we provide using plain language and in a range of formats".[731] The ombudsman is particularly rarely accessed by young offenders, but reports that these "appeared to have less distrust of the system, relying, for the most part, on a good support system in the young offender institution to deal with most of their complaints"[732] which consists of "a personal officer assigned to each offender [who were] con-

---

727 Here and in the following: Prisons and Probation Ombudsman for England and Wales, Business Plan 2011-12, p. 9 – c.f. fn. 685

728 Postage costs will be met, c.f. Terms of Reference Document, p. 3 – c.f. fn. 675

729 Here and in the following: Seneviratne (2010), pp. 7f

730 Prisons and Probation Ombudsman for England and Wales, Business Plan 2011-12, p. 6 – c.f. fn. 685

731 Prisons and Probation Ombudsman for England and Wales, Business Plan 2011-12, p. 12 – c.f. fn. 685

732 Report for the Prisons and Probation Ombudsman on the Relevance and Effectiveness of their current publicity materials, 2008. Available from ppo.gov.uk (last accessed Dec 12th, 2011) p. 1

sidered [to] be the best person to talk to about any problems." The Ombudsman consequently indicates that "[t]here seemed to be less of a need to use the official complaints system amongst young offenders".[733]

The outcome of a complaint is left to the discretion of the ombudsman, who "in the course of a complaint [...may] seek to resolve the matter in whatever way the Ombudsman sees most fit, including by mediation."[734] The former office-holder, Shaw, considered "the restorative approach to problem solving [to be] particularly well-suited to complaints in a prison context."[735] He reasons that financial compensation is rarely appropriate unless there is direct evidence of material loss on the one hand, and on the other hand it helps to "break down the "them and us" mentality both between prisoners and prison staff, and between prisoners and wider authority". The restorative approach has the potential to render a full investigation and the issuing of a formal report unnecessary.[736] Wherever this is impossible, the ombudsman "may make recommendations to the authorities within remit, the Secretary of State for Justice, the Home Secretary or the Secretary of State for Children, Schools and Families, or to any other body or individual that the Ombudsman considers appropriate given their role, duties and powers."[737] The addressed authorities "will normally reply within four weeks to recommendations from the Ombudsman. The Ombudsman should be informed of the reasons for any delay. The Ombudsman will advise the complainant of the response to the recommendations." Shaw attests to an acceptance rate of proffered recommendations following complaints investigation of nearly ninety-eight per cent.[738] This shows quite an improvement from the early days when "as many as one in five recommendations was rejected by the Prison Service".

The accountability of the Prisons and Probation Ombudsman for England and Wales is defined by its reporting arrangements which are set out in the Terms of Reference Document[739] as follows:

"The Ombudsman will publish an annual report, which the Secretary of State will lay before Parliament. The report will include: anonymised examples of complaints investigated; recommendations made and responses received; selected anonymised

---

733   Report for the Prisons and Probation Ombudsman on the Relevance and Effectiveness of their current publicity materials, 2008. Available from ppo.gov.uk (last accessed Dec 12th, 2011) p. 7

734   Here and in the following: Terms of Reference Document, pp. 8f – c.f. fn. 675

735   Here and in the following: Shaw (2004), p. 129

736   Seneviratne (2002), p. 94

737   Here and in the following: Terms of Reference Document, pp. 8f – c.f. fn. 675

738   Here and in the following: Shaw (2004), p. 128

739   Terms of Reference Document, pp. 1f – c.f. fn. 675

summaries of fatal incidents investigations; a summary of the number and type of investigations mounted and the office's success in meeting its performance targets; a summary of the costs of the office. The Ombudsman may publish additional reports on issues relating to his investigations, which the Secretary of State will lay before Parliament upon request. The Ombudsman may also publish other information as considered appropriate".

These reports are expressly aimed at influencing "the practice of the organizations whose actions [the Prisons and Probation Ombudsman for England and Wales] oversee[s]: the National Offender Management Service NOMS – that is, prisons and probation – and the UK Border Agency."[740] The possible impression of the ombudsman's work as a one-way road is counteracted by the Prisons and Probation Ombudsman for England and Wales' sixth statement of values, which concerns accountability and reads "We will take responsibility for our actions and be open to learning from constructive criticism."[741]

In his work, the Prisons and Probation Ombudsman for England and Wales interacts with many separate institutions, amongst them the Ministry of Justice, Parliament and individual MPs, the Parliamentary and Health Service Ombudsman and other prison service institutions.

The most intensive interaction takes place between the Prisons and Probation Ombudsman for England and Wales and the MoJ. Its details are set out in the Framework Document in sections 3.1-3.2[742]. Its most important functions are the setting of the Prisons and Probation Ombudsman for England and Wales' budget and the monitoring of the corporate performance by the Permanent Secretary. In everyday life, these functions, including sponsorship, which covers the policy and administrative arrangements as well as the funding of the Prisons and Probation Ombudsman for England and Wales' office, will be delegated to the Director General of the Criminal Justice, who will meet with the Ombudsman at least quarterly.

The MoJ is committed to consulting the Prisons and Probation Ombudsman for England and Wales on any policy proposals which are relevant to the institution's work and will invite the Ombudsman's views on the development of strategy and policy where appropriate. The ombudsinstitution also regularly meets with the organisations whose work it oversees, namely the NOMS Agency (including HM Prison Service and the Probation Service) and the UK Border Agency of the Home Office. During these meetings, the agencies should be in-

---

740 Prisons and Probation Ombudsman for England and Wales, Business Plan 2011-12, p. 7 – c.f. fn. 685

741 Prisons and Probation Ombudsman for England and Wales, Business Plan 2011-12, p. 12 – c.f. fn. 685

742 Framework Document, pp. 4-7 - c.f. fn. 675

formed of any proposed changes to the Ombudsman's practice which are relevant to them.

Sections 3.1.1 and 3.3.1 of the Framework Document set out the Ombudsman's relationship with Parliament to be mediated by the Secretary of State and the sponsorship team.[743] The former "is accountable to Parliament for matters relating to the discharge of the Ombudsman's remit and for laying the Ombudsman's annual report before Parliament" while the latter for example collects the Prisons and Probation Ombudsman for England and Wales' replies to Parliamentary. Both the Permanent Secretary and the Ombudsman are liable to be summoned before the Public Accounts Committee or Justice Select Committee with regards to their respective responsibilities. There is also room for direct communication between the Prisons and Probation Ombudsman for England and Wales and individual MPs on matters relating to the Ombudsman's responsibilities.

In addition, some interaction exists with the Parliamentary and Health Service Ombudsman. The PHSO knows only one officeholder for the two combined posts of the PCA and the Health Service Ombudsman. Prisoner complaints have never formed a major part of PCA caseload, which was supposedly due to a conglomerate of reasons including the MP-filter, a large backlog of cases within that institution, "the lack of knowledge about this institution among prisoners and the fact that the PCA could only investigate allegations of maladministration and not consider the merits of decisions taken without maladministration".[744] Nevertheless, the remit of the PCA includes all those cases handled by the Prisons and Probation Ombudsman for England and Wales that are concerned with maladministration. If one of these cases reaches the PCA, it will be passed on to the Prisons and Probation Ombudsman for England and Wales for initial consideration. This is in part due to the fact that the timescale of about a year on which the PCA operates is too long for many short or medium term prisoners.[745] If the prisoner is not satisfied with the handling of the case by the Prisons and Probation Ombudsman for England and Wales, the PCA will consider the case.[746] In a way, the PCA's remit may be considered to be slightly broader than that of the Prisons and Probation Ombudsman for England and Wales as it extends to complaints from third parties referred through an MP.

---

743 Framework Document, pp. 5, 7 - c.f. fn. 675
744 Seneviratne (1994), p. 43; here and in the following: Seneviratne (2001), p. 95
745 Ryan/Ward (1993), p. 40
746 Seneviratne (2010), p. 14 even speaks of thirteen complaints about the Prisons and Probation Ombudsman for England and Wales made to the PCA

The Prisons and Probation Ombudsman for England and Wales also interacts with other institutions such as the Independent Monitoring Boards[747], the
Independent Police Complaints Commission[748], HM Chief Inspectorate of Prisons and the media. The Ombudsman may share information with these governmental institutions as long in compliance with the Data Protection legislation,
"and may work jointly with them where this is considered to be of mutual benefit".[749] The Prisons and Probation Ombudsman for England and Wales' relations
with the Prisons Inspectorate, which unlike the ombudsinstitution gained a statutory basis in 1982 which supposedly reduced ministerial involvement[750], are of a
special quality in that there has lately been an influx of staff members from the
Inspectorate to such prominent positions as the Ombudsman, the Deputy Ombudsman of the Deaths in Custody and the Central Services Deputy.[751] This exchange seems rather useful as it allows for a combination of the structural examination of the penal system with a more individualized approach – as demonstrated by this interview quote: "[…] we do use Inspectorate reports. So we have
got a complaint about this issue. We look through the inspection notes to see if
this has been a concern for them as well."[752] This difference between the two
institutions also explains why the relations of the Prisons and Probation Ombudsman for England and Wales with the ECPT are limited to a number of
meetings whilst the main liaison work is left to the Inspectorate: the latter's approach of unannounced visits being identical to that of the ECPT.[753]

The communication with the media is currently channelled through the MoJ
Press Office, which may request the reasonable provision of information.[754] Although sensitive or controversial matters should be passed on to the Secretary of
State or the Departmental Sponsor prior to publication, the Prisons and Probation Ombudsman for England and Wales "[i]n accordance with the practice applying throughout government departments, […] will follow the Government's

---

747 Neff/Avebury (2000), p. 671f
748 Here and in the following: Framework Document, p. 8 – c.f. fn. 675
749 C.f. Protocol on working arrangements between HMCIP and the Prisons and Proba-
     tions Ombudsman for England and Wales, 2010, available from ppo.gov.uk (last ac-
     cessed June 6th, 2012)
750 Fowles (1989), p. 30
751 p. 15 of the interview conducted on April 2nd, 2012 with Assistant Ombudsman, Oliv-
     ia Morrison-Lyons. Full transcript available through this study's author.
752 p. 7 of the interview conducted on April 2nd, 2012 with Assistant Ombudsman, Olivia
     Morrison-Lyons. Full transcript available through this study's author.
753 here and in the following: p. 13 of the interview conducted on April 2nd, 2012 with
     Assistant Ombudsman, Olivia Morrison-Lyons. Full transcript available through this
     study's author.
754 Here and in the following: Framework Document, p. 8 – c.f. fn. 675

policy that official information should be made available unless it is clearly not in the public interest to do so."[755]

II. The Justizvollzugsbeauftragter des Landes Nordrhein-Westfalen

In the following section, the local framework surrounding the Justizvollzugs-beauftragter des Landes Nordrhein-Westfalen will be described by means of a country survey. The section will then go on to analyse the process and outcome of the implementation of the office of Justizvollzugsbeauftragter des Landes Nordrhein-Westfalen.

1. Country survey

This country survey on the Justizvollzugsbeauftragter des Landes Nordrhein-Westfalen serves the same purpose as that of the Prisons and Probation Ombudsman for England and Wales: it sets out to describe the institutional setting of the Justizvollzugsbeauftragter des Landes Nordrhein-Westfalen within its home country. The information provided will outline the current state of research on the institution and offer a brief overview over the history of imprisonment in Germany – particularly North Rhine-Westphalia – as well as the latter's inmate population and characteristics. An overview over the legal basis of imprisonment and the current prison organisation will be given, whilst special attention will be paid to the available external and internal grievance channels. Please note that this country survey is strictly limited to the background information relevant to an understanding of this study's argument.[756]

a) Current state of research

The earliest proof for discussions around a possible introduction of a specialist prison ombudsman in Germany by academics and politicians are a series of essays which appeared in the journal *Mensch und Staat* in the late 1960s (N.N. 1965; Reigrotzki, 1970). Although the journal was strongly connected with a society that called itself "Aktionsgemeinschaft Deutscher Ombudsmann" (Ac-

---

755 Terms of Reference Document, pp. 1f – c.f. fn. 675
756 For an in-depth discussion of the German penal system please turn to the appropriate literature such as Kaiser/Schöch (2002) or Laubenthal (2011). A useful comparison of the penal systems in the UK and Germany is available from Koeppel (1999) and Lazarus (2004).

tion Group German Ombudsman), the published articles only campaigned for the introduction of general ombudsmen and strictly disapproved of specialist ombudsmen such as the *Wehrbeauftragte des Bundestages* (German Military Ombudsman).[757] It is interesting that whilst no direct mention of any proposal for the introduction of a prison ombudsman can be found, multiple authors found it necessary to disavow its usefulness and proclaimed its incompatibility with the general principle of rehabilitation.[758] However, a suggestion for its introduction appears to have been discussed as an aside at the 48th Biannual Conference of the German Legal Association's Annual Meeting (Deutscher Juristentag, DJT) where it was rejected for potential constitutional problems, unnecessary competency quarrels as well as a confusing doubling of competences. In 1973, Münchbach, who had been present at the DJT, wrote that a prison ombudsman was no replacement for a Board of Visitor as its function of increasing public faith in the penal system was only a small part of the function of the boards.[759] If the then newly introduced boards were to fail to meet these expectations, a prison ombudsman might be considered.

Before the introduction of the Ombudsmann für den Justizvollzug Nordrhein-Westfalen there were only three essays - two older papers (Redeker, p. 1300; Kühler, 1970) and one newer piece of research (Kretschmer 2005) – campaigning for the introduction of an ombudsman in German prisons. Since the introduction of the Ombudsmann für den Justizvollzug Nordrhein-Westfalen in 2007 there have been no books and only few essays on the Ombudsmann für den Justizvollzug Nordrhein-Westfalen specifically – the exception being an interview with the first incumbent of the office by Sanker in 2007.[760] The literature is limited to passing mentions of the introduction of an ombudsinstitution in North Rhine-Westphalia (Rotthaus 2008, Neubacher 2008) or the acknowledgement of the continued existence of said institution (Ritter 2009). Although the German standard textbooks on the penal system mention the *Ombudsmann für den Justizvollzug Nordrhein-Westfalen*'s existence, its description rarely takes up more than two pages.[761] A thorough description of the institutions legal basis and work has yet to appear in academic literature.

---

757   Reigrotzki (1968), p. 7
758   Reigrotzki (1970), p. 82
759   Here and in the following: Münchbach (1973), p. 85
760   Sanker (2007), p. 52ff
761   Kaiser/Schöch (2002), p. 152; Laubenthal (2011), p. 500f; Schwind (2009), p. 820

b) Brief history of imprisonment in North Rhine-Westphalia

The state and history of imprisonment in North Rhine-Westphalia has generally coincided with the imprisonment in Western Germany.

Only the development after WWII will be described here.[762] The post-Nazi restructuring of the German penal system commenced on November 12th, 1945 with the enactment of the 19th directive of the control council called "Grundsätze für die Verwaltung der deutschen Gefängnisse und Zuchthäuser" (Fundamental principles for the administration of German prisons and jails).[763] In Western Germany, a reconnection with the humanizing reform principles of the Weimar period was begun that led to the first calls for a homogenous penal system based on federal laws. The greater importance attached to the reform of the criminal code delayed any attempts at this through the fifties and sixties. The StVollzG was introduced in January 1977 in response to a verdict[764] by the *Bundesverfassungsgericht* (Federal Constitutional Court (FCC)) which determined the so called *besonderes Gewaltverhältnis* (special power relationship) to not present a sufficient legal basis and subsequently ordered proper legislation to be passed.[765] One of the most important elements of the constitution is the legality of administrative action. This basic principle is defined in Art. 20 III *Grundgesetz* (GG, German Basic Law) as the *Vorrang des Gesetzes* (priority of law) and the *Vorbehalt des Gesetzes* (provisio of the law). Both of these were not adequately fulfilled under the *besonderes Gewaltverhältnis*. In 2006, the legislative competence for penal law was transferred to the states.[766] These may now act upon their new competence. North Rhine-Westphalia has so far chosen not to do so and instead continues to rely on the StVollzG.

The German prison system had to come a long way before it deserved its name.[767] Whether the German penal system will continue to deserve it, is a question of the future development and the continued humanization process in particular.[768]

---

762 For details on the historic development during the Kaiserreich, Weimar Republic and Nazi-time, see Laubenthal (2008), pp. 60-66; for detailed (comparative) description of the historic development of the German prison system see Lazarus (2004)

763 Here and in the following: Laubenthal (2008), pp. 66 ff

764 BVerfGE 33, pp. 1ff

765 Here and in the remainder of this paragraph: Kaiser/Schöch (2002), pp. 20f, 28f

766 Laubenthal (2008), p. 70

767 Bohlen (2008), pp. 169ff, 306ff

768 Hoffmann (2000), p. 253

c) Inmate population and characteristics

In 2010, there were 37 prisons in North Rhine-Westphalia with 18,390 prison places, which housed 14,554 prisons and 148 persons on extended term of imprisonment (*Sicherungsverwahrte*).[769] Overcrowding also poses a challenge in North Rhine-Westphalia. In 2000, 5,102 of the prison spaces were part of the so called "open" regime in which the prisoners spend only the nights and weekends on the premises.[770] These experienced an overcrowding rate of 106.7%. About 5% of all prisoners were women and 30% were foreigners. One recent trend is the increase in the proportion of prisoners with long sentences.[771] 7% of the ADP serve an alternative sentence for failure to pay a fine; the rate is much higher if one were to count prison receptions. The associated administrative effort is considered an inconvenience.[772] As a consequence of the aspects outlined above, prison life is today dominated by prisoners with very short or very long sentences. This is especially problematic since in some prisons up to every second inmate spends 23 hours in lock-up.[773]

The age breakdown of adult prisoners (12,366) is as follows: 10% below 25 years, 23.3% between 25 and 30 years, 39.6% between 30 and 40 years, 17.9% between 40 and 50 years and 9.2% were above 50 years of age.[774] For those prisoners that fall into the preventive custody category (75), the age average is rather different with 52% of inmates above the age of 50. In addition, the younger the prisoner, the more likely he is sentenced for property offences.

Regarding marital status, it can be noted that only 22.4% of the male and 31.9% of the female prisoners in 2000 were married. Finally, the daily cost of imprisonment in Northrhine-Westphalia in 1999 stood at 141.65 DM (~70€).[775]

---

769   Laubenthal (2011), pp. 24, 40

770   Dieckmann (2000), p. 22. The data quoted here is slightly dated. It has been used, however, since it directly and in details refers to Northrhine-Westphalian and not the entire German penal system. For newer data for Germany see Laubenthal (2011), pp. 43ff

771   For details on reception, induction, accommodation, recreation, searches, mandatory drug testing, food, clothing, work, education, facilities and privileges please see Dieckmann (2000), pp. 24-91, Kaiser/Schöch (2002), pp. 113-219 and 257-332.

772   Kaiser/Schöch (2002), pp. 68f

773   c.f. http://mobil.derwesten.de/dw/politik/cdu-wirft-kutschaty-massives-fuehrungsversagen-vor-id6420114.html?service=mobile Article first published online March 2nd, 2012 (last accessed June 6th, 2012)

774   Here and in the following: c.f. Dieckmann (2000), pp. 106f

775   For newer data for Germany see Kaiser/Schöch (2002), pp. 315ff

d) Legal basis of imprisonment

The legal basis for the closed prison regime may be found in the StVollzG as well as in the *Jugendgerichtsgesetz* (German Juvenile Court Act), the *Wehrstrafgesetz* (German Military Penal Code) and the *Strafprozessordnung* (Code of Criminal Procedure). While the GG gives the State competence to imprison criminal offenders (Art. 74 GG), asserts a right to personal liberty (Art. 2 II 2 GG) and habeas corpus (Art. 104 II, III GG), and lays out criteria by which a person may be punished (Art. 103 II GG), detained, or sentenced to imprisonment (Art. 104 GG), it does not explicitly state how prisons should be administered or which rights prisoners should hold after conviction. Instead, this is set out in the StVollzG.[776] This law had no impact on the basic rights of the prisoners, which bind the penal institutions and courts alike. The StVollzG rather defines the legal status of prisoners, the conditions for action as well as the provisional obligations of the institutions and the organizational and staff requirements of the penal regime.

Prisoner's Rights have been debilitated by compromises made during the drafting of the Prison Act, the persistent resistance of state administrators against the ideals of the Act, "the initial restraint of the Higher Regional Courts in structuring and checking prison administrative discretion, the failure of Prison Courts to fulfil the expectation of reformers, the refractory culture of prison administrators, and the lack of prisoners' access to legal support".[777] The extent of the administrative discretion is caused by so called *unbestimmte* (undetermined) legal terms contained within the StVollzG, which have to be interpreted in light of the constitutional rights of the prisoners. These undetermined legal terms constitute one of the first points of critique against the StVollzG itself. This critique arose as early as during the legislative process and claimed that the multitude of these terms minimized the basic rights position of prisoners.[778] Another point frequently criticized are the transitional clauses (§§198-201), which suspend many innovative parts of the StVollzG such as inclusion of the prisoners in the social insurance system. In 1977, Müller-Dietz claimed that these clauses left the StVollzG a mere torso. 15 years later he said the financial restrictions on the federal budget, which were claimed to make the on-going suspension necessary, leave the StVollzG a ruin.[779]

---

776   Lazarus (2004), p. 33
777   Lazarus (2004), p. 124
778   Müller-Dietz (1994), p. 49
779   Müller-Dietz (1992), p. 27

e) Current prison organisation

There exist drastic differences between prison facilities depending on their status as open or closed facilities, their age or their location within the Federal Republic. Many of these distinguishing factors apply even within the smaller context of North Rhine-Westphalia. Consequently, the current system of prison organization applied in North Rhine-Westphalia can only be described in a generalized manner. This section will include general information on the executional aim, the manner of execution and administrative structure, personnel structure, living conditions as well as disciplinary and control measures.

German Prisoners have a right to re-socialization as elaborated by the FCC (BVerfGE 45, 187, 239), which is derived from Art. 1 I, 2 I and 20 GG.[780] The executional aim of the StVollzG aligns with this constitutional re-socialization requirement by providing a clear and unitary statement on the purpose of imprisonment (§2 StVollzG), including special provisions on substantive positive rights for prisoners which furthered the right to re-socialization.[781] The drafters of the StVollzG – mostly academics and politicians – were "particularly concerned to establish administrative guidelines aimed at countering the damaging institutional effects of imprisonment and the entrenched culture of prison administration".[782] For this purpose they included three guiding principles (§3 StVollzG): the adjustment principle (*Angleichungsgrundsatz*), counter-measures principle (*Gegensteuerungsgrundsatz*) and integration principle (*Integrationsgrundsatz*). These do not directly constitute prisoners' rights.[783]

The manner of execution is structured as follows. The direct supervisory control of legal and substantive issues (*Dienst- und Fachaufsicht*) is located with the *Justizvollzugsämter* (Prison Offices) in the Rhineland and Westphalia-Lippe for their respective areas.[784] The *Fachaufsicht* is provided for the Prison Offices by specially trained personnel such as doctors, psychologists, social workers, educational and library staff. The highest level of *Dienst- und Fachaufsicht* is organized by a special prison department within the North Rhine-Westphalian Ministry of Justice. The work of the Ministry of Justice and the prison administration is subject to political supervision through the *Landtag* (North Rhine-Westphalian parliament), the temporary committees of enquiry (*Untersuchungsausschuss*), the petition committee and the prison committee (*Strafvollzugskommission*) as a subdivision of the law committee, see *Geschäftsordnung des*

---

780   For details see Lazarus (2004), pp. 38-49
781   Lazarus (2004), p. 49
782   Lazarus (2004), p. 84
783   Kaiser/Schöch (2002), p. 130
784   Here and in the following: Dieckmann (2000), p. 9

Landtages §107 GO LT NRW.[785] The prison committee may act upon transfer of a petition by the petition committee or upon own-motion initiative, §107 II GO LT. In consultation with the Ministry of Justice, the prison committee may visit the prisons without advance notice, §107 III GO LT. Another competence of the prison committee is to report on the work of the petition committee and to make recommendations, §107 IV GO LT. The petition committee will then discuss the outcome of this review and may include the recommendations in its report to the Landtag (parliament). The prison committee is made up by seven members, §107 V GO LT, and the head of the petition committee is necessarily also the head of the prison committee.

Inside the institutions, the execution is designed similarly to all other German state penal systems.[786] One of the specialties of the North Rhine-Westphalian penal system is that it provides the opportunity for long-time visits of a prisoner's family.[787] The experience made with this tool has been entirely positive – with no abuse and a significant reduction in prisoner aggressiveness.

The staff of the penal institutions influence the design of prison life as a comprehensive field for communication and interaction. With §154 StVollzG, the German prison act contains a mandatory cooperation clause forcing all those working in prison to join their efforts in fulfilling their work. This includes officers, as well as extra official staff, supervisory committees and NGOs. The staff infrastructure involves the cooperation of the prisoners, who are not only required to participate in their treatment, but also carry responsibility collectively, §160 StVollzG. The different professions represented in prison are named in §155 II StVollzG. The majority of those employed in prisons are charged with custodial functions.[788] The governor of an institution holds an official function according to §156 I 1 StVollzG and does not have to hold a law degree – though many do –, but could also for example be a psychologist or social worker.

The upholding of discipline and order is regulated in §§ 81ff StVollzG and includes preserving security, averting escapes, preventing threats or danger towards staff, prisoners and objects.[789] §82 StVollzG contains general rules for the conduct within the prison community. All security measures such as body and cell searches are described in §84-87 StVollzG. Direct force may be applied under the conditions of §94-98 StVollzG and disciplinary measures against prisoner misconduct can be applied according to §102 I StVollzG.

---

785 Koeppel (1999), pp. 116, 119ff
786 Since there are no significant deviations, please refer to Kaiser/Schöch (2002), pp. 255-334; Laubenthal (2008), pp. 171-408
787 Eder (2008), pp. 157ff
788 Laubenthal (2011), p. 146
789 For details see Kaiser/Schöch (2002), pp. 220-30

f) External and internal grievance channels

In this section on external and internal grievance-mechanisms in North Rhine-Westphalia, only those which are specific to Germany will be discussed in any detail. For those grievance channels available to all European prisoners please refer to chapter B II. 1.

The internal grievance channels available to a prisoner in Germany are: (1) submitting a complaint within the prison either to prison staff or (2) to the supervisory authority during one of their representatives' visits or (3) applying to the inmate board or (4) prison board. The right to complain to the staff of a prison is governed by §108 I StVollzG, which reads: "The Prisoner is afforded the opportunity to address the governor with wishes, suggestions and complaints in all matters pertaining to himself. Regular clinics will be instituted."[790] Complaints may be made in writing or those unable or unwilling to produce a written complaint may complain orally during one of the governor's clinics. §156 II 2 StVollzG allows for the transferal of responsibilities to other staff. Accordingly, the lower tiers of staff are also allowed to hear complaints. This affords a speedier and more local solution of most complaints. In his 1981 study titled "Rechtsmittel im Strafvollzug", Diepenbruck established that the prisoners for the most part prefer the oral complaint to the governor and that this grievance-channel has seen the highest historic success rate (34%).[791]

§108 II StVollzG gives the right to complain to representatives of the supervisory authority while those are present at the facility. It reads: "Whenever a representative of the supervisory authority visits the institution it is to be ensured that he may be approached by the prisoner with matters pertaining to himself."[792] This grievance channel allows for written and oral complaints. In order to facilitate the possibility for prisoners to complain to the supervisory authority's representative orally, the prison will inform the inmates of upcoming visits and take down the names of those prisoners interested in complaining.

Another internal grievance mechanism is to apply to the prison board. Their implementation is not mandatory by law. However, §160 StVollzG speaks of the "prisoners' joint responsibility" and reads: "The prisoners and institutionalised are to be offered the opportunity to share in the responsibility for matters of common interest, which are due to their character and the assignment of the institution suited for participation."[793] Thus, §160 StVollzG may be considered a

---

790   Own translation
791   Diepenbruck (1981), pp. 12, 206
792   Own translation
793   Own translation

legal basis for the implementation of inmate boards. How such boards operate and can be approached by prisoners may differ depending on the institutional design of the individual prison facility.

The last internal grievance-channel available to prisoners in Germany is the prison boards. Their legal basis is to be found in §§162ff StVollzG. §164 I 1 and II StVollzG regulate the complaint procedure and read: "The members of the board may receive wishes, suggestions and complaints. [...] The members of the board may visit the prisoners and institutionalised in their rooms. Discussion and correspondence will not be monitored." Accordingly, prisoners may address the prison board through written or oral complaints.

External grievance-channels available to prisoners in Germany which have specific characteristics are the courts (including the FCC), petition committees, general ombudsmen and religious caregivers. §§109ff StVollzG regulate the prisoners' appeal to the courts which is guaranteed by Art. 19 IV GG. The extent of the prisoner's legal protection largely depends on the legal arrangement of the constitutional guarantees.[794] Its strongest mode is the legal entitlement while other forms are for example the requirement of provisions by the penal institution or rules providing the latter with so called "evaluative leeway".

The design of the appeal is borrowed mostly from the proceedings before the administrative courts augmented by some elements from criminal procedures, which is due to the differences between prisoners and free citizens.[795] A pre-condition for the admissibility of §§ 109ff StVollzG is the existence of a provision by the prison administration that is aimed at regulating a specific event, such as factual or lawful living conditions. The appeal may be filed by any person injured in their rights, such as prisoners themselves, relatives, advocates or members of the prison council. It must be filed within two weeks from the time of the provision or denial thereof (§112 StVollzG). According to §115 I StVollzG, the court decides without a hearing – although the court may call one where this would clarify the case at hand – by means of an enactment.[796] Filing an appeal has no suspensory effect, but wherever the realization of a right of the injured party may be foiled or hampered and is not opposed by a higher ranking interest, a suspensory effect maybe declared by the court (§114 I and II StVollzG). When first introduced, it was generally expected that the judges of these courts would visit "their" prisons regularly and keep in on-going contact

---

794   Here and in the following: Dünkel (1996b), p. 522
795   Koeppel (1999), p. 7
796   Lazarus (2004), p. 96

with the administration, staff and inmates alike and thus impact prison life directly. However, none of these anticipations have become reality.[797]

The court's decision may be appealed within one month by both the prisoner and the administration before the *Oberlandesgericht* (Higher Regional Court), § 116, 118 StVollzG. Problematic for the prisoner are the large margins of regression opened by the StVollzG to the administration, which cannot be surmounted by court action. This explains the reluctance Diepenbruck noted for prisoners to take legal action. In fact, only 12% of prisoners ever use this option, with the success rate at about 3%.[798] Frequently, the judges charged with deciding prisoner suits have no taste for or experience in this line of work, which is depreciated as can be seen by the quota lists.[799] A common problem of all court proceedings is the time necessary for completion.[800] Additionally, prisoners with on-going lawsuits are treated differently by the prison administration. There are also cases in which the administration refuses to implement court orders.[801] However, the strongest determinative cause for the low success rate arises from the so called evaluative leeway provided by the StVollzG itself. Despite the exacting standards stipulated by the FCC, these undefined legal terms do not meet with sufficiently rigorous scrutiny by the courts. "The resultant unpredictability which prisoners experience in the vindication of these positive rights is said to exacerbate prisoners' alienation from the prison administration and to undermine their general readiness to co-operate in their resocialization".[802]

If the prisoner is not satisfied with the decision of both the primary court and, if applicable, the Higher Regional Court, an additional judicial grievance channel open to prisoners in Germany would be taking legal action before the FCC. The legal basis for this is as for all citizens provided through Art. 93 I Nr. 4A GG, §§ 90ff BVerfGG (Law on the Federal Constitutional Court). In the past, the FCC has proven influential for changes in prison administration. Notably, in 1993 the success rate for prisoners' appeals peaked at 9%, with an overall success rate of citizens' appeals at 1,2%.[803] This has led to the declaration that

---

797   C.f. Rotthaus (2008), p. 387
798   Diepenbruck (1981), pp. 206 and 210; Lesting/Feest (1987), p. 393; in a similar study Kamann (1991) finds that 15-20% of prisoners take legal action at least once with a success rate of 9.8%, pp. 156, 162, 194
799   Koeppel (1999), pp. 26f; Kamann (1991), p. 8
800   Which for a suit before the primary court and the Higher Regional Court takes an average of 15 months, c.f. Feest et al. (1997), p. 121
801   Lesting/Feest (1987), p. 390; for details see Koeppel (1999), pp. 18, 30f
802   Lazarus (2004), p. 104; for details concerning the matter of evaluative leeway see Dünkel (1996b), p. 523
803   Koeppel (1999), p. 33

the Federal Constitutional Court is the only true ally in the permutation of the reform spirit of the 1977 StVollzG into the real world.[804] However, due to long delays there usually is no individual benefit for the suing prisoner involved who may frequently be already discharged before any decision is made. All in all, the assessment that with few exceptions all true judicial successes gained by prisoners have been won before the FCC still rings true today.[805] Overall, the success rate of the legal action taken by prisoners averages around 1%.[806]

Three other external grievance channels are available for prisoners in Germany: religious caregivers, petition committees and general ombudsmen. §53 StVollzG allows prisoners to turn to a religious caregiver, who is part of the obligatory cooperation between all persons working within the institution. This permits intercession on the prisoner's behalf. For all religious prisoners with access to religious caregivers of their denomination, this may be a low-threshold complaint mechanism while for all non-believers this may not even come to mind as a method for complaining.

Another channel that is accessible and widely known and used by prisoners is petitions to the parliaments. Their legal basis may be found within the constitution of either the *Bund* or the *Länder*. Since prisons are institutions of the German *Länder*, petitions are usually addressed to their parliaments. Nevertheless, the federal parliament, the Bundestag, also receives petitions from prisoners. All parliaments have mandatory petitions committees to process the petitions. Mail addressed to them may not be monitored by the prison administration, § 29 II StVollzG, and may not be stopped by the governor, §31 IV StVollzG. Diepenbruck found that 7% of all prisoners submit at least one petition.[807] The explanation for this high submission-rate is held to be a combination of the success rate of 23% and the fact that petitions are free of charge.[808] This is augmented by the members of parliament's personal involvement and their access to the media, which offsets the drawback that they may not make their decisions binding for the prison administration.

Some German *Länder* have introduced general ombudsmen, who function as an assistant to the petitions committees in parliament. As such, they are independent of the executive, but dependent on the legislative.[809] Therefore, the petition committees may call for the general ombudsman's presence at their meetings. In North Rhine-Westphalia, petitions from prisoners are handled almost

---

804   c.f. Süddeutsche Zeitung, March 8th 1995, p. 3
805   Koeppel (1999), p. 35; Diepenbruck (1981), 231
806   Dünkel (1996a), p. 31
807   Diepenbruck (1981), p. 210
808   Diepenbruck (1981), p. 206; Koeppel (1999), p. 35
809   Here and in the following: Koeppel(1999), p. 113, 115

exclusively according to Art. 41a of the Constitution of North Rhine-Westphalia. Here, the reporting MP together with a representative of the administration will confer personally with the prisoner, the governor and other staff about the case at hand. This method is popular due to its avoiding long written reports in favour of personal discussion.

2. How was the Justizvollzugsbeauftragter des Landes Nordrhein-Westfalen implemented?

The country survey is now complemented by an in-depth analysis of the implementation process and outcome of the Justizvollzugsbeauftragter des Landes Nordrhein-Westfalen.

a) The process of implementation: History of the Justizvollzugsbeauftragter des Landes Nordrhein-Westfalen

The section on the implementation process of the Justizvollzugsbeauftragter des Landes Nordrhein-Westfalen first outlines the history of the institution before laying a particular focus on the Justizvollzugsbeauftragter des Landes Nordrhein-Westfalen as a legal transplant.

aa) History of institution

The history of the North Rhine-Westphalian prison ombudsinstitution can only be properly understood if placed into the larger context of the German prison ombudsman debate. About thirty years before the introduction of the *Ombudsmann für den Justizvollzug Nordrhein-Westfalen*, academics in Germany first considered the merits of prison ombudsmen.[810] The calls for the introduction of a prison ombudsman were muted by the introduction of the German prison act, the StVollzG, as the newly established legal remedies including for example boards of visitors underwent a trial period. When they were found to be lacking in efficiency during the 1980s, the debate about the introduction of a prison ombudsman recommenced.[811]

Although prison ombudsman may be translated into *Strafvollzugsombudsmann*, this has never been the term of choice in the German prison ombudsman debate. There has been a long-standing traditional preference for the technical

---

810   Schäfer (1985), p. 9; Lesting (1993), p. 52; Kaiser/Schöch (2002), p. 152; Gerken (1986), p. 283
811   Lesting (1993), pp. 52; Kretschmer (2005), p. 220

term *Beauftragte* in Germany.[812] Wild believes the word to be derived from the second part of the ombudsman's double function: the protection of individual (citizen) rights. Consequently, *Strafvollzugsbeauftrager* has been the preferred generic German term. Thus, the original appellation of the "Ombudsmann für den Justizvollzug Nordrhein-Westfalen" was somewhat surprising, but can be traced to a purposeful decision of Roswitha Müller-Piepenkötter, then Minister of Justice, who states:

> "This was important to me! Because it's different from a 'Beauftragter' for anybody who thinks about it! The term is just as known in Germany and makes it clear that he is the contact person for all those affected by the penal system and not some 'Beauftragter' for the penal system by the *Land* government or *Land* parliament. This is why it was particularly important to me personally not to create a 'Beauftragter'".[813]

However, this conviction did not carry over to the next government. Hence, the 2010 adaptations to the office were accompanied by a renaming of the institution to Justizvollzugsbeauftragter des Landes Nordrhein-Westfalen, thus reaffirming the German *Beauftragten*-tradition.

Although there had been no precedent in Germany for the introduction of a prison ombudsman, there was a tradition in North Rhine-Westphalia for handling prisoners' complaints orally.[814] This was implemented under the direction of the petitions committee through an MP who attended a hearing of a prisoner in the presence of a prison representative. Rotthaus attested the advantages of this method to be very similar to that of a prison ombudsman and consequently suggested placing an ombudsman at the apex of the petition system handling prisoner grievances.[815]

That this suggestion was finally taken up however was completely independent of any academic suggestions. Instead, the first prison ombudsman in one of the German *Länder* owes its existence to the occurrence of what has quickly become to be known as the "Siegburger Foltermord" (Torture Homicide

---

812   Following this tradition: Kempf (1976); Kretschmer (2005), p. 217; Kruse (2006), who holds that the legal structure of the *Beauftragten* draws on both the German *Kommissar* as well as the Scandinavian ombudsman concept and merges them to an organizational form sui generis, p. 174; breaking the tradition: Wild (1970), p. 8

813   p. 12 of the interview conducted on February 7th, 2012 with the former Minister of Justice, Roswitha Müller-Piepenkötter. Full transcript available through this study's author.

814   Here and in the following: Rotthaus (2008), p. 381

815   Rotthaus (2008), p. 382

of Siegburg Penitentiary).[816] During the incident, which occurred on November 11th, 2006 in the Siegburg Penitentiary, three cell-inmates tortured and raped the fourth inmate repeatedly over a period of 12 hours and in the sixth attempt succeeded in their effort for a forced suicide. This occurred although two guards (one called by means of the alarm button pressed by the victim and one called by inmates of neighbouring cells) checked-up on the cell mates – regrettably without ever entering the cell or discovering the proceedings within.

In the aftermath of this event, the parliamentary opposition heavily criticized MP Müller-Piepenkötter, then Minster of Justice for the governing party, the Christian Democratic Union (CDU), and called for her resignation due to her political responsibility for the inmate's death.[817] In her defence, the Minister recalled incidents from 2002 a time at which the social democrats were governing in a coalition with the green party. As a result of the controversy, the North Rhine-Westphalian *Landtag* instated a congressional investigation committee comprised of eleven members mandated to discover possible deficits within the penitentiary and the Ministry of Justice during the period of 2003-2006.[818] The final report was discussed in the Landtag on June 19th 2008.[819] While the opposition claimed that the Minister had behaved negligently in ignoring events hinting at rising levels of brutality in North Rhine-Westphalian prisons, the majority vote by the governing coalition of CDU and Liberals declared that the Siegburger Foltermord had been an "unparalleled, rationally not understandable event".[820]

---

816   Sanker (2007), p. 52; c.f. Spiegel from August 1st, 2007 www.spiegel.de/panorama /justiz/0,1518,497725,00.html; c.f. Spiegel from November 17th, 2007 www.spiegel. de/panorama/justiz/0,1518,449208,00.html; Stern from August 1st, 2007 222. stern.de/panorama/foltermord-in-der-jva-siegburg-keiner-wollte-dasweichei-sein-594333.html, RP online from April 24th, 2009 www.rep-online.de /panorama/deutschland/prozess-um-siegburger-foltermord-neu-aufgerollt-1.2018284

817   Here and in the following: Kölner Stadtanzeiger from December 6th, 2006, www.ksta.de/html/artikel/1165385193305.shtml (last accessed June 6th, 2012)

818   Einstimmiger Einsetzungsbeschluss des Untersuchungsausschusses Drs 14/4011 aus der 57. Sitzung des Landtages am 28. März 2007; NGO online Internetzeitung from March 28th, 2007 www.ngo-online.de/2007/03/28/gefangnis (last accessed June 6th, 2012)

819   For details see www.landtag.nrw.de/portal/WWW/GB_I/I.1/PUA/PUA_I/aufgaben.jsp (last accessed June 6th, 2012)

820   Teilabschlussbericht Drs. 14/6900 vom 19. Juni 2008 available from www.landtag.nrw.de/portal/WWW/GB_I/I.1/ PUA/ PUA_I/aufgaben.jsp; Nealine from June 17th, 2008 www.nealine.de/news/Politik/koalition-und-opposition-weiter-uneins-ueber-siegburger-foltermord-1937766469.html (all online resources last accessed June 6th, 2012)

Quite some time before the issuing of the final report, the Ministry of Justice took executive action in form of a package of measures which included:

- short-term reactions (temporarily prohibiting the placement of more than three prisoners to a cell), – medium-term reactions (employing more pedagogues) and
- as a long- term reaction, an *Allgemeinverfügung* (AV; a ministerial decree) which instated the Ombudsmann für den Justizvollzug Nordrhein-Westfalen (Ombudsman for the penal system in North Rhine-Westphalia).[821] Consequently, the 2007 budget was amended to include funding for the Ombudsmann für den Justizvollzug Nordrhein-Westfalen in the position "Einzelplan 04, Kapitel 04 020, Titelgruppe 70".[822] The introduction of the Ombudsmann für den Justizvollzug Nordrhein-Westfalen was met with a defensive demeanour by the MPs of all parties[823] and criticized by the opposition as a superfluous ad-hoc decision.[824] Especially members of the petitions committee understood it as concision of their foremost duty. With the first annual report, which was well received by the MPs, the protest quieted – especially when it was found that no decline in the number of petitions could be observed.[825]

As early as 2008, the social democratic opposition brought forth the motion of placing the ombudsman on a statutory footing that was to include own-motion powers.[826] The legislative basis was intended to guarantee independence from the executive without raising the ombudsman above the station of a helpmeet of parliament, whose directives the new ombudsinstitution was to be subjected to.[827] A constitutional basis was expressly not the intent of the social democratic motion which explicitly drew on reported positive experiences of the Prisons

---

821   Here and in the following: AV d. JM from March 14th, 2007 – 4400 – IV. 396, Justizministerialblatt, Issue 8 from April 15th, 2007, pp. 87ff

822   Vorlage 14/1045 from July 20th, 2007

823   LT-Drs. 14/45. Here and in the following: pp. 6, 7, 11f of the interview conducted on February 7th, 2012 with the former Minister of Justice, Roswitha Müller-Piepenkötter. Full transcript available through this study's author.

824   Plenarprotokoll 14/93 Section 12 to Drs. 14/6866 from May 27th, 2008, p. 11079

825   pp. 12f of the interview conducted on February 7th, 2012 with the former Minister of Justice, Roswitha Müller-Piepenkötter. Full transcript available through this study's author. The same quieting of the opposition is also noted by Christian Möbius, MP (CDU) in LT-Ausschussprotokoll 14/459, p. 20 and demonstrated in LT-Plenarprotokoll 14/93 p. 11076 by the MPs Sichau (SPD) and Giebels (CDU) and on 11077 MPs Orth (FDP) and Düker (Bündnis 90/Die Grünen)

826   Drs. 14/6866 from May 27th, 2008

827   Here and in the following: Plenarprotokoll 14/93 Section 12 to Drs. 14/6866 from May 27th, 2008, pp. 11075f

and Probation Ombudsman for England and Wales. The CDU, then ruling party, and its Minister of Justice acknowledged the Ombudsmann für den Justizvollzug Nordrhein-Westfalen as a unique success within Germany but insisted on a longer trial period before establishing a more permanent basis for the institution.[828] It is very interesting to note that during the continuing consultation, Monika Düker, speaking for the green party, recommended Article 3 of the OP-CAT as the basis upon which to establish the Ombudsmann für den Justizvollzug Nordrhein-Westfalen.[829] This would designate the latter as a NPM – a suggestion which has also met with frequent support in academic writing.[830] Without further consultation in the law commission or the plenum, but with a delay of almost two years, the motion was rejected.[831]

After the 2010 elections placed a coalition of social democrats and the green party in government, they returned to the basic idea of this motion. As the pre-determined term of office of the Ombudsmann für den Justizvollzug Nordrhein-Westfalen incumbent had just expired, the new Minister of Justice, Thomas Kutschaty, commenced the search for a candidate. After some rejections, he found a willing candidate in Prof. em. Michael Walter, a former professor of criminology at the University of Cologne.[832] The latter was nominated without any advertisement of the vacancy, application procedure or involvement of the parliament – a course of action that Prof. Walter has hence come to recommend.[833] Nevertheless, he lays claim to full independence from the Minister and the Ministry citing his age, his lack of a party membership, his three-year contract interminable on the part of the Ministry, and the public knowledge of his positions on the penal system.[834]

---

828 Here and in the following: Plenarprotokoll 14/93 Section 12 to Drs. 14/6866 from May 27th, 2008, pp. 11076, 11079

829 Here and in the following: Plenarprotokoll 14/93 Section 12 to Drs. 14/6866 from May 27th, 2008, p. 11076

830 Rotthaus (2008), p. 383; Carl (2012a), p. 108

831 Drs. 14/0866 from March 22, 2010

832 Here and in the following: pp. 26f of the interview conducted on April 25th, 2012 with the Justizvollzugsbeauftragter des Landes Nordrhein-Westfalen, Prof. Michael Walter.

833 For the recommendation of changes to the constitution to allow election of the Justizvollzugsbeauftragter des Landes Nordrhein-Westfalen by members of parliament – c.f. p. 26 of the interview conducted on April 25th, 2012 with the Justizvollzugsbeauftragter des Landes Nordrhein-Westfalen, Prof. Michael Walter.

834 The appointment to office for a term of three years seems to have been continued without consideration during the transformation of the Ombudsmann für den Justizvollzug Nordrhein-Westfalen into the Justizvollzugsbeauftragter des Landes Nordrhein-Westfalen. p. 29 of the interview conducted on April 25th, 2012 with the Justizvollzugsbeauftragter des Landes Nordrhein-Westfalen, Prof. Michael Walter. The

It is interesting to note that Prof. Walter's assent to the post was tied to a revision of the Ombudsmann für den Justizvollzug Nordrhein-Westfalen's office which was supposed to involve a shift in the job description which stressed planning and conceptualization.[835] Similar requests had already been made by the previous officeholder, Söhnchen, who lamented finding his hands tied upon recognizing and mentioning a structural problem in his annual report. A former staff member of the Ombudsmann für den Justizvollzug Nordrhein-Westfalen and current staff member of the Justizvollzugsbeauftrager des Landes Nordrhein-Westfalen notes: „The ombudsman as well always found it unsatisfactory that he could not do more, but was always limited to intercessional activities. He often recognized a problem and then was not allowed to do more. He mentioned more than once to the committee on legal affairs that he regretted not having this opportunity."[836] Walter approached this problem by presenting the Minister and the permanent secretary with a paper recommending corresponding changes to the AV. He later described their positive reaction saying:

"Back then the Minister and the permanent secretary recognized that this [conceptual element] adds all the zest [and allows] the commissioner to take action and make recommendations. Of course, [...] we can only convince with our arguments. But the Ministry has to look into it [...] and that's the main point, I think".[837]

At the end of the revision of the Ombudsmann für den Justizvollzug Nordrhein-Westfalen stood a new AV that included Prof. Walter's recommendations and renamed the institution to Justizvollzugsbeauftragter des Landes Nordrhein-

---

former Minister of Justice, Müller-Piepenkötter, would agree with Prof. Walter's position on his independence as she is convinced: "It is important how independent the officeholder is. Personally, I regard it in the same manner as judicial independence: the person has to be independent. This was clearly provided for by the AV. A law would only cause a shift of ombudsman's dependence [from the Ministry] to the parliament." – c.f. p. 11 of the interview conducted on February 7th, 2012 with the former Minister of Justice, Roswitha Müller-Piepenkötter. Full transcript available through this study's author. See also Tätigkeitsbericht des Justizvollzugsbeauftragten des Landes Nordrhein-Westfalen, p. 25

835   Here and in the following: p. 23. Prof. Walter claims to have already considered the Ombudsmann für den Justizvollzug Nordrhein-Westfalen's lack of a conceptualization component at the time of his introduction in 2007, c.f. p. 19 of the interview conducted on April 25th, 2012 with the Justizvollzugsbeauftragter des Landes Nordrhein-Westfalen, Prof. Michael Walter.

836   For the hear-say evidence see p. 23 of the interview conducted on April 25th, 2012 with the Justizvollzugsbeauftragter des Landes Nordrhein-Westfalen, Prof. Michael Walter. For Söhnchen's personal statement see LT-Ausschussprotkoll 14/908, p. 7

837   p. 24 of the interview conducted on April 25th, 2012 with the Justizvollzugsbeauftragter des Landes Nordrhein-Westfalen, Prof. Michael Walter.

Westfalen (Commissioner for the penal system of North Rhine-Westphalia).[838] This alteration was also advocated by Prof. Walter in an attempt to underscore the changes made to the institution and prevent misgivings about his future work approach.[839] The selection of the new appellation emanated from inside the Ministry and was expressly motivated by purging the exotic term ombudsman from the institution's title in favour of reconnecting with the German tradition of *Beauftragte*.[840] On December 20th, 2010 the Minister of Justice appointed Walter the new officeholder calling the instatement of an independent Justizvollzugsbeauftragter an important step towards the optimization of the North Rhine-Westphalian prison system[841]. He declared the establishment of the Justizvollzugsbeauftragter des Landes Nordrhein-Westfalen to constitute an advancement of the Ombudsmann für den Justizvollzug Nordrhein-Westfalen-based idea reasoning that while the latter was solely charged with handling individual grievances, the Justizvollzugsbeauftragter des Landes Nordrhein-Westfalen was also mandated to care for those inmates who are not complaining themselves[842] and would place an additional focus on the penal system as a whole.[843] The latter involves a continual analysis of the organizational and structural conditions of the penal system resulting in concise recommendations for its improvement. This arrangement of two complimentary roles was immediately questioned by Robert Orth, a liberal MP (FDP), who holds that providing advice

---

838   AV d. JM from December 13th, 2010, 4400 – IV. 396
839   p. 24 of the interview conducted on April 25th, 2012 with the Justizvollzugsbeauftragter des Landes Nordrhein-Westfalen, Prof. Michael Walter.
840   Interviewer: "And the word *Beauftragter*, was this your choice?" Walter: "No. That was not my idea. I made some suggestions. This came from the Ministry. Incidentally out of the consideration: we do not want exotic terminology. There always were *Beauftragte* such as the *Datenschutzbeauftragter* [Data Protection Commissioner] [...] the *Wehrbeauftragter* [German Military Ombudsman]. They said, there are examples [...] I then signaled my agreement." – c.f. p. 24 of the interview conducted on April 25th, 2012 with the Justizvollzugsbeauftragter des Landes Nordrhein-Westfalen, Prof. Michael Walter.
841   Here and in the following press release of the Ministry of Justice from December 20th, 2010 available from
       www.justiz.nrw.de/JM/Presse/PresseJM/archiv/2010_02_Archiv/10-12-20/index.php
842   C.f. Ausschussprotokoll 15/102, p. 15
843   Kaminski (2012), p. 286 shows Prof. Walter's complete agreement with the Minister's statement. Considering the former's influence on the new AV this is hardly surprising – c.f. pp. 22ff of the interview conducted on April 25th, 2012 with the Justizvollzugsbeauftragter des Landes Nordrhein-Westfalen, Prof. Michael Walter

to the Minister whilst at the same time gaining the trust of the prisoners and staff was mutually exclusive.[844]

It will be interesting to observe the future development of the Justizvollzugsbeauftragter des Landes Nordrhein-Westfalen under the strong influence of the new incumbent. Much impact can be expected from the first annual report, which was presented in the summer 2012 and includes so called "Leitlinien für den Strafvollzug" (Guidelines for the penal system). The latter might amount to the passing of a North Rhine-Westphalian penal law which – if Prof. Walter's speculations should materialize – could place the Justizvollzugsbeauftragter des Landes Nordrhein-Westfalen on a statutory footing.[845] This would make the Justizvollzugsbeauftragter des Landes Nordrhein-Westfalen the second prison ombudsman to gain a legislative basis after the Canadian Correctional Investigator in 1992 and the third legislative prison ombudsman overall (the Michigan Legislative Corrections Ombudsman was implemented in law from its outset in 1975). This legislative footing would represent a considerable step towards strengthening the Justizvollzugsbeauftragter des Landes Nordrhein-Westfalen's influence and independence and quite an accomplishment considering that the Prisons and Probation Ombudsman for England and Wales has unsuccessfully campaigned for a statutory footing for a much longer time than the Justizvollzugsbeauftragter des Landes Nordrhein-Westfalen and his predecessor have even been in existence.

bb) The Ombudsmann für den Justizvollzug Nordrhein-Westfalen as a product of cross-fertilization

The above discussion of the history of the Justizvollzugsbeauftragter des Landes Nordrhein-Westfalen functions as the framework for the analysis of the Justizvollzugsbeauftragter des Landes Nordrhein-Westfalen as a potential product of cross-fertilization. This analysis will be done in two steps. In a first step, the history of the Ombudsmann für den Justizvollzug Nordrhein-Westfalen will be examined for the occurrence of a cross-fertilization process. The second step will be an analysis of the history of the Justizvollzugsbeauftragter des Landes Nordrhein-Westfalen pertaining to additional processes of inter-legal-system learning.

The Minister of Justice at the time of the introduction of the Ombudsmann für den Justizvollzug Nordrhein-Westfalen, Müller-Piepenkötter, confirms that

---

844 http://www.fdp-mg.de/?wc_c=28517&wc_lkm=0&id=939 (last accessed June 6th, 2012)

845 p. 27 of the interview conducted on April 25th, 2012 with the Justizvollzugsbeauftragter des Landes Nordrhein-Westfalen, Prof. Michael Walter

"[y]es, this was a new idea [within the Ministry]".[846] However, the specific wording of the AV, which confirms that the Ombudsmann für den Justizvollzug Nordrhein-Westfalen was not a direct copy of any single other institution, shows that "[p]ast policies constrain agents as to both what can be transferred and what agents look for when engaging in policy transfer".[847]

This leads to the questions of where and how the idea originated. The question of the how asks after the driving factors for the introduction of a prison ombudsman and includes a time and an agency element.[848] De Jong et al.[849] try to describe the timing factor as "[s]pecial periods of regime transformation characterised by a sense of emergency and urgency (e.g. system upheaval, nation building or national financial performance crisis) [that] create policy windows and critical junctures that facilitate the transplantation process". A glance at the institutional history set out above proves that the occurrence of the "Siegburger Foltermord" (Torture Homicide of Siegburg Penitentiary) produced a sense of urgency entailing at least some element of systemic upheaval. This created a window of opportunity, which served as the motivational factor spurring quick policy action from the Minister of Justice.[850] Müller-Piepenkötter later confirmed this stating "Of course it was political – it [the Siegburg incident] was being heavily debated".[851] She also acknowledged that this was a time of acute pressure on the North Rhine-Westphalian penal system and that this motivated and expedited the implementation process of the prison ombudsman.

However, the Minister does not stop at the acknowledgment of the existence of a catalyst, which would create an expectation of calculating rationality for the implementation process that would be diametrically opposed to a typical cross-fertilization process. The latter, as Dolowitz and Marsh point out, "is not inevitably, or perhaps even usually, a rational process. Rather, it is often a messy pro-

---

846 p. 6 of the interview conducted on February 7th, 2012 with the former Minister of Justice, Roswitha Müller-Piepenkötter. Full transcript available through this study's author.

847 Dolowitz/Marsh (1996), p. 353

848 c.f. chapter B III. 4.

849 Here and in the following: De Jong et al. (2002), p. 291

850 Sanker (2007), p. 54; for a comprehensive analysis of the incident see Walter (2007) and (2009) – c.f. p. 150 for the mention of the consequential introduction of a prison ombudsman; p. 5 of the interview conducted on April 25th, 2012 with the Justizvollzugsbeauftragter des Landes Nordrhein-Westfalen, Prof. Michael Walter

851 Here and in the following: pp. 8f of the interview conducted on February 7th, 2012 with the former Minister of Justice, Roswitha Müller-Piepenkötter. Full transcript available through this study's author.

cess in which different policy, solution, and problem streams need to combine at the appropriate moment for a policy to develop".[852]

Three interrelated quotes by Müller-Piepenkötter particularly stand out, namely her references pertaining to

- the catalytic incident (Q1)
- her reaction to it (Q2)
- and the element of time involved (Q3).

With her claim that

"[p]olitically this was not an unparalleled incident – other countries have previously experienced similar situations – but it was so drastic that it was necessary to make it clear to the outside: we will not simply go back to normal, which after all was not our intent".[853] (Q1)

she creates a greater context by affirming the inevitability and – at least to some degree – normalcy of such incidents. At the same time however, this hides the repeated occurrence of similar non-fatal incidents in the very same penitentiary over quite some time of her being in office.[854]

Concerning her reaction, the Minister tries to assure that

"I cannot claim that we would not have had the idea otherwise [without the Siegburg incident] as at the time there was already an inquiry being conducted on prison incidents, reasons for those incidents and possible preventive measures."

and goes on to say that

"[a]s far as the question 'How do I handle this?' is concerned, it was mostly business-like: How can I do the best for the penal system and how can I best assist prisoners with problems?"[855] (Q2).

The element of time involved between the incident and the reaction is well described by this interview quote:

| Interviewer: | "When was the ombudsman idea first presented to the public and the parliament?" |

852 Dolowitz/Marsh (1996), p. 356
853 p. 8 of the interview conducted on February 7th, 2012 with the former Minister of Justice, Roswitha Müller-Piepenkötter. Full transcript available through this study's author.
854 See Walter (2009), p. 150 for details; LT-Drucks. 14/6900, pp. 72f confirms 21 incidents in the Siegburg penitentiary requiring medical assistance mostly burns and head-wounds (such as lacerations, fractured jaws and permanent eye damage).
855 Here and in the following: pp. 6, 8ff of the interview conducted on February 7th, 2012 with the former Minister of Justice, Roswitha Müller-Piepenkötter. Full transcript available through this study's author.

Müller-Piepenkötter:	"Relatively fast, but I am not sure anymore".
Interviewer:	"Mhm".
Müller-Piepenkötter:	"Well, you have to consider: we thought of it on Sunday and Tuesday or Wednesday we held a press conference. And I believe the [designated candidate for the office of] ombudsman was already present".[856] (Q3)

In these three quotes, the Minister exhibits rationalizing behaviour typical for cross-fertilization processes in which the "[p]olicy makers act to reduce the possibility of incurring electoral defeat".[857] In this case, Müller-Piepenkötter had to combat three possible kinds of electoral defeat:

- P1: to avoid being personally removed from office, a demand heatedly made by the opposition[858],
- P2: to reduce possible points of attack against her political party, the CDU, which was heading towards four important *Länder* elections in 2008, and
- P3: to avoid potentially losing face over failing to put draft legislation through parliament due to dissenting votes from her own party.

The former two problems (P1 and P2) explain her claim that the catalytic incident was not such a singular occurrence (Q1). Her failure to avoid the death of a prisoner should not result in her personal loss of office or in being allotted a share of the blame in her party's potential electoral defeat as such incidents regrettably but unfailingly occur in all penal systems.

The third problem (P3) of potentially losing face relates to the reluctance of MPs, even within the Minister's own party, to pass a bill introducing a prison ombudsman. This explains her attempts to rationalize her reaction to the incident in Q3 by trying to present the introduction of the prison ombudsman as something that could have occurred even without the Siegburg incident, and as being predominantly led by "business-like" considerations of improving the penal system.[859]

---

856   p. 11 of the interview conducted on February 7th, 2012 with the former Minister of Justice, Roswitha Müller-Piepenkötter. Full transcript available through this study's author. The great speed with which the ombudsman idea was presented is also proven in LT-Ausschussprotokoll 14/308. This protocol dates from November 23rd, 2006 (the Siegburg incident happened on November 11th, 2006) and on p. 20 contains questions by the opposition about the reasonableness of the ombudsman suggestion.

857   Dolowitz/Marsh (1996), p. 356

858   LT-Drs. 14/45, pp. 5025, 5038

859   Here and in the following: pp. 6, 7, 9f, 11f of the interview conducted on February 7th, 2012 with the former Minister of Justice, Roswitha Müller-Piepenkötter. Full transcript available through this study's author.

All three problems (P1-3) serve to explain the sense of urgency evident in her fast resolution upon a deflective course of action-notably the prompt implementation of a prison ombudsman (c.f. Q3). The problems driving this necessity for immediate action also had an impact on the acquisition and implementation phase of the cross-fertilization process. Let us first turn to the acquisition phase: During this stage of cross-fertilization, the usual minimum standard of information gathering for the knowledge transfer between legal systems involves site visits as "an especially common source of information, along with information gleaned from contacts with officials of other countries [... whilst] knowledge of domestic debates over programs, program evaluations, or research comparing the strengths and weaknesses of various program designs" is frequently lacking.[860] In the case of the Ombudsmann für den Justizvollzug Nordrhein-Westfalen, the limited amount of time available due to P1-3 had a direct impact on the effort made. Site visits were neglected.[861] Academic writings on the topic – as was well as documented evidence on the subject such as by the DJT, were disregarded as irrelevant academic skirmishes.[862] However, the following quote by the Minister demonstrates that some information was gathered on the ombudsman concept in general, as well as on some of the particular models available.

| Interviewer: | "How did you go about informing yourself about the institution once the idea came up?" |
| Müller-Piepenkötter: | "We checked: What happens in Scandinavia? What happens in England? How did they organize it? And then there are also ombudsmen in other fields: in the economy, in the Chamber of Crafts etc. That we checked out as well".[863] (Q4) |

This orientation towards existing models is typical for the acquisition phase of cross-fertilization processes. While the Minister's quote reveals that the Ombudsmann für den Justizvollzug Nordrhein-Westfalen had no single, distinct role model, this does not negate the occurrence of a cross-fertilization process. In

---

860 Mossberger/Wolman (2003), p. 432
861 pp. 7f of the interview conducted on February 7th, 2012 with the former Minister of Justice, Roswitha Müller-Piepenkötter. Full transcript available through this study's author.
862 p. 10 of the interview conducted on February 7th, 2012 with the former Minister of Justice, Roswitha Müller-Piepenkötter. Full transcript available through this study's author.
863 p. 7 of the interview conducted on February 7th, 2012 with the former Minister of Justice, Roswitha Müller-Piepenkötter. Full transcript available through this study's author.

fact, a study by De Jong et al. has lately presented evidence that "considering only one definite model makes the transplantation process less easy" and that "[l]oosely defined models, or even lesson drawing from different models at the same time, provide domestic actors more leeway to make combinations that fit their desires and circumstances".[864] What Q4 does attest to, however, is the randomness of the model selection based on the pool of potential role models. The Minister only explicitly mentions German private sector ombudsmen as well as the Scandinavian and English models. Besides these, the information gathering could have extended to the German public sector ombudsmen such as the *Wehrbeauftragte des Deutschen Bundestages* (German Military Ombudsman) and the Data Commissioners and *Bürgerbeauftragte* of multiple German *Länder*[865] on the one hand, and on the other hand could have aimed to include the six other prison ombudsmen that were already in existence in the US (3), the UK (2) and Canada.

Interestingly, with her reference to checking "what happens in England?", the Minister refers to the most likely model for the Ombudsmann für den Justizvollzug Nordrhein-Westfalen. This would have been the Prisons and Probation Ombudsman for England and Wales for two main reasons: first, the German focus is frequently restricted to Europe. Within Europe (here: limited to England and Wales and Northern Ireland), the choice was more likely to fall on England and Wales, as the latter still has a special status where human rights are concerned due to its recent history of civil war. In addition, while the Prisoner Ombudsman for Northern Ireland was only introduced in 2005, the Prisons and Probation Ombudsman for England and Wales had been adopted in 1994 and had thus successfully operated for more than a decade by the time the North Rhine-Westphalian counterpart was designed.

However, it will be shown that no in-depth study of the English model was carried out, will be shown during the examination of the implementation phase. This is also manifest in the following quote:

Interviewer:	"And did you at this stage established actual contact to prison ombudsmen or similar institutions?"
Müller-Piepenkötter:	"No, no".
Interviewer:	"No personal conversations or visits abroad then?"
Müller-Piepenkötter:	"No".
Interviewer:	"Nothing. Mhm. And..."

---

864   De Jong et al. (2002), p. 288
865   For details see above at B I. 1.

Müller-Piepenkötter: "We did not want to make the time".[866] (Q5)

Both Q4 and Q5 give evidence to the superficial nature of the information gathering process. While the previously cited comment by Mossberger and Wolman attests to this being typical for a cross-fertilization process, the minimal extent of prior research exhibited here is nevertheless remarkable. Consequently, the acquisition phase can be described as severely stinted concerning both the amount of time invested and the amount of knowledge transferred. Mossberger and Wolman characterize this form of information "as a preeminent form of policy making by anecdote rather than analysis".[867]

However, the consequences of the perceived need for prompt action caused by P1-3 and demonstrated by Q3 are not limited to the acquisition phase of this cross-fertilization process. Instead, the most permanent impact must be noted in the implementation phase were it forced the Minister's hand as to the selection of the implementation form. Indeed, it caused her to opt for the introductory method of a ministerial decree, an AV, instead of a law, which she personally preferred.[868] The Minister confirms this saying: "The willingness to legally install an ombudsman was not very large [P3] and we deliberated for quite some time whether it could be done as an AV because of the sensitive nature of data protection and internal knowledge. But we came to the conviction that it could be done ..." and adds "... a legislative procedure takes time. There are the readings, the committees, negotiations; this easily takes a year until implementation. By choosing an AV we passed it in, I believe, two months [need for quick action caused by [P1-3]". This quote shows the strong interrelation between the problems involved in the acquisition phase and their direct impact – the time element – on the implementation phase of the cross-fertilization process. One could graphically depict the process as below:

---

866   pp. 7f of the interview conducted on February 7th, 2012 with the former Minister of Justice, Roswitha Müller-Piepenkötter. Full transcript available through this study's author.

867   Mossberger/Wolman (2003), p. 434

868   Here and in the following: pp. 7, 9, 12 and especially 10 of the interview conducted on February 7th, 2012 with the former Minister of Justice, Roswitha Müller-Piepenkötter. Full transcript available through this study's author.

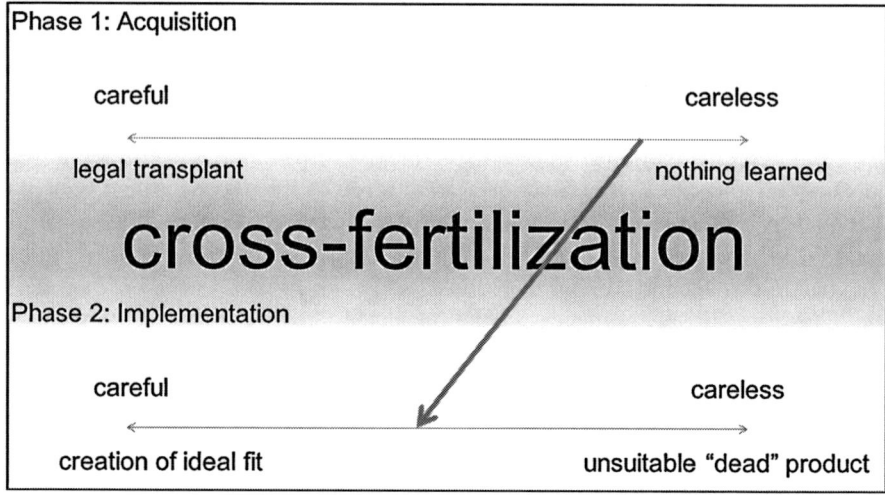

Figure 10: *The Ombudsmann für den Justizvollzug Nordrhein-Westfalen as a product of cross-fertilization*

This ministerial choice cast the Ombudsmann für den Justizvollzug Nordrhein-Westfalen as an institution within the Ministry of Justice with the office-holder being appointed by the Minister of Justice and the staff being employed by the Ministry. Consequently, the Ombudsmann für den Justizvollzug Nordrhein-Westfalen was created as an executive specialty (single-purpose) ombudsman. While chapter B I. 6. has revealed this implementation form to be inferior to an implementation on a legislative or constitutional basis, this does not necessarily equate with an inferior performance of the institution itself. Nevertheless, after a mere few months in existence, Müller-Piepenkötter once more considered placing the Ombudsmann für den Justizvollzug Nordrhein-Westfalen on a statutory footing.[869] She explains her lack of success by saying "I only ever made one penal law, the youth penal code and in this we installed the Ombudsmann für den Justizvollzug Nordrhein-Westfalen as an institution. But everything else remained in the AV".[870]

It is interesting to note – especially reconsidering Q4 and Q5 – that this concern about the preferential implementation form came up in the North Rhine-

---

869 Meant here are the six months between the passing of the AV and the passing of the Youth Penal Code on November 20th, 2007.

870 p. 10 of the interview conducted on February 7th, 2012 with the former Minister of Justice, Roswitha Müller-Piepenkötter. Full transcript available through this study's author.

Westphalian deliberations independently of similar discussions in prior ombudsinstitutions. In fact, there is no evidence that the limited amount of information gathering mentioned above had led to the discovery of Rowat's prominent struggle against executive ombudsmen or the on-going quest for statutory footing for the Prisons and Probation Ombudsman for England and Wales[871]. Consequently, it must be a direct result of P3.

Another feature common to cross-fertilization process is that of agency.[872] In both phases of the cross-fertilization process examined here, the Minister, as a politician, and the Ministry of Justice, made up of bureaucrats, were heavily involved as agents of transfer.[873] Especially without the action of Müller-Piepenkötter the introduction of the Ombudsmann für den Justizvollzug Nordrhein-Westfalen would have been unthinkable.

Overall, the evidence on the acquisition and the implementation phase gathered here combined with the weighty indicator of the agency element indicates the Ombudsmann für den Justizvollzug Nordrhein-Westfalen to be a product of a cross-fertilization process.

cc) The Justizvollzugsbeauftrager des Landes Nordrhein-Westfalen as a product of cross-fertilization

Since the Ombudsmann für den Justizvollzug Nordrhein-Westfalen is the direct predecessor of the Justizvollzugsbeauftragter des Landes Nordrhein-Westfalen, this necessarily makes the latter a product of cross-fertilization as well. However, the process of recasting the Ombudsmann für den Justizvollzug Nordrhein-Westfalen into the Justizvollzugsbeauftragter des Landes Nordrhein-Westfalen also provides an additional source for potential cross-fertilization processes. There are two points to highlight in this context: first, the fact that a remodeling occurred after such a short period of time; and second, that during a remodeling the knowledge transfer can never flow as freely as during the original cross-fertilization process.

Concerning the danger of a quick remodeling of institutions, Offe observed that designers of institutions frequently purposefully deny their creative role in institutional creation in an attempt to avoid the suspicion "of trying to impose his particular interest or normative point of view upon the broader community".[874] This is due to the fact that said suspicion "may invalidate the recognition and respect of the new institution" and "will invite others to attempt a different

---

871   For further information on Rowat c.f. chapter B I. 6. For the Prisons and Probation Ombudsman for England and Wales' struggle c.f. above chapter D I. 2. a) aa)

872   Evans/Davies (1999), p. 382; Marsh/Sharman (2009), p. 275

873   C.f. Evans (2009a), p. 244

874   Here and in the following: Offe (1994), pp. 14f

design, the consequence being an overload of contingency, complexity, and uncertainty which contradicts the essence of what we mean by an institution". However, this clearly is not the case where the Ombudsmann für den Justizvollzug Nordrhein-Westfalen was concerned. At the Ombudsmann für den Justizvollzug Nordrhein-Westfalen first incumbent's introductory press conference, Minister Müller-Piepenkötter actually stated that if the parliament were to demand it, they could become directly involved in the selection process.[875] In doing so, Müller-Piepenkötter purposefully tried to invite the opposition to attempt a different design closer to her own personal preference for a legal basis.[876] It may therefore be said that the Minister's dissatisfaction was at the root of the new cross-fertilization process.

The successfully baited opposition entered a parliamentary motion in 2008 requesting a statutory footing for the Ombudsmann für den Justizvollzug Nordrhein-Westfalen modeled on the German Military Ombudsman.[877] It is therefore not surprising that when this opposition was elected into government it commenced a remodeling of the Ombudsmann für den Justizvollzug Nordrhein-Westfalen. What is surprising, however, is that the new government did not place the institution on statutory footing despite this having previously been demanded in order to ensure its independence from the Ministry and strengthen its efficiency – instead again basing it on an AV.

This ties in with the second point regarding the more constrained flow of knowledge transfer during a remodeling as compared to the original cross-fertilization process. As Rose previously pointed out: "Policy makers are inheritors before they are choosers; as a condition of taking office they swear to uphold the laws and programs that predecessors have set in place ... new programs cannot be constructed on green field sites. Instead, they must be introduced into a policy environment dense with past commitments".[878] What this means is that "[p]ast policies constrain agents as to both what can be transferred and what

875   Kölner Stadtanzeiger, 16.04. 2007
876   This stands in no opposition to her defence of the Ombudsmann für den Justizvollzug Nordrhein-Westfalen's executive basis in LT-Plenarprotokoll 14/93 p. 11079. Her statement then must be seen as 1. defending her own position against claims of influencing the Ombudsmann für den Justizvollzug Nordrhein-Westfalen by stating that the office worked successfully (c.f. p. 10078) and 2. Müller-Piepenkötter did favour a longer trial period for the Ombudsmann für den Justizvollzug Nordrhein-Westfalen as mentioned on p. 11076 and in the article referred to in fn. 875. That she upheld her mid-term preference of a statutory footing is expressly protocolled on p. 11079.
877   Here and in the following: LT-Drs. 14/6866; note that the German Military Ombudsman's legal basis is the German Basic Law and as such constitutional.
878   Rose (1993), p. 78

agents look for when engaging in policy transfer".[879] This in fact happened to the opposition MPs cum government in case of the Ombudsmann für den Justizvollzug Nordrhein-Westfalen as highlighted by the following quote by Prof. Walter:

| Interviewer: | "Did you recommend to the government, now the former government, that it should be placed on a legislative basis?" |
| Walter: | "I mentioned it asking why it was an AV. Then I was instructed how this came about. I did not know why this was an AV and not a law – especially since it is included in the Youth Penal Code. And this is also why I know about the constitutional problem. [...] back then it was not necessary [to make it a law] in order to make it work and secondly, it is difficult reaching the necessary majority for a constitutional amendment if you are a minority government".[880] |

The constitutional problematic is mentioned here:

| Walter: | It turns out that according to our *Länder* constitution – note that I am not a constitutional lawyer – if a person shall be elected by parliament, this can only be decreed by the constitution. A simple law is not enough. I believe that somehow, if he is to be elected by parliament, which would basically be a sensible idea, than that has to be in the constitution. This would probably necessitate a constitutional amendment."[881] |

When the opposition found itself elected to government, it must have viewed the entire problematic with new eyes recognizing that ruling by ministerial decrees is much more convenient and easier than passing laws let alone constitutional amendments. This is especially true for a minority government, as Prof. Walter correctly points out. Another factor may have been the timing, as the AV was enacted shortly after the elections and may well have been the first legislative proposal brought forth by the minority government not to be passed by the parliament. The controversy around the remodeling of the Ombudsmann für den Justizvollzug Nordrhein-Westfalen into the Justizvollzugsbeauftragter des Landes Nordrhein-Westfalen can be deduced from the heated consultation pro-

---

879   Dolowitz/Marsh (1996), p. 353
880   p. 32 of the interview conducted on April 25th, 2012 with the Justizvollzugsbeauftragter des Landes Nordrhein-Westfalen, Prof. Michael Walter.
881   p. 28 of the interview conducted on April 25th, 2012 with Justizvollzugsbeauftragter des Landes Nordrhein-Westfalen, Prof. Michael Walter.

tocols upon the incumbent, Prof. Michael Walter's, induction.[882] It will be interesting to see whether the legislative basis that Prof. Walter already hinted at in the conducted interview will be delivered in a North Rhine-Westphalian penal law now that the minority government has become a majority government on May 13th, 2012.[883]

The renaming of the office to Justizvollzugsbeauftragter which represents a return to the strong German *Beauftragten*-tradition once again conforms to Rose and Dolowitz/Marsh's observations that legislators are "inheritors before they are choosers" and are limited "as to what can be transferred" and what they "look for when engaging in policy transfer".[884]

So far, this argument amounts to proof of the occurrence of learning processes within the North Rhine-Westphalian legal system across time. Rose also recognized this as a cross-fertilization process, saying "The past has two faces: history-as-continuity and history-as-intelligence [...]. The continuity of history is often a constraint [...]. History as intelligence seeks to make use of past times and places [...]. History as intelligence offers a wide choice of lessons that may apply in the present".[885] What the minority government produced in this case is a combination of history-as-continuity and history-as-intelligence. On the one hand, they recognized the Ombudsmann für den Justizvollzug Nordrhein-Westfalen's limitation – assisted by Prof. Walter – and added a conceptual component[886]. On the other hand, they returned to the German *Beauftragten*-tradition, which extends to institutions that are clearly public sector ombudsmen. They also maintained the previously criticized implementation of the ombudsoffice through an AV.

Although this could be considered a process of cross-fertilization, at least according to Rose's "guide to leaning across time and space" – Evans and Davies would consider this evidence of a non-transfer which they declare to occur whenever "[e]lements of an idea or a programme [...] are found to have been borrowed from domestic antecedents".[887] While we see clear evidence of copying from domestic antecedents, this does not exclude the possibility of simultaneous additional learning processes occurring from geographically further removed institutions such as the Prisons and Probation Ombudsman for England and Wales. This relates to Dolowitz and Marsh's

---

882   Ausschussprotokoll 15/102, pp. 14-25
883   See above at F II. 2. a) aa)
884   For proof please see at F II. 2. a) aa)
885   Rose (1993), p. 78
886   See above at F II. 2. a) aa)
887   Evans/Davies (1999), p. 382

"basic assumption in drawing lessons from other nations [...] that: 'similarities are greater within a given program across national boundaries than among different programs within a country.' When drawing lessons across nations, geographic propinquity does not equate with policy transfer because ideological and resource similarities are necessary preconditions to adapt lessons from one country to another and neighbouring countries do not always meet these conditions".[888]

Indeed, further information concerning the remodeling of the Ombudsmann für den Justizvollzug Nordrhein-Westfalen into the Justizvollzugsbeauftragter des Landes Nordrhein-Westfalen indicates exactly that. During the consultations on the motion brought forth by the social democrats, Frank Sichau, MP (SPD), mentioned in his plenary speech that the motion was expressly based upon reported positive experiences from abroad.[889] He even quotes an academic article relating the positive experiences made with the Prisons and Probation Ombudsman for England and Wales. However, this paper fails to mention the continued fight for a statutory footing for the Prisons and Probation Ombudsman for England and Wales'.[890] Sichau, nevertheless, knew that the international standard required the ombudsinstitution to be independent from the executive.[891] However, the limited nature of his understanding of the ombudsman concept can be seen from his comments on the idea of using the German Military Ombudsman as a model, saying:

"Our motion does not aim at placing the ombudsman on a constitutional basis like the German Military Ombudsman. This is not our intent, although this would definitely strengthen the institution. We want that the ombudsman [...] becomes a helpmeet for parliament. Besides transparency, protection and control of the executive it is important to us that the ombudsman is independent of the executive".[892]

Art. 45b GG declares the German Military ombudsman to be exactly that: a partner and advisor of parliament concerning the supervision of the armed forces. Nevertheless, Sichau has certainly made his mark as the most knowledgeable North Rhine-Westphalian MP (at least within the SPD) in matters concerning prison ombudsmen.

This episode proves that after the introduction of the Ombudsmann für den Justizvollzug Nordrhein-Westfalen, knowledge about prison ombudsmen continued to grow. In this instance, the inter-legal-system learning occurred by means of academic writings. Sichau's public comments further disseminated this

---

888 Dolowitz/Marsh (1996), p. 353
889 Here and in the following: Plenarprotokoll 14/93 Section 12 to Drs. 14/6866 from May 27th, 2008, p. 11076
890 Kretschmer (2005), pp. 217ff
891 Plenarprotokoll 14/93, p. 11080
892 Plenarprotokoll 14/93, pp. 11075f

knowledge amongst his MP colleagues, many of which became part of the government in 2010 and as such were in a position to influence the remodeling of the Ombudsmann für den Justizvollzug Nordrhein-Westfalen into the Justizvollzugsbeauftragter des Landes Nordrhein-Westfalen.[893] The fact that only his quest for more independence was taken up in the new AV while his recommendation of a statutory footing was not carried over to the government might be attributed to the problems resulting from minority government as well as Sichau not being re-elected as an MP in 2010.

Overall, the subtle combination of impulses from similar institutions exiting at home and abroad together with the first-hand experiences made with the Ombudsmann für den Justizvollzug Nordrhein-Westfalen as a predecessor model add up to a constant undercurrent of influences on the formulation and development of new laws.[894] Unlike the process of knowledge transfer for the Ombudsmann für den Justizvollzug Nordrhein-Westfalen which was initiated by dissatisfaction and conflict, the acquisition phase for the Justizvollzugsbeauftragter des Landes Nordrhein-Westfalen can be attributed to discourse pull.[895] As such, the new prison ombudsman variation represented by the Justizvollzugsbeauftragter des Landes Nordrhein-Westfalen may be considered the product of a weak act of inter-temporal and inter-locational cross-fertilization.[896]

b) The outcome of implementation: Structures of the Justizvollzugsbeauftragter des Landes Nordrhein-Westfalen

The outcome of the implementation focuses on the structures of the Justizvollzugsbeauftragter des Landes Nordrhein-Westfalen.

aa) Legal basis and categorization

The legal basis of the Justizvollzugsbeauftragter des Landes Nordrhein-Westfalen is mostly determined by a ministerial decree, the AV. [897] However, this legal basis is complemented by §97 JStVollzG NRW, the youth penal law, which mentions the prison ombudsman as a potential grievance channel. Before the dissolution of the North Rhine-Westphalian *Landtag* on March 14th, 2012, the coalition formed of social democrats and the green party had been working

---

893 Sichau's co-author for the motion LT-Drs. 14/6866, Hannelore Kraft, in 2010 become Ministerpräsident of the North Rhine-Westphalian parliament.

894 C.f. Leyland (2002), p. 217

895 C.f. B I. 4. d) and there especially Figure 8

896 Thus, the above mentioned discrepancy between Rose (1993) and Evans/Davies (1999) concerning cross-fertilization across time only does not have to be resolved.

897 AV d. JM from December 13th, 2010, 4400 – IV. 396; for critique by Dr. Robert Orth see Ausschussprotokoll 15/102, p. 18 Dr. Robert Orth

on a new penal law, which might have included a statutory footing for the Justizvollzugsbeauftragter des Landes Nordrhein-Westfalen.[898] In light of the election results on May 13th, 2012, this effort might now be recommenced. This motion is supported by the current office-holder, Prof. Walter, who emphasizes the legal-cultural benefit, whilst admitting to the every-day sufficiency of the AV. Personally, he would favour a constitutional amendment to afford the possibility of parliamentary election of the incumbent and to thereby guarantee the broadest possible legitimation basis and greatest independence.

According to the AV, the Justizvollzugsbeauftragter des Landes Nordrhein-Westfalen is a ministerial appointee whose staff members are employees of the Ministry of Justice. The latter also provides the funding and staffing according to the general budget. The officeholder is required to work in tight consultation with the permanent secretary where staff issues are concerned. However, according to section 1 II of the AV, the Justizvollzugsbeauftragter des Landes Nordrhein-Westfalen is independent in the execution of his duties – limited only by positive law.[899] This is a much greater degree of independence than its predecessor, the Ombudsmann für den Justizvollzug Nordrhein-Westfalen, enjoyed.[900] Despite this improvement and the mention in the Youth Penal Law, the lack of a legal basis marks the Justizvollzugsbeauftragter des Landes Nordrhein-Westfalen - like the Prisons and Probation Ombudsman for England and Wales – as an executive specialty ombudsman.[901] Unlike the Prisons and Probation Ombudsman for England and Wales, who is also charged with overseeing the probation service, the Justizvollzugsbeauftragter des Landes Nordrhein-Westfalen is a single-subject executive ombudsman.[902]

bb) Role and remit

The role of the Justizvollzugsbeauftragter des Landes Nordrhein-Westfalen comprises two components. The Justizvollzugsbeauftragter des Landes Nordrhein-Westfalen as prison ombudsman is in charge of complaint handling, which

---

898 c.f. here and in the following: pp. 27f of the interview conducted on April 25th, 2012 with the Justizvollzugsbeauftragter des Landes Nordrhein-Westfalen, Prof. Michael Walter.

899 Ausschussprotokoll 15/102, p. 15

900 The ministerial decree AV d. JM from March 14th, 2007, 4400- IV. 396 JMBl. NRW, p. 87f makes no mention of any independence of the Ombudsmann für den Justizvollzug Nordrhein-Westfalen. This is criticized in Plenarprotokoll 14/93, p. 10076.

901 Without a legislative basis any ombudsman can be eliminated by a simple ministerial decree upon inopportune behavior. For details see above at B. VII. 2.

902 For details see above at B. VII. 4.

makes up about 40% of his workload.[903] The other 60% of his role are taken up with providing conceptual advice to the Ministry of Justice by means of developing recommendations for penal policy. This presents a notable shift in institutional focus – especially considering that this occurred without any increase in staff.[904]

Compared to the Ombudsmann für den Justizvollzug Nordrhein-Westfalen, the Justizvollzugsbeauftragter des Landes Nordrhein-Westfalen's responsibilities (see section 3 of the AV) have been given a shorter wording, reading:

> "The Justizvollzugsbeauftragter des Landes Nordrhein-Westfalen contributes to a penal system aligned with the human rights as well as the fundamental principles of a social state under the rule of law. He advises the Ministry of Justice on fundamental issues concerning the penal system, especially concerning its continuous development. He is also contact person for all persons concerned with the North Rhine-Westphalian penal system and functions at the same time as "Ombudsperson for the penal system in North Rhine-Westphalia" according to §97 II JStVollzG".[905]

While the only Ombudsmann für den Justizvollzug Nordrhein-Westfalen officeholder, Rolf Söhnchen, primarily understood his role as spokesperson for all those concerned with the North Rhine-Westphalian prison system[906], the Justizvollzugsbeauftragter des Landes Nordrhein-Westfalen officeholder, Prof. Michael Walter, considers his role to include more of a creative element.[907] He emphasizes section 3 of the AV, which regulates the involvement of the Justizvollzugsbeauftragter des Landes Nordrhein-Westfalen with the future progress of the penal system. [908] Walter states that the insights into the penal system gained from his ombudsfunction are intended for the development of criminal policy.

Section 6 of the AV grants the Justizvollzugsbeauftragter des Landes Nordrhein-Westfalen the right of initiative. There is no legally binding obligation forcing the Justizvollzugsbeauftragter des Landes Nordrhein-Westfalen to consider a grievance addressed to his/her office. Walter considers this essential to

---

903   c.f. p. 12 of the interview conducted on April 25th, 2012 with the Justizvollzugsbeauftragter des Landes Nordrhein-Westfalen, Prof. Michael Walter.

904   In agreement Orth (MP, FDP) and Giebels (MP, CDU) c.f. LT-Ausschussprotokoll 15/102, p. 21 as well as Kaminski (2012), p. 288, who holds: "I am under the impression, that your scope of duties shifts away from the work of an ombudsman as a friend and helper with individual concerns [and] towards conceptual work, where our penal system is in need of improvement."

905   Own translation

906   C.f. Sanker (2007), p. 54

907   Here and in the following: interview with Prof. Michael Walter in Der Vollzugsdienst (2011), p. 42

908   AV d. JM from December 13th, 2010, 4400 – IV. 396

his work as it provides a sensible tool for dealing with perpetual complainers that would otherwise swamp his office.[909] This option is for example not available to judges. Section 6 II allows for an organizational design placing the handling of grievances solely under the charge and oversight of a staff member. Although Prof. Walter personally insisted upon the inclusion of this section into the AV when he has was inaugurated, it has not been put into action since a purposeful reduction of grievances has rendered the discussion of the less than 500 individual submissions amongst the full staff of four possible.[910] This reduction was accomplished by retiring formal replies made up of text modules and reference numbers requesting further information in favour of a more direct, interpretative approach on incoming complaints.

The Justizvollzugsbeauftragter des Landes Nordrhein-Westfalen has full access to all facilities and persons as well as all necessary documents within the legal rights for his investigation.[911] Upon request, the penal administration has to provide information to the Justizvollzugsbeauftragter des Landes Nordrhein-Westfalen. This duty to give information works well in the praxis, but may – depending on the prison involved – face slight delays.[912] Additionally, the Justizvollzugsbeauftragter des Landes Nordrhein-Westfalen may request a meeting with the Ministry of Justice at any time.

The Justizvollzugsbeauftragter des Landes Nordrhein-Westfalen may also access all knowledge within the *Kriminologischer Dienst Nordrhein-Westfalen.* A productive collaboration with the Justizvollzugsbeauftragter des Landes Nordrhein-Westfalen requesting information for his recommendations, focal points and analyses has already been established.[913] The outcome of this collaboration serves the Justizvollzugsbeauftragter des Landes Nordrhein-Westfalen in his structural advice to the Ministry of Justice for the future development of the penal system.

---

909   c.f. p. 13 of the interview conducted on April 25th, 2012 with the Justizvollzugsbeauftragter des Landes Nordrhein-Westfalen, Prof. Michael Walter.

910   c.f. here and in the following: p. 16f of the interview conducted on April 25th, 2012 with the Justizvollzugsbeauftragter des Landes Nordrhein-Westfalen, Prof. Michael Walter.

911   Section 7 of the AV d. JM from December 13th, 2010, 4400 – IV. 396

912   c.f. p. 12 of the interview conducted on April 25th, 2012 with the Justizvollzugsbeauftragter des Landes Nordrhein-Westfalen, Prof. Michael Walter.

913   c.f. p. 18 of the interview conducted on April 25th, 2012 with the Justizvollzugsbeauftragter des Landes Nordrhein-Westfalen, Prof. Michael Walter.

cc) Execution

There are two key standard sources which provide information around the execution of duties by the Justizvollzugsbeauftragter des Landes Nordrhein-Westfalen – the AV as the legal basis and the annual report. Theoretical information on the execution of duties can also be drawn from the rules of internal procedures, which the Justizvollzugsbeauftragter des Landes Nordrhein-Westfalen has published in accord with section 2 IV of the AV.[914] In these rules, the Justizvollzugsbeauftragter des Landes Nordrhein-Westfalen asserts his intent to cooperate with the prison facilities as well as the "Kriminologische Dienst" and arranges to discuss any publicity measures with the Ministry of Justice in advance of publication.[915] Of particular interest is section 3 which shows that the selection of submissions for investigation depend either on considerations connected to the particular submission, or on their coinciding with the Justizvollzugsbeauftragter des Landes Nordrhein-Westfalen's core areas of interest. In the former case, the Justizvollzugsbeauftragter des Landes Nordrhein-Westfalen may refrain from investigation where

- the *Länder* administration has no legal influence,
- the case is pending at the Office of Public Prosecution or at a court or where a court decision has already been given,
- the case is or was subject of a committee of inquiry or petition committee.

The Justizvollzugsbeauftragter des Landes Nordrhein-Westfalen may also refuse to investigate where

- the internal complaints channels have not been completed,
- the submission does not bare name and address of the complainant or is at least partly unreadable,
- the submission contains no specific concern or is at least partly incomprehensible,
- the submission is slanderous or constitutes a crime or
- the submission does not contain any new information compared to previous submissions.

The extent of practical information available stems from the three annual reports of the Ombudsmann für den Justizvollzug Nordrhein-Westfalen (2007/2008, 2008/2009, 2009/2010), which are of limited use as a basis of information on its institutional successor, and the first annual report of the Justizvollzugsbeauftrag-

---

914 AV d. JM from December 13th, 2010, 4400 – IV. 396
915 Here and in the following: c.f. http://www.justizvollzugsbeauftragter.nrw.de/ Rechtliche_Grundlagen/Gesch__ftsordnung/index.php (last accessed June 6th, 2012)

ter des Landes Nordrhein-Westfalen. The *Tätigkeitsbericht* (annual report) 2011 was completed in accordance with section 8 of the AV for presentation on March 31st, 2012, but has been delayed due to the dissolution of the North Rhine-Westphalian Landtag. The report has since been presented unchanged to the re-elected Minister of Justice, Thomas Kutschaty, soon after his induction in the summer of 2012.[916]

The annual report begins with an explanation of how the work of the Justizvollzugsbeauftragter des Landes Nordrhein-Westfalen will deviate from that of the Ombudsmann für den Strafvollzug and which aspects will be continued. The actual reports are set out in six sub-sections, which describe the (1) conceptual work, (2) work on core areas, (3) grievance-handling, (4) site visits, (5) meetings with representatives of the occupational groups and (6) individual problems and questions. Of particular interest and potential impact is section (1) which includes structural advice on the development of the penal system, the so called *Leitlinien für den Strafvollzug* (guidelines for the penal system), which have been requested by the previous government for potential use in creating a North Rhine-Westphalian penal code. With the former minority government consisting of a coalition of SPD and *Bündnis 90/Die Grünen* (the Greens) gaining a majority in the elections on May 13th, 2012, the chances for acceptance and implementation of the recommendations and particularly the *Leitlinien* seem rather good.

Besides the *Tätigkeitsbericht,* interviews given or articles written by the current incumbent, Prof. Walter, function as primary sources for practical information on Walter's approach to both of the components of the Justizvollzugsbeauftragter des Landes Nordrhein-Westfalen's role: namely, as an external, independent grievance channel on the one hand, and an advisor to the Minister of Justice on the structural development of the penal system on the other hand.[917]

As a grievance channel, the Justizvollzugsbeauftragter des Landes Nordrhein-Westfalen handles so called submissions, which by section 5 of the AV are legally defined to include all complaints, suggestions, observations and directions by anyone as long as they relate to the penal system.[918] In 2011/2012,

---

916 pp. 13, 16 of the interview conducted on April 25th, 2012 with the Justizvollzugsbeauftragter des Landes Nordrhein-Westfalen, Prof. Michael Walter and c.f. here and in the following: Annual Report/*Tätigkeitsbericht* of the Justizvollzugsbeauftragten des Landes Nordrhein-Westfalen. The Leitlinien can be found on pp. 27ff.

917 Der Vollzugsdienst (2011); Kaminski (2012); Walter (2012, in print) or the interview conducted on April 25th, 2012 with the Justizvollzugsbeauftragter des Landes Nordrhein-Westfalen, Prof. Michael Walter.

918 For a visualization of the grievance-handling process of the Justizvollzugsbeauftragter des Landes Nordrhein-Westfalen please view p. 9 Annual Report/*Tätigkeitsbericht* of the Justizvollzugsbeauftragten des Landes Nordrhein-Westfalen.

the Justizvollzugsbeauftragter des Landes Nordrhein-Westfalen received 476 such submissions, 25 of which were ineligible as they either concerned the penal facilities of *Länder* besides North Rhine-Westphalia or did not pertain to the penal system at all.[919] Of these 476 submissions, 64 were made by staff, 311 by prisoners and 101 by others, which are mainly submissions by prisoner relatives and as such are veiled prisoners' complaints.

Table 2: Submissions received by the Justizvollzugsbeauftragter des Landes Nordrhein-Westfalen in 2011/2012

SUBMISSIONS	In writing only	Oral only	Combined written and oral	Total
Staff	26	11	27	64
Prisoners	232	4	75	311
Others	69	1	31	101
Total	327	16	133	476

Table 2[920] shows that about half of the submissions by staff or relatives reach the Justizvollzugsbeauftragter des Landes Nordrhein-Westfalen via email or telephone, whilst prisoners' submissions are usually submitted in the form of handwritten letters. Prisoners in open prison facilities may also submit grievances by phone, but if doing so are regularly asked to provide some written statement to ease the handling process.[921]

Prof. Walter acknowledges that one of the unsolved problems concerns accessibility of the Justizvollzugsbeauftragte for illiterate prisoners or those not capable of German.[922] The accessibility for foreigners could be improved by providing the easily understandable explanatory brochure on the Justizvollzugsbeauftragter des Landes Nordrhein-Westfalen, currently only available in German, in multiple languages. With his expectation of written submissions, the

---

919 p. 7 of the interview conducted on April 25th, 2012 with the Justizvollzugsbeauftragter des Landes Nordrhein-Westfalen, Prof. Michael Walter and Annual Report/*Tätigkeitsbericht* of the Justizvollzugsbeauftragten des Landes Nordrhein-Westfalen, pp. 201ff especially pp. 212f

920 Table adapted from Walter (2012, in print) and p. 215 of the Annual Report/*Tätigkeitsbericht* of the Justizvollzugsbeauftragten des Landes Nordrhein-Westfalen.

921 pp. 10f of the interview conducted on April 25th, 2012 with the Justizvollzugsbeauftragter des Landes Nordrhein-Westfalen, Prof. Michael Walter.

922 C.f. Kaminski (2012), p. 291; pp. 10f of the interview conducted on April 25th, 2012 with the Justizvollzugsbeauftragter des Landes Nordrhein-Westfalen, Prof. Michael Walter.

Justizvollzugsbeauftragter des Landes Nordrhein-Westfalen deviates from a praxis established by his predecessor. The Ombudsmann für den Justizvollzug Nordrhein-Westfalen also set out with the expectation that prisoners would write, but recognized this to present too much of an obstacle and consequently emphasized the importance of regular visits to the facilities by members of his staff.[923] The Justizvollzugsbeauftragter des Landes Nordrhein-Westfalen explains the discontinuation of this approach saying that even with one full staff member charged with regular prison visits, a sufficient level of accessibility could not be achieved.[924]

This does not mean that the Justizvollzugsbeauftragter des Landes Nordrhein-Westfalen does not conduct personal visits to the prisons. He and his staff visit each of the 37 North Rhine-Westphalian prisons once per year on average.[925] 40 such visits were carried out in 2011/2012.[926] Almost all of these visits are announced in advance and are conducted according to a jointly agreed upon schedule. Walter describes this procedure saying:

> "We have a specific schedule for our visits that is made known to the local prison administration in advance. It is not predetermined what house we visits, that we decide on the spot, but we arrange that we will first talk to the Governor, than the heads of staff, the specially trained staff [therapists, social workers, priests etc.], then the staff council, some representatives of the uniformed staff [the guards], the control staff, the prison council, the board of visitors and then all prisoners or staff members who ask for an appointment".

---

923   pp. 5-6 of the interview conducted on February 7th, 2012 with the former Minister of Justice, Roswitha Müller-Piepenkötter. Full transcript available through this study's author. For Prof. Söhnchen's statement of his abandoning his expectation of receiving written complaints and instead relying on prison visits, c.f. LT-Ausschussprotokoll 14/459, p. 20.

924   Annual Report/*Tätigkeitsbericht* of the Justizvollzugsbeauftragten des Landes Nordrhein-Westfalen, pp. 6f and 206-11; c.f. Walter's quote in the interview with Kaminski (2012), p. 290: "In the annual report I set out an extensive argument concerning this approach to increased presence in specific prisons by means of an AVD-staff member employed by the ombudsman. Here only so much: Particularly after carefully reading the field report I am not convinced of this approach. It did make the ombudsman (more widely) known, but besides this did not result in any worthwhile gain. Besides, the prisoner wanting to make an oral submission, rarely has the patience to wait weeks or even months to do so." See also Annual Report/*Tätigkeitsbericht* of the Justizvollzugsbeauftragten des Landes Nordrhein-Westfalen, pp. 235ff

925   Here and in the following: pp. 4ff of the interview conducted on April 25th, 2012 with the Justizvollzugsbeauftragter des Landes Nordrhein-Westfalen, Prof. Michael Walter.

926   Here and in the following: Annual Report/*Tätigkeitsbericht* of the Justizvollzugsbeauftragten des Landes Nordrhein-Westfalen, pp. 221-31

On average, the Justizvollzugsbeauftragter des Landes Nordrhein-Westfalen speaks to five prisoners per visit, which includes prison council members. Due to his focus on discovering structural deficits and his knowledge that these visits – whether carried out by the Justizvollzugsbeauftragter des Landes Nordrhein-Westfalen, the German NPM under the OPCAT called "Nationale Stelle zur Verhütung von Folter" or even the ECPT – can easily be manipulated, the Justizvollzugsbeauftragter des Landes Nordrhein-Westfalen conducts these visits without any great expectation of finding anything to criticize concerning the buildings, cells or sanitation.[927]

Walter holds that "a rigid style of control clashes with the intent of recognizing weak spots and developing solutions in cooperation with the praxis".[928] This does not mean that the Justizvollzugsbeauftragter des Landes Nordrhein-Westfalen does not make a point of visiting for example especially secured cells, but refers to Walter's expectation that more insight can be derived from the information exchange, which these visits afford. For him, this idea is connected with the scheduled list of communication partners:

> "The idea behind listening to all these different groups and representatives is that together the different perspectives will produce a coherent picture, much like a mosaic. [...] If we try to investigate upon own-motion, we will not find anything scandalous [...]. German prisons are not that bad. The problems arise from human interaction. Those you cannot simply uncover – you can only trace them. This is why we make such an effort in this area and quite a bit comes to light".[929]

Consequently, Walter's workload also includes regular meetings with specific occupational groups in the Justizvollzugsbeauftragter des Landes Nordrhein-Westfalen's facilities.[930] It is much easier for staff members to approach the Justizvollzugsbeauftragter des Landes Nordrhein-Westfalen during a visit than for a prisoner as they can draw on a greater number of available communication channels, which are both unsupervised by the prison administration and can be used without adhering to any internal chain of command.[931] Walter describes the rather different situation for the prisoners saying:

---

927 Here and in the following: p. 21 of the interview conducted on April 25th, 2012 with the Justizvollzugsbeauftragter des Landes Nordrhein-Westfalen, Prof. Michael Walter.

928 Kaminski (2012), p. 292

929 p. 5 of the interview conducted on April 25th, 2012 with the Justizvollzugsbeauftragter des Landes Nordrhein-Westfalen, Prof. Michael Walter.

930 Here and in the following: Annual Report/*Tätigkeitsbericht* of the Justizvollzugsbeauftragten des Landes Nordrhein-Westfalen, pp. 21f and 231-4

931 p. 6 of the interview conducted on April 25th, 2012 with the Justizvollzugsbeauftragter des Landes Nordrhein-Westfalen, Prof. Michael Walter.

"Talks with prisoners involve particular problems as we do not know who is admitted under what condition. The procedures between prisons differ as well. Apparently it is not always appreciated if a prisoner wants to talk to the [Justizvollzugsbeauftragter des Landes Nordrhein-Westfalen]. Some prisoners have actually asked us to break-off established contact, because the backlash on the part of some individual staff members was too fierce. Of course this is a first class flare! But so far all our efforts to follow-up on this have proven difficult and turned up no success".[932]

Consequently, the Justizvollzugsbeauftragter des Landes Nordrhein-Westfalen tries to accommodate prisoners wishing to make an oral submission during a visit as much as possible noting that "[f]or prisoners it is much easier to voice their wishes and demands in small groups that present assurance and stability. During an interview individual prisoners often appear lost – at the mercy of an unassailable superior power".

Once a submission has reached the Justizvollzugsbeauftragter des Landes Nordrhein-Westfalen, it is shared at a round table discussion between the members of staff. Once it has been settled which issues will be taken up, the prisoner will be informed about the commencement of activity and requested to return a data protection consent form.[933] Prof Walter explains: "This is sent right away. According to our experience, the patience of prisoners is rather limited. The more precisely one describes the intended course of action, the better will later be the feedback." Concerning those issues, which the Justizvollzugsbeauftragter des Landes Nordrhein-Westfalen refuses to take up, the prisoner will receive an explanatory note with a recommended course of action. Due to the subsidiarity of the prison ombudsman, this may include trying to settle the issue within the prison first and, if unsuccessful, to take it up again with the ombudsman.[934] Partially, this is done to protect the prisoner from unnecessary backlash within the institution.

While the Justizvollzugsbeauftragte handles all incoming submissions, he freely admits to being especially interested in those revealing underlying structural problems.[935] Consequently, the Justizvollzugsbeauftragter des Landes Nordrhein-Westfalen is always happy if prisoners re-state their submissions af-

---

932   Here and in the following: Kaminski (2012), p. 291
933   Here and in the following: pp. 8f of the interview conducted on April 25th, 2012 with the Justizvollzugsbeauftragter des Landes Nordrhein-Westfalen, Prof. Michael Walter.
934   C.f. Kaminski (2012), p. 286; here and in the following: p. 11 of the interview conducted on April 25th, 2012 with the Justizvollzugsbeauftragter des Landes Nordrhein-Westfalen, Prof. Michael Walter.
935   pp. 7, 21 of the interview conducted on April 25th, 2012 with the Justizvollzugsbeauftragter des Landes Nordrhein-Westfalen, Prof. Michael Walter.

ter failing to settle them internally as this is an easy way to gather information about internal structural problems.[936]

Once the Justizvollzugsbeauftragter des Landes Nordrhein-Westfalen has taken up investigations concerning a submission, he/she makes use of the prison administration's duty to give information according to section 7 I and II of the AV. Section 7 IV then allows the Justizvollzugsbeauftragter des Landes Nordrhein-Westfalen to present the prison administration with a recommendation. It is important to note that not every submission will be concluded by giving a recommendation.[937] If this is the case, however, the prison administration is requested to make a reply and provide information about their compliance with the recommendation.[938] Prof. Walter confirms that whilst there are differences in correspondence time and enthusiasm, he knows of no case in which the prison administration has not made a reply.[939] In the 2011 *Tätigkeitsbericht,* the Justizvollzugsbeauftragter des Landes Nordrhein-Westfalen acknowledges that it is at least extremely difficult if not impossible to evaluate the success of his recommendations – "most cases are closed without statements about precise results being possible".[940] The *Tätigkeitsbericht* also emphasizes that the number of submissions or recommendations is not an ideal criterion to measure success.[941]

Recommendations of a structural nature are included in the annual report.[942] Both kinds of recommendations are released directly either to the prisoner or to the public in the annual report with no advance warning being given either to the Governor or the Minister. Walter notes:

> "The recipients are usually cooperative. At the same time, we seriously try to avoid giving an impression of degrading the prison in the eyes of the prisoners. We are always fair. If a prisoner is in the right, the Governor will receive a copy of our reply.

---

936   p. 18 of the interview conducted on April 25th, 2012 with the Justizvollzugsbeauftragter des Landes Nordrhein-Westfalen, Prof. Michael Walter.

937   Examples are: satisfaction of the prisoner's wish, release from prison in the meantime, etc. Here and in the following: pp. 8f of the interview conducted on April 25th, 2012 with the Justizvollzugsbeauftragter des Landes Nordrhein-Westfalen, Prof. Michael Walter.

938   C.f. Annual Report/*Tätigkeitsbericht* of the Justizvollzugsbeauftragten des Landes Nordrhein-Westfalen, p. 10

939   p. 10 of the interview conducted on April 25th, 2012 with the Justizvollzugsbeauftragter des Landes Nordrhein-Westfalen, Prof. Michael Walter.

940   here and in the following: Annual Report/*Tätigkeitsbericht* of the Justizvollzugsbeauftragten des Landes Nordrhein-Westfalen, p. 219

941   Annual Report/*Tätigkeitsbericht* of the Justizvollzugsbeauftragten des Landes Nordrhein-Westfalen, p. 12

942   here and in the following: Annual Report/*Tätigkeitsbericht* of the Justizvollzugsbeauftragten des Landes Nordrhein-Westfalen, pp. 235ff

This is done so he knows what we have written the prisoner and to guarantee transparency. Fairness and the avoidance of setting anyone down is of the highest priority. Our aim is to improve the penal system".

The *Tätigkeitsbericht* 2011 includes recommendations on medical care, drugs, treatment of HIV-positive prisoners, sentence planning, visitations and phone calls, use of electric devices, illegal control of prisoners' mail and the manner of grievance handling by the governors.

Besides the grievance-handling role, the Justizvollzugsbeauftragter des Landes Nordrhein-Westfalen also has a conceptual role, which makes up 60% of his workload.[943] Prof. Walter emphasizes that

"For us it is quite important, that we are not limited to handling submissions, but are also involved in conceptual work: the future development of the penal system. For that we have to define core areas [...] such as victim-related penal enforcement, discipline in youth penal institutions, the further development of prison boards".[944]

Once a selection of core areas of developmental focus has been made, the Ministry of Justice becomes involved in the process of information gathering. In his annual report, the Justizvollzugsbeauftragter des Landes Nordrhein-Westfalen makes recommendations concerning these core areas in accordance with section 3 of the AV. In 2011, the core areas were victim-related sentence planning, occupational training, education and discipline of juvenile delinquents, prison boards and the avoidance of imprisonment for failure to pay a fine.[945]

The Justizvollzugsbeauftragter des Landes Nordrhein-Westfalen also regularly conducts analyses of the penal system for the Ministry, although this does not necessarily coincide with his conceptual focus on core areas. In 2011/2012, the analysis pertained to such large projects as the development of the *Leitlinien* but also included advice on social therapy or the proper size of a prison facility. The latter analysis was one of several, which had been officially requested by the internally undecided Ministry.[946]

Section 3 of the AV relates to both the core areas and the analyses, and declares that the Justizvollzugsbeauftragter des Landes Nordrhein-Westfalen contributes to "the alignment of the penal system with the human rights and the so-

---

943 C.f. Kaminski (2012), p. 286, 288; c.f. Tätigkeitsbericht des Justizvollzugsbeauftragten des Landes Nordrhein-Westfalen, pp. 27-200

944 Here and in the following: pp. 8, 14 of the interview conducted on April 25th, 2012 with the Justizvollzugsbeauftragter des Landes Nordrhein-Westfalen, Prof. Michael Walter.

945 c.f. Annual Report/*Tätigkeitsbericht* of the Justizvollzugsbeauftragten des Landes Nordrhein-Westfalen, pp. 43-200

946 Here and in the following: pp. 15f of the interview conducted on April 25th, 2012 with the Justizvollzugsbeauftragter des Landes Nordrhein-Westfalen, Prof. Michael Walter.

cial and legal principles". Walter explains this mandate as follows: "Obviously, the penal system should always be in accord with the legal principles. To us this is a matter of course. What is meant here is that we are continuously involved in re-establishing this rule of law, which in the penal system can never be taken for granted. It has to be re-won every day".[947] Accordingly, the Justizvollzugs-beauftragter des Landes Nordrhein-Westfalen acts especially fast whenever there is a potential threat to the human rights of a prisoner. In this context, the Justizvollzugsbeauftragter des Landes Nordrhein-Westfalen in 2011/2012 made inquiries into health care, treatment of pregnant prisoners and restrictions of physical contact during family visits.

In fulfilment of his duties Justizvollzugsbeauftragte cooperates with a number of institutions. Walter recognizes that "from the perspective of the Justi-zvollzugsbeauftragter des Landes Nordrhein-Westfalen, all other checks on the penal system appear to be 'competition'. Yet, it makes no sense to compete with other well-functioning institutions. An ancillary approach focusing on areas where a suitable contact person for critique and improvements was lacking, is much more sensible."[948]

The Justizvollzugsbeauftragter des Landes Nordrhein-Westfalen cooperates primarily with the Ministry of Justice. This is due to Section 3 of the AV which demands that the Justizvollzugsbeauftragter des Landes Nordrhein-Westfalen advise the Ministry of Justice concerning the future development of the penal system, and Section 7 V of the AV which gives the Justizvollzugsbeauftragter des Landes Nordrhein-Westfalen the right to report to the Ministry at any given time. The Justizvollzugsbeauftragter des Landes Nordrhein-Westfalen also co-operates with the parliament in so far as the Ministry of Justice tables his annual report for the perusal of MPs. During the discussion session, the Permanent Sec-retary and/or the Justizvollzugsbeauftragter des Landes Nordrhein-Westfalen may appear before the *Landtag* to give further insights and explanations. The Justizvollzugsbeauftragter des Landes Nordrhein-Westfalen also cooperates with the petitions committee, other prison services and the "Kriminologischer Dienst" of North Rhine-Westphalia. Walter also reports including the control check-list of the ECPT in his prison visits in order to "inspect all points considered to be of a sensitive nature by them".[949]

---

947   Here and in the following: p. 19 of the interview conducted on April 25th, 2012 with the Justizvollzugsbeauftragter des Landes Nordrhein-Westfalen, Prof. Michael Walter and Annual Report/*Tätigkeitsbericht* of the Justizvollzugsbeauftragten des Landes Nordrhein-Westfalen, pp. 235-54 and 265-9

948   Walter (2012, in print)

949   Kaminski (2012), p. 292

The Justizvollzugsbeauftragter des Landes Nordrhein-Westfalen performs the workload described above assisted by three permanent staff members: a crown prosecutor functioning as deputy Justizvollzugsbeauftragter des Landes Nordrhein-Westfalen, a judge functioning as assistant to the Justizvollzugsbeauftragter des Landes Nordrhein-Westfalen and one secretarial staff. The Justizvollzugsbeauftragter des Landes Nordrhein-Westfalen's budget matches that of the Ombudsmann für den Justizvollzug Nordrhein-Westfalen [950] and amounts to 50,000€ in material expenses. As the costs for staffing are neither listed in the North Rhine-Westphalian Parliament's Annual Budget nor the Ombudsmann für den Justizvollzug Nordrhein-Westfalen or Justizvollzugsbeauftragter des Landes Nordrhein-Westfalen's annual report, they can only be estimated based on an educated guess to range somewhere around 200,000€ p.a.[951]. Consequently, the budget should be estimated at about 250,000€. This matches the equally staffed Michigan Legislative Corrections Ombudsman (256,000€ p.a.) rather well and as such might be assumed to be reasonable approximation.[952]

III. Synthesis

Following the above analysis of the Prisons and Probation Ombudsman for England and Wales and the Justizvollzugsbeauftragter des Landes Nordrhein-Westfalen, the general research outcome will be summarized graphically using an adapted version of Evans and Davies' model of transfer processes.[953] This provides the groundwork for a combination of the individual findings required for the verification of the hypotheses previously stated in Chapter A.

---

950   Ausschussprotokoll 15/102, p. 22

951   This estimate is based on the assumed average monthly income of 2000€ for the secretarial staff, 5000€ for the judge, 3000€ for the crown prosecutor. Since the Ministry of Justice will presumably have at least matched the income of the former university professor, an average monthly income of 6000€ was assumed for Prof. Walter. The projected personnel costs p.a. should therefore at least amount to 192,000€. Since this estimate is probably rather low, it has been rounded up.

952   C.f. the table included in chapter B II. 6.

953   Adapted in Figure 8 of chapter B III. 4. Please also note Evans/Davies (1999), p. 377, Figure 2

Process of transfer: PPO					
1 **Recognition**	**2** **Search**	**3** **Contact**	**4** **Emergence of** **Information Feeder** **Network**	**5** **Cognition &** **Reception**	**6** **Emergence of** **Transfer Network**
conflict (Hull Riot); dissatisfaction; discourse pull; conflict (riots in Strangeways Penitentiary and others)	international (Canada; Scandinavia etc.); national (PCA)	none	academicians; JUSTICE; All-Party Penal Affairs Group; Association of the Members of the Boards of Visitors; Prison Trust; Woolf Report	Ministry White Paper	within Ministry
$\longrightarrow$	$\longrightarrow$	$\longrightarrow$	$\longrightarrow$	$\longrightarrow$	$\longrightarrow$
7 **Elite & Cognitive** **Mobilization**	**8** **Interaction**	**9** **Evaluation**	**10** **Decision Enters** **Policy Stream**	**11** **Process**	**12** **Outcome**
academicians; JUSTICE; All-Party Penal Affairs Group; Association of the Members of the Boards of Visitors; Prison Trust; Woolf Report; in cooperation with Ministry	by participants of number 7	only superficial; except for exclusion of PCA as a potential model	announcement by Home Secretary Kenneth Clark	Ministry deliberates implementation mode, settles on and creates Terms of Reference document	Ministry passes Terms of Reference document; instates first incumbent Sir Peter Woodhead
$\longrightarrow$	$\longrightarrow$	$\longrightarrow$	$\longrightarrow$	$\longrightarrow$	

Figure 11: The chain of events during the Prisons and Probation Ombudsman for England and Wales' transfer process

Process of transfer: OJNW					
1 **Recognition**	**2** **Search**	**3** **Contact**	**4** **Emergence of** **Information Feeder** **Network**	**5** **Cognition &** **Reception**	**6** **Emergence of** **Transfer Network**
conflict: incident in Siegburg Penitentiary	very short (less than a week); exclusively Ministry conducted; national and international	none	within Ministry only	within Ministry only	within Ministry only; led by Minister of Justice
$\longrightarrow$	$\longrightarrow$	$\longrightarrow$	$\longrightarrow$	$\longrightarrow$	$\longrightarrow$
7 **Elite & Cognitive** **Mobilization**	**8** **Interaction**	**9** **Evaluation**	**10** **Decision Enters** **Policy Stream**	**11** **Process**	**12** **Outcome**
of MPs, who did not favor the idea	between Minister and MPs	only superficial; MPs questioned necessity of institution	announcement by Minister of Justice Müller-Piepenkötter	Ministry deliberates implementation mode, settles on and creates AV	Ministry passes AV; instates first incumbent Rolf Söhnchen
$\longrightarrow$	$\longrightarrow$	$\longrightarrow$	$\longrightarrow$	$\longrightarrow$	

Figure 12: The chain of events during the Ombudsmann für den Justizvollzug Nordrhein-Westfalen's transfer process

Process of transfer: JBNW					
1 **Recognition** dissatisfaction of Minister of Justice (Müller-Piepenkötter)	2 **Search** international (PPO); national (German Military Ombudsman); regional (OJNW)	3 **Contact** none	4 **Emergence of Information Feeder Network** opposition (SPD); especially Sichau, MP	5 **Cognition & Reception** within newly staffed Ministry only	6 **Emergence of Transfer Network** within newly staffed Ministry; assisted by Prof. Walter
→	→	→	→	→	→
7 **Elite & Cognitive Mobilization** Prof. Walter; former MPs of opposition now in government	8 **Interaction** Prof. Walter; Minister of Justice; permanent secretary and MPs	9 **Evaluation** only superficial; positive evaluation of OJNW as predecessor by MPs of all parties	10 **Decision Enters Policy Stream** announcement by Minister of Justice Kutschaty	11 **Process** Ministry deliberates implementation mode, settles on and creates AV assisted by Prof. Walter	12 **Outcome** Ministry passes AV; instates Prof. Michael Walter as first incumbent
→	→	→	→	→	

Acquisition Phase (rows 1–6); *Implementation Phase* (rows 7–12)

Figure 13: The chain of events during the Justizvollzugsbeauftragter des Landes Nordrhein-Westfalen's transfer process

Table 2 and Figures Figure 11 to Figure 13 summarize why both prison ombudsinstitutions were classified as products of cross-fertilization. Note especially the similarity of the respective

- catalysts (category 1 of Table 1 and Figures Figure 4Figure 5)
- transfer processes (categories 2, 3, 6 and 9)
- and outcome (categories 10-12).

These findings, accumulated during the grounded research on two examples, compare favourably with the original hypotheses set out in chapter A, which held that

- Prison ombudsmen are only introduced during times of acute pressure on the host penal system.
- Their implementation happens via cross-fertilization.
- This frequently results in executive ombudsmen.

The nature of the catalysts (category 1) in the selected examples – conflict and dissatisfaction in or with the host penal system, creating the element of time pressure –, satisfies the first hypothesis. As section D I. 2. a) revealed, the Prisons and Probation Ombudsman for England and Wales was implemented in the aftermath of the 1990 Prison Disturbances in Strangeways Penitentiary and other institutions. While these riots extended to multiple prisons, their classification as a conflict, which created system upheaval renders them comparable to the incident in Siegburg Penitentiary, which section II. 2. a) has shown to be the underlying conflict leading to the introduction of the Ombudsmann für den Justizvollzug Nordrhein-Westfalen as the direct predecessor of the Justizvollzugs-beauftragter des Landes Nordrhein-Westfalen. Consequently, the Prisons and Probation Ombudsman for England and Wales and the Ombudsmann für den Justizvollzug Nordrhein-Westfalen/Justizvollzugsbeauftragter des Landes Nord-rhein-Westfalen were introduced during times of acute pressure on the respec-tive host penal systems.

Further examination of the implementation processes of the two examples – performed in sections D I. 2. a) bb) and D II. 2. a) bb) and cc) – has confirmed the second hypothesis that the implementation of prison ombudsmen happens via cross-fertilization. The implementation analysis of the Prisons and Probation Ombudsman for England and Wales and the Ombudsmann für den Justizvollzug Nordrhein-Westfalen/Justizvollzugsbeauftragter des Landes Nordrhein-Westfalen allows the description of their transfer processes as unbroken, con-sistent chains (c.f. Table 1 and Figures Figure 4Figure 5). Especially noteworthy is the discovery of a marked similarity in some of the transfer stages such as the diffuse nature of the search for a suitable model (category 2), the lack of contact (category 3), the limitations of the transfer network (category 6) and the superfi-ciality of the evaluation (category 9).

The analysis of the implementation outcome (categories 10-12) of the two selected examples – conducted in sections I. 2. b) aa) and II. 2. b) aa) – meets the expectation of the third hypothesis: namely, it can bee seen that the studied cross-fertilization processes led to the implementation of executive prison om-budsmen. To this day, both the Prisons and Probation Ombudsman for England and Wales and the Justizvollzugsbeauftragter des Landes Nordrhein-Westfalen remain executive in nature despite the continuous effort by the officeholders to gain a statutory footing.

That the two selected examples satisfy all three hypotheses is not surprising considering that this study made use of grounded theory as a methodology. As outlined in the methodology review, grounded theory is one that is "inductively derived from the study of the phenomenon it represents".[954] The process of data collection and analysis follows a systematic set of procedures including purpose-ful direction by means of pre-selected research questions, which allows the iden-tification of the underlying concepts of a so far little-studied phenomenon. Gla-ser holds that "once the GT researcher lets the meaning emerge and sees the pat-tern, he/she will feel 'sure' that this is what is going on".[955] This accurately de-scribes the process of discovery of the cross-fertilization pattern in this study. By applying the methodological procedures of grounded theory, the collected

---

954   Strauss/Corbin (1990), pp. 23f
955   Glaser (2007), p. 2

findings verifying the hypotheses serve as a basis for abstraction from which a coherent, integrated theory may be developed.

Chapter B I. and II. exposed prison ombudsmen as a modification of general purpose ombudsmen, which evolved in response to a need for independent grievance channels in modern penal systems. This need becomes apparent through the occurrence of catalytic events such as conflict and dissatisfaction creating acute pressure and system upheaval. At these times, local actors deliberate prison ombudsmen as potential foreign solutions to their local problems, thereby activating the processes of knowledge transfer in between legal systems described in chapter B III. The institutional transfer itself is achieved by means of cross-fertilization. The element of time pressure accompanying the catalytic event influences the local actors' choice of implementation mode in favour of executive ombudsmen.

IV. Brief Overview of further cases

The selection of two examples for analysis was necessary in this study for purposes of scientific economy. The theory derived from it by means of grounded methods, however, raises the claim of generalizability. This chapter will therefore be supplemented with a brief overview of further cases. To this end, the table included in chapter B II. 6. is retrofitted with the additional categories "categorization" and "catalyst for introduction".

Please note the consistent fulfilment in all further cases of the first hypothesis (namely, that prison ombudsmen are only introduced during times of acute pressure on the host penal system) and equally of the third hypothesis (frequent implementation as executive ombudsmen). The legislative implementation mode of the Michigan Legislative Corrections Ombudsman – while constituting an exception – does not so much countermand the rule as affirm the possibility of a statutory footing as a direct implementation outcome.

Consequently, the table fortifies the claim this study makes as to the generalizability of hypotheses 1 and 3. Even if further analysis of the individual implementation processes of the five other existing ombudsmen would be necessary for an affirmative statement, the information compiled in the table seems to confirm that prison ombudsmen are frequently implemented as executive ombudsmen during times of acute pressure on the host penal system by means of cross-fertilization.

Table 3: Extended overview of prison ombudsmen in existence

Name	Year	Country	Staff	Annual Budget (in T €)	Catego-rization	Catalyst for Introduction
Canadian Correctional Investigator	1973; statutory footing 1992	Canada	30	2,808	Legisla-tive	1971 Kingston Penitentiary Riot
Indiana Department of Corrections Ombudsman Bureau	1973-1981; 2003	US, Indiana		98	Execu-tive	Aryan Broth-erhood mur-dering black prisoners
Kentucky Corrections Ombudsman	1975	US, Michigan	4	256	Execu-tive	Prison riots
Michigan Legislative Cor-rections Om-budsman	1982	US, Kentucky	2	69	Legisla-tive	Class action law suit
Prisons and Probation Ombudsman for England and Wales	1994	UK, England and Wales	113.7 (50.2 inves-tigating complaints)	6,388	Execu-tive	Riots in Strangeways Penitentiary and other prisons
The Prisoner Ombudsman for Northern Ire-land	2005	UK, Northern Ireland	11	777	Execu-tive	Tensions in prisons
Justizvollzugs-beauftragter des Landes Nord-rhein-Westfalen	2007; extension of remit 2010	Germany, North Rhine-Westphalia	4 (1 exclu-sively in-vestigating complaints)	250	Execu-tive	Forced suicide in the Sieg-burg Peniten-tiary

E Conclusion

This chapter provides a compilation of the study's results and highlights their impact on praxis and research. A critical analysis of the research constraints will be conducted. A description of future prospects in this field rounds this study off.

I. Compilation and potential impact of research results

Any compilation of research results has to answer the question: what – if anything – was learned? This researcher set out to challenge the assumption of institutional success at the heart of the prison ombudsman spread. To this end the structures, forms, and means of proliferation and implementation of prison ombudsmen were examined with the intent to provide comprehensive insights from which to develop a primary academic understanding of prison ombudsmen. During the examination of two selected examples, two alternate but comparable "perceptions of the world and justice" with their individual approaches to "solving practical problems by accommodating competing interests as well as meeting the prerequisites of substantive justice" were discovered.[956]

This was achieved using the method of grounded theory. The pursuit of any interesting leads, as demanded by this methodology, motivated this researcher to examine prison ombudsmen in the context of the development of the ombudsman concept. A comparable synopsis explicating the demand, structures and operational modes has so far not been available at a comparable level of detail, degree of systematization or with as general an applicability to all prison ombudsmen. Equally innovative is the attempt of presenting an exhaustive list of all offices currently in existence, which directly relates to the focus of this study on the why and how of prison ombudsman proliferation and implementation. This sparked the examination of the possibility of learning processes occurring between different legal systems, which led to the discovery of cross-fertilization as a two-step implementation process unique to prison ombudsmen. The comparative analysis of the Prisons and Probation Ombudsman for England and Wales and the Ombudsmann für den Justizvollzug Nordrhein-Westfalen/ Justizvollzugsbeauftragter des Landes Nordrhein-Westfalen as the two primary examples of prison ombudsmen provided research results confirming this study's hypotheses that

---

956 Melissaris (2004), p. 76

- Prison ombudsmen are only introduced during times of acute pressure on the host penal system.
- Their implementation happens via cross-fertilization.
- This frequently results in executive ombudsmen.

The inductive process prescribed by the grounded theory methodology allowed an integrated theory of prison ombudsmen to develop from the conducted research. This theory comprehends prison ombudsmen as an evolutionary derivative of general purpose ombudsmen. This research highlights that the variant developed in recognition of the need for independent grievance channels as a particular void in modern penal systems – a need that becomes apparent whenever penal systems experience times of acute pressure such as conflict or dissatisfaction. During these times, transfer agents consider prison ombudsmen as ready-made foreign solutions to their local problems – thus allowing learning processes to occur in between legal systems. The institutional transfer of prison ombudsmen is achieved by means of cross-fertilization. The element of time pressure accompanying the catalytic event affects the local actors' preference of executive ombudsmen as an implementation mode.

This proves the assumption of institutional success at the heart of the prison ombudsman spread wrong. Local systemic pressure dominates the mind of state key-holders. Institutional success abroad is neither required nor evaluated prior to local implementation – otherwise executive ombudsmen would in all probability not be the dominant implementation mode.

II. Potential impact on research and praxis

The discussed research results have implications for research as well as praxis. An effect on the research may be expected concerning both prison and general ombudsmen: On the former in so far as a structured understanding of the prison ombudsman as an institution and its implementation process and outcome is now available. This will provide a framework for any comparative analysis of individual prison ombudsinstitutions. The impact also extends beyond prison ombudsmen to general ombudsmen as the assumption of institutional success at the heart of the ombudsman spread may now be challenged for general ombudsmen in the same manner. Research undertaken on the comparable merits of executive and legislative implementation modes may draw on the identification of cross-fertilization as the concept behind these institutional implementation outcomes.

In terms of practical implications, prison ombudsmen may use the provided research results to capitalize on their claim for improvement of the outcome of the cross-fertilization processes. The placement of the Canadian Correctional Investigator on a statutory footing almost twenty years after its introduction illustrates one possibility. The structural and historical analysis of the Prisons and Probation Ombudsman for England and Wales and the Ombudsmann für den Justizvollzug Nordrhein-Westfalen/the Justizvollzugsbeauftragter des Landes Nordrhein-Westfalen provides valuable examples for possible extensions of a prison ombudsman's remit. In addition, the detailed comparison of existing structures and implementations available through the table included in chapter B II. 6. may prove beneficial when campaigning for an increase in funding or staffing.

A different form of potential impact entirely is that on local transfer agents such as politicians, administrators etc. Although this study has established that prison ombudsmen are only implemented during times of acute pressure on the host penal system, the analysis of the two selected examples has proven that some local, national and international search is conducted whilst personal contact was considered superfluous or at least impossible time-wise. In the future, any search will be able to draw on the results of this research which provides local transfer agents not only with a comprehensive overview of all existing prison ombudsmen, but also with their typical structures and some advice on possible modes of implementation. Dolowitz and Marsh suggest that "the more information agents have about how a programme operates in another location [… and] the more easily outcomes can be predicted the easier a programme is to transfer".[957]

III. Critical analysis of the constraints of the research

The critical analysis of the constraints of this research draws on Evans "logical framework for assessing the utility of policy transfer research for public action".[958] While this framework provides rigorous parameters for research assessment, its suitability to this critical analysis is limited in two ways: On the one hand, this study was not specifically designed to be used for public action, which is part of the reason why the potential impact of this study on local trans-

---

957   Dolowitz/Marsh (1996), p. 353
958   here and in this entire section: Evans (2009a), p. 264, there Table 1– complemented by Champion (2009), pp. 500, 503

fer actors has been tentatively formulated.[959] On the other hand, this study makes use of grounded theory, which does not form part of the research designs which Evans had in mind when drafting his framework. However, his questions for research assessment may be adapted to suit a grounded theory approach and may be considered a helpful structuring forthe critical analysis of this study's research constraints. This is in line with Strauss and Corbin's observation that grounded theorists share the conviction of qualitative researchers "that the usual canons of 'good science' should be retained, but require redefinition in order to fit the realities of qualitative research, and the complexities of social phenomena that we seek to understand".[960]

The first step in a grounded theory study must be the assessment of the suitability of the approach. Despite earlier criticism of all qualitative methods as unscientific and the on-going differences between Glaser and Strauss, grounded theory may today be considered a tried and trusted qualitative method without an inherent bias, which allows for the development of a verifiable theory.[961]

The data upon which this theory is built was drawn from such diverse and trustworthy sources as the existing expert literature, local transfer agents and officeholders. Unfortunately, nuanced information such as the extent of the "recognition of differences in setting" and the extent to which "the information gathered in the process of considering policy transfer actually enter[ed] into the decision making" was unavailable in case of the Prisons and Probation Ombudsman for England and Wales as nearly two decades after its introduction the original policy makers could not be located for interviews – a problem that is recognized by Mossberger and Wolman as common to policy transfer studies.[962] Despite this drawback, the evidence generated in interview transcripts alone amounts to 69 pages, while the literature gathered following the leads provided by the grounded theory approach spans 14 binders (more than a full meter) and

---

959   see section above

960   Strauss/Corbin (1990), pp. 249f

961   For a discussion of the differences and the method see chapter C. I. 1; for the extent of acceptance of this method see Mey/Mruck (2007a), p. 7 and (2007b), pp. 12, 14, who declare grounded theory methodology to be "one of the most prominent approaches" in sociology as well as other disciplines.

962   Mossberger/Wolman (2003), p. 435; for the discussion of the Justizvollzugsbeauftragter des Landes Nordrhein-Westfalen's quality as a product of cross-fertilization this author was able to conduct an interview with an original policy maker: Roswita Müller-Piepenkötter, then Minister of Justice. For the grounded theory approach, Glaser (2007), p. 8, puts this into perspective saying "Learned informants may be valuable in a research, but they must constantly be checked on by other data; must saturate by theoretical sampling of many other participant incidents."

more than 250 pages in memos.[963] The data has been integrated with different sources using the grounded theory method of "constant comparison". This resulted in evidence for systematically related concepts concerning the two examples of this study that were selected for the greatest possible richness of comparative data.[964]

The description of the Prisons and Probation Ombudsman for England and Wales supports the previous research on this prison ombudsman conducted by Seneviratne; the gathered evidence on the Justizvollzugsbeauftragter des Landes Nordrhein-Westfalen meets with the very few existing publications – most of which stem from the first incumbent, Prof. Walter. While Glaser might consider the rich description of the two institutions undertaken in chapter D contrary to grounded theory and more in line with the kind of qualitative research performed in the social sciences, it was a necessary step of data collection unavoidable in order to ensure coding all incidents for the process of theory building.[965]

The entirety of the assembled evidence is generalizable within the limits described in chapter D III. and IV. The same holds true for the theory developed from this evidence. This limitation of generalizability is due to the purpose of grounded theory, which is specifying conditions "that give rise to specific sets of action/interaction pertaining to a phenomenon and the resulting consequences".[966] A grounded theory is never right or wrong in the traditional sense, it just has more or less fit, relevance, workability and modifiability.[967] The concepts of the theory closely fit with the incidents they are representing and deal with a real concern of both prisoners and local actors. The theory performs well in this context as it explains the proliferation and implementation of prison ombudsmen with much variation permitting alteration when new relevant data, taken from the world of observation for example via the analysis of the implementation process and outcome of any or all of the other five prison ombudsmen currently in existence, is compared to existing data.

Elements of the research that would have been relevant for practice include the selection or – if none were to be found – the creation of an ideal legal statute and the development of a comprehensive evaluation methodology suitable to ombudsmen or at least prison ombudsmen. However, as this study was not specifically designed for its utility for public action, the exclusion of these aspects

---

963   For the importance of memoing to the grounded theory method and the precise procedures see Strauss (2007), p. 75 and Strauss/Corbin (1990), pp. 197ff respectively.
964   For details on the selection process please see chapter C I. 4.
965   Boychuck Duchscher/Morgan (2004), p. 610
966   Strauss/Corbin (1990), p. 251
967   Glaser (1998), p. 18; Strauss/Corbin (1990), p. 249-58

for reasons of scientific economy as well as on grounds of feasibility seems justifiable. The research results themselves will be accessible for public use.

IV. Future prospects for research in this field

The research undertaken for this study revealed additional prospects for future research in the field of ombudsmen generally and prison ombudsmen in particular. In different ways, all of them relate to the matter of evaluation.

Throughout the history of (prison) ombudsmen, it has been repeatedly claimed that their introduction would reduce litigation and thus court costs for both the state and the complainants.[968] This hypothesis has never been proven. However, it should not be too difficult to gain access to, for example, data from the North Rhine-Westphalian government on the amount of incoming prisoner litigation in the *Strafvollstreckungskammern* before and after the introduction of the local prison ombudsman in 2007. A similar approach may also be elected concerning prisoner petitions to the parliamentary petition committee in order to once and for all rebut the objection by MPs that prison ombudsmen detract from their constitutional role as the intercessors of their constituents.[969]

Another claim concerning the usefulness of prison ombudsmen as NPM is of a more recent nature.[970] This, of course, is due to the fact that the OPCAT only entered into force on June 22nd, 2006. The research conducted for this study has revealed that while many ratifying nations have designated their ombudsmen or human rights commissions as NPMs, this has so far not been extended to their prison ombudsmen – despite the UK for example designating no less than eighteen bodies.[971] The fact that prison ombudsmen are generally worthy of consider-

---

968   see chapter B. I. 6; Moore (1968b), p. 72; Brakel (1982), p. 131; Lesting (1993), p. 54; Owen (1993), p. 5; Kempf/Mille (1993), p. 197; Jacobs (2004), p. 301; Alarcón (2007), p. 59

969   This argument is still used by British MPs to retain the PCA's MP-filter, c.f. Giddings (2001), p. 14; Morris/Henham (1999), p. 375; Seneviratne (1994), p. 43; Shaw (2004), p. 123. The groundlessness of this objection is suggested by the former North Rhine-Westphalian Minister of Justice, who stated: "As far as I know did neither the petition committee nor the courts watch [... for a fluctuation in incoming petitions/litigation] – we didn't statistically affirm this, but the petition committee did not have any less petitions." p. 13 of the interview conducted on February 7th, 2012 with the former Minister of Justice, Roswitha Müller-Piepenkötter. Full transcript available through this study's author.

970   Carl (2012a), p. 108; Rotthaus (2008), p. 373

971   For the NPMs designated so far see

ation for designation derives from the particular sensitivity of the prison system to human rights infractions. Whether the OPCAT-cause would derive a benefit from their designation that extends beyond the utility gained from the NPMs hitherto designated remains to be proven.

The research conducted for this study also touched upon the long-standing discussion of the comparative qualities of executive and legislative ombudsmen.[972] While much has been averred as to their respective success, impact and efficiency, a comparative analysis has yet to be produced.

This question of performance measurement of ombudsinstitutions is not limited to the comparative merits of the two implementation modes. Although the necessity for evaluation has been well acknowledged, the ombudsman concept *in toto* as well as most individual ombudsinstitutions have never been properly evaluated.[973] Mossberger and Wolman explain that "[i]n many policy areas, what passes for evaluation is a recommendation for best practice based on received wisdom or process evaluation rather than concrete evidence of success".[974] Gellhorn's previously cited dictum that "[t]he Ombudsman has in recent years been so rapturously regarded abroad that [... w]hat he is supposed to accomplish is taken as the equivalent of what he has in fact accomplished" still stands.[975] This fits with Mossberger and Wolman's further observation that "[a]ssessing program performance is especially difficult when program goals are unclear and when there are a variety of program designs operating under a single policy label". The quick hybridization of the ombudsman concept is likely to be the root of the problems regarding any attempt to try to establish criteria for measuring ombudsman success.[976] However, this study removes the argument of a lack of programmatic clarity as a reason for the lack of evaluation, at least for the field of prison ombudsmen.

---

http://www2.ohchr.org/english/bodies/cat/opcat/mechanisms.htm (last accessed June 6th, 2012)

972   Fitzharris (1973); Adamoleku (1984); Rowat (1993); Ayeni (1995)

973   Holt et al. (1980); Danet (1987); Ayeni (1999); Ayeni (2000); Aufrecht/Hertogh (2000); Hyson (2006); Buck et al. (2011a). For the few exceptions containing examples of ombudsman evaluation – c.f. Lux (1993); Hertogh (1998, 2001); Male (1999); Harrison (2004); van Roosbroek/van de Walle (2008); Fowlie (2008)

974   Here and in the following: Mossberger/Wolman (2003), p. 433

975   Gellhorn (1966b), p. 239

976   c.f. chapter B. I.; Uppendahl (1986), p. 191ff; Seneviratne (1994), pp. 13f; Buck et al. (2009a), pp. 99ff

References

Abedin, Najmul (2011), "Conceptual and Functional Diversity of the Ombudsman Institution: A Classification", *Administration & Society* 20(10): 1-34

Abraham, Ann (2008), "The ombudsman and 'paths to justice': a just alternative or just an alternative?", *Public Law* Spring: 1-10

Abraham, Ann (2009), "Good Administration: Why We Need it more than ever", *The Political Quarterly* 80(1): 25-32

Adamoleku, Ladipo (1984), "The Nigerian ombudsman experience", *International Review of Administrative Sciences* 50: 227-9

Alarcón, Arthur (2007), "A Prescription for California's Ailing Inmate Treatment System: An Independent Corrections Ombudsman", *Hastings Law Journal* 58(3): 591-621

Allen, Richard (1974), "International Bar Association Biennial Conference Draws Lawyers from Around the World to Vancouver, British Columbia", *American Bar Association Journal* 60: 1077-80

American Bar Association, (2001), *Standards for the Establishment and Operation of Ombudsman Offices.* Available from: http://www.usombudsman.org/documents/ MSWord/References/ABA/ABA_Standards.doc (last accessed June 6th, 2012)

Ancel, Marc (1971), *Utilité et methods du droit compare: Eléments d'introduction générale à l'étude comparative des droits.* Neuchâtel: Edition Ides et Calendes

Anderson, Stanley (1968), "Proposals and Politics" in Stanley V. Anderson (ed.), *Ombudsmen for American Government?*, pp. 136-159. Englewood Cliffs, NJ: Prentice-Hall, Inc.

Anderson, Stanley (1975a), "Comparing Classical and Executive Ombudsmen" in Alan Wyner (ed.), *Executive Ombudsman in the United States*, pp. 307-313. Berkley: Institute of Governmental Studies

Anderson, Stanley (1975b), "The Prison Ombudsman", *The Center Magazine*, November/December: 6-8

Anderson, Stanley (1978) "Ombudsmen and Prisons in Scandinavia", *Nordisk tidsskrift for kiminalvidenskab* 66 (3-4): 211-246

Anderson, Stanley (1981a), "The Corrections Ombudsman" in David Fogel and Joe Hudson (eds.), *Justice as Fairness*, pp. 252-69. Cincinnati, Ohio: Anderson Publishing Company

Anderson, Stanley (1981b) "The Prison Work of the New Zealand Ombudsman", *The Ombudsman Journal* 1: 25-40

Anderson, Stanley (1983), "The Ombudsman in Correctional Institutions. A. The Corrections Ombudsman in the United States" in Gerald E. Caiden (ed.), *International Handbook of the Ombudsman. Evolution and Present Function*, pp. 137-147. Westport, Conn.: Greenwood Press

André, Kerstin (2009), "Inspections as a Pro-Active Method of Combating Maladministration", The Stockholm 2009 Conference Papers, http://www.theioi.org/publications/the-stockholm-2009-conference-papers (last accessed June 6th, 2012)

Arnott, Hamish et al. (2000), *Prisoners, Deaths in Custody and the Human Rights Act*. London: Prisoners Advice Service and Inquest

Ascher, Charles (1967), "The Grievance Man or Ombudsmania", *Public Administration Review*, 27: 174-8

Ashworth, Andrew (2010), *Sentencing and Criminal Justice*. Cambridge: Cambridge University Press

Atalay, Nail (2000), "The historical development of the Institution of KADI: Ombudsmen during the Islamic and/or Ottoman periods" in Ludo Veny and Rita Passemiers (eds.), *Looking for Ombudsman Standards*, pp. 47-58. Gent: Mys and Breesch

Atteslander, Peter (2008), *Methoden der empirischen Sozialforschung*. Berlin: Erich Schmidt Verlag

Aufenanger, Stefan (1991), „Qualitative Analyse semi-struktureller Interviews – ein Werkstattbericht" in Detlef Garz and Klaus Kraimer (eds.), *Qualitative-empirische Sozialforschung. Konzepte, Methoden, Analysen*. pp. 35-59. Opladen: Westdeutscher Verlag GmbH

Aufrecht, Steven and Hertogh, Marc (2000), "Evaluating Ombudsman Systems" in Roy Gregory and Philip Giddings (eds.), *Righting Wrongs. The Ombudsman in Six Continents,* pp. 389-402. Amsterdam: IOS Press

Ayeni, Victor (1995), "Defining ombudsman institutions: a re-assesment", *Politeia*, 14(1): 72-85

Ayeni, Victor (1999), "Evaluating Ombudsman Programmes" in Linda C. Reif (ed.), *The international Ombudsman Anthology*, pp. 169-94 The Hague: Kluwer Law International

Ayeni, Victor (2000), "The Ombudsman around the world: Essential Elements, Evolution and Contemporary Issues" in V. Ayeni and L. Reif (eds.), *Strengthening Ombudsman and Human Rights Institutions in Commonwealth Small and Island States*, pp. 98-116. London: Commonwealth Secretariat

Ayeni, Victor (2001), "The Ombudsman in the Achievement of Administrative Justice and human rights in the new millenium", *The Ombudsman Yearbook* 5: 32-61

Ayeni, Victor (2009), "Ombudsmen as Human Rights Institutions: The New Face of a Global Expansion" International Ombudsman Institute Workshop

Baqwa, Selby (2000), "Systemic and System-Wide Investigations" in V. Ayeni and L. Reif (eds.), *Strengthening Ombudsman and Human Rights Institutions in Commonwealth Small and Island States*, pp. 98-116. London: Commonwealth Secretariat

Barbour, Bruce (2002), 'What are the Essential Features of an Ombudsman?' in Robin Creyke & John McMillan (eds.) *Administrative Law: the Essentails*, pp. 53-63. Canberra: Australian Institute for Administrative Law

Barton, Preston (1983), "The Ombudsman in Correctional Institutions. B. Ombudsmanship in corrections: The Power of Presence on the Premises" in Gerald E. Caiden (ed.), *International Handbook of the Ombudsman. Evolution and Present Function*, pp. 147-151. Westport, Conn.: Greenwood Press

Bauer, Fritz (1964a), "Brauchen wir einen Ombudsmann?", *Gewerkschaftliche Monatshefte* 227-30

Bauer, Fritz (1964b), *Die neue Gewalt*. München: Verlag der Zeitschrift RUF UND ECHO

Bell, John (2006), "Comparative Administrative Law" in Mathias Reimann and Reinhard Zimmermann (eds.), *The Oxford Handbook of Comparative Law*, pp. 1259-86 . Oxford: Oxford University Press

Birkinshaw, Patrick (1985), "An ombudsman for prisoners" in Mike Maguire, Jon Vagg et al. (eds.), *Accountability and Prisons. Opening up a closed world*, pp. 165-74

Blaikie, Norman (1991), "A Critique of the Use of Triangulation in Social Research", *Quality & Quantity*. 25(2): 115–136

Bohlen, Anneke (2008), *Möglichkeiten und Grenzen einer gesetzlichen Steuerung des Strafvollzuges.*, Ph.D. Dissertation. University of Cologne, Germany.

Bottoms, Anthony (1987), "Limiting Prison Use: Experience in England and Wales", *The Howard Journal of Criminal Justice* 26(3): 177-202

Boychuck Duchscher, Judy and Morgan, Debra (2004), "Grounded theory: reflections on the emergence vs. forcing debate", *Journal of Advanced Nursing* 48(6), 605-12

Brakel, Samuel (1982), "Administrative Justice in the Penitentiary: A Report on Inmate Grievance Procedures", *American Bar Foundation Research Journal* 111-140

Buck, Trevor et al. (2011a), *The ombudsman enterprise and administrative justice*. Farnham, England: Ashgate Publishing

Buck, Trevor et al. (2011b), "Time for a 'Leggatt-style" review of the Ombudsman system?", *Public Law*. Spring:20-29

Burbridge, Charles (1974) "Problems of Transferring the Ombudsman Plan", *International Review of Administrative Sciences* 40: 103-108

Busck, Lars (1995), "The History and Development of the Institution of Ombudsman" in Hans Gammeltoft-Hansen and Flemming Axmark (eds.), *The Danish Ombudsman*, pp. 23-33. Copenhagen: Djøf Publishing

Caiden, Gerald (1983), "Introduction" in Gerald E. Caiden (ed.), *International Handbook of the Ombudsman. Evolution and Present Function*, pp. xvii-xviii. Westport, Conn.: Greenwood Press

Caiden, Gerald et al. (1983), "The Institution of Ombudsman" in Gerald E. Caiden (ed.), *International Handbook of the Ombudsman. Evolution and Present Function*, pp. 3-23. Westport, Conn.: Greenwood Press

Cameron, Alastair (2001) "The Ombudsmen: Time for a Jurisdictional Expansion. The Case for Extending the Jurisdiction of the Statutory Ombudsmen to Cover the Exercise of Public Power in the Private Sector", *Victoria University of Wellington Law Review* 32: 549-71

Carl, Sabine (2012a), "Ombudsman und Strafvollzug. Eine Übersicht über die weltweit tätigen Justizvollzugsbeauftragten.", *Forum Strafvollzug* 61(2): 106-108

Carl, Sabine (2012b), "Toward a Definition and Taxonomy of Public Sector Ombudsmen", *Canadian Public Administration* 55(2): 203-20

Champion, Dean (2009), *Research Methods for Criminal Justice and Criminology*. Upper Saddle River, New Jersey: Pearson Prentice Hall

Chapman, Brian (1960), "The Ombudsman", *Public Administration* 38(4), 303-310

Charmaz, Kathy (2006), *Constructing Grounded Theory. A Practical Guide Through Qualitative Analysis*. London: Sage

Chidiac, Marie-José (2004) "Administrative Mediation and Ombudsmen: An Encounter with Internormativity", *International Ombudsman Yearbook*. 8: 85-90

Colby, Ann and Kohlberg, Lawrence (1987), *The measurement of moral judgement. Two volumes*. New York: Cambridge University Press

Coleman, Wiliam (1994), "Policy convergence in banking: a comparative study", *Political Studies* XLII:274-92

Committee of Inquiry into the United Kingdom Prison Services (1979), Report Presented to Parliament by the Secretary of State for the Home Department, the Secretary of State for Scotland, the Secretary of State for Northern Ireland by Command of Her Majesty ("May Committee Report") Cmnd. 7673. London: HMSO

Cotterrell, Roger (2000), "Seeking similarity, appreciating difference: comparative law and communities" in David Nelken (ed.), *Contrasting criminal justice: getting from here to there*, pp. 33-54, Burlington: Ashgate

Council of Europe (1985) Recommendation No. R (85) 13 of the Committee of Ministers of the Member States on the Institution of Ombudsman

Council of Europe (2005), *Principles governing the institution of the Ombudsman/Ombudsperson at local and regional level*. Strasbourg: Council of Europe Publishing

Cromwell Jr., Paul (1974), "A Vote for the Jail Ombudsman", *Federal Probation*, 54-56

Curran, Vivian (1998), "Cultural Immersion, Difference and Categories in U.S. Comparative Law", *American Journal of Comparative Law* 46: 43-87

Danet, Brenda (1978) "Toward a Method to evaluate the Ombudsman Role", *Administration and Society* 10(3): 335-70

Dannemann, Gerhard (2006), "Comparative Law: Study of Similarities or differences?" in Mathias Reimann and Reinhard Zimmermann (eds.), *The Oxford Handbook of Comparative Law*, pp. 383-420. Oxford: Oxford University Press

De Asper Y Valdés, Daisy (1999), "The self-perceptions of the Ombudsman: Comparative and Longitudinal Survey" in Linda C. Reif (ed.), *The international Ombudsman Anthology*, pp. 227-70. The Hague: Kluwer Law International

De Jong, Martin (1999), *Institutional Transplantation. How to adopt good transport infrastructure decision-making ideas from other countries?* Delft, Netherlands: Eburon

De Jong, Martin et al. (2002) "Two contrasting perspectives on institutional transplantation" in Martin De Jong et al. (eds.), *The Theory and Practice of Institutional Transplantation*, pp. 283-300. Dordrecht, Netherlands: Kluwer

Der Vollzugsdienst (2011) „Prof. Walter sieht sich der Weiterentwicklung des NRW-Strafvollzuges verpflichtet", *Der Vollzugsdienst* 3: 42-45

Dieckmann, Jochen (2000), *Strafvollzug in Nordrhein-Westfalen*. Düsseldorf: Justizministerium NRW

Diepenbruck, Karl-Heinz (1981), *Rechtsmittel im Strafvollzug*. PhD. Dissertation, University of Göttingen

DiMaggio, Paul and Powell, Walter (1991), "The Iron Cage Revisted: Institutional Isomorphism and Collective Rationality in Organizational Fields" in Walter Powell and Paul DiMaggio (eds.), *The New Institutionalism in Organizational Analysis*, pp. 63-82, Chicago: University of Chicago Press

Dolowitz, David and Marsh, David (1996), "Who Learns What from Whom: a Review of the Policy Transfer Literature", *Political Studies*, XLIV: 343-57

Douglas, Gillian (1984), "Dealing with Prisoners' Grievances", *British Journal of Criminology* 24(2): 150-67

Dünkel, Frieder & van Zyl Smit, Dirk (1991), "Conclusion" in Dirk Van Zyl Smit & Frieder Dünkel (eds.), *Imprisonment Today and Tomorrow*, pp. 712-30. Deventer, The Netherlands: Kluwer Law and Taxation Publishers

Dünkel, Frieder (1996a), *Empirische Forschung im Strafvollzug*. Bonn/Mönchengladbach: Forum Verlag Godesberg

Dünkel, Frieder (1996b), „Die Rechtsstellung von Strafgefangenen und Möglichkeiten der rechtlichen Kontrolle von Vollzugsentscheidungen in Deutschland", *Goldtammer's Archiv für Strafrecht* 518-38

Eady, Dennis (2007), "Prisoners' Rights since the Woolf Report", *The Howard Journal of Criminal Justice* 46(3): 269-75

Ebert, Kurt (1968), *Der Ombudsman in Großbritannien*, Tübingen: J.C.B. Mohr (Paul Siebeck)

Eder, Ulrike (2008), „Langezeitbesuche im Nordrhein-Westfälischen Strafvollzug" in Frieder Dünkel et al. (eds.), *Humanisierung des Strafvollzugs – Konzepte und Praxismodelle*, pp. 157-163. Mönchengladbach: Forum Verlag Godesberg

Eklundh, Claes (2002), "The Independence of the Ombudsman" in Lisbeth Garly Andersen and Thomas Trier Hansen (eds.), *The Work and Practice of Ombudsman and National Human Rights institutions,* pp. 13-7. Copenhagen: Danish Ministry of Foreign Affairs

Evans, Malcom and Haenni-Dale, Claudine (2004), "Preventing Torture? The Development of the Optional Protocol to the UN Convention Against Torture", *Human Rights Law Review*, 4(1): 19-55

Evans, Mark (2009a), "Policy transfer in critical perspective", *Policy Studies*, 30(3): 243-68

Evans, Mark (2009b), "Editorial: New directions in the study of policy transfer", *Policy Studies*, 30(3): 237-41

Evans, Mark and Davies, Jonathan (1999), "Understanding Policy Transfer: A Multi-Level, Multi-Disciplinary Perspective", *Public Administration*, 77(2): 361-85

Farrell-Donaldson, Marie (1999), "Will the Real Ombudsman come Forward?" in Linda C. Reif (ed.), *The international Ombudsman Anthology*, pp. 411-21. The Hague: Kluwer Law International

Feest, Johannes and Lesting, Wolfgang (2009), "Contempt of court. Zur Wiederkehr des Themas der renitenten Strafvollzugsbehörden." in *festschrift für Ulrich Eisenberg*, pp. 675-90. München: Verlag C. H. Beck

Feest, Johannes et al. (1997), *Totale Institution und Rechtsschutz*. Opladen: Westdeutscher Verlag

Fielding, Nigel and Fielding, Jane (1986), *Linking data: The Articulation of Qualitative and Quantitative Methods in Social Research*. London: Sage

Fitzharris, Timothy (1973), *The Desirability of a Correctional Ombudsman*. Berkeley: Institute of Governmental Studies, University of California, Berkeley.

Flick, Uwe (2002), *Qualitative Sozialforschung. Eine Einführung*. Reinbek: Rowohlt

Fliflet, Arne (2009), "Ombudsman and Prisons Oversight", The Stockholm 2009 Conference Papers, http://www.theioi.org/publications/the-stockholm-2009-conference-papers (last accessed June 6th, 2012)

Fowles, A. J. (1989), *Prisoners' Rights in England and the United States*. Hants, England: Gower Publishing Company

Fowles, Tony and Wilson, David (2011), "Penal Policy File No. 129", *The Howard Journal of Criminal Justice*, 50:203-224

Fowlie, Frank (2008), "A Blueprint for the Evaluation of an Ombudsman's Office: A Case Study of the ICANN Office of the Ombudsman", Ph.D. dissertation, La Trobe University, Bundoora, Victoria, Australia

Fowlie, Frank (2005) "The Ombudsman and Client Satisfaction: Observations on the Relationship between Jurisdiction, Outcome, and Satisfaction", *The International Ombudsman Yearbook* 9: 3-9

Frank, Bernard (1975), "The Ombudsman – Revisited", *International Bar Journal* May: 48-61

Fuchs, Michael (1985), *"'Beauftragte' in der öffentlichen Verwaltung"*, Berlin: Duncker und Humblot

Fulmer, Richard (1981), "The Prison Ombudsman", *Social Service Review* 300-313

Gadamer, Hans-Georg (1989), "Text and Interpretation" in Diane P. Michelfelder and Richard E. Palmer (eds.), *Dialogue and Deconstruction: The Gadamer-Derrida Encounter*, pp. 21-51. Albany: State University of New York Press

Gadamer, Hans-Georg (1990). *Hermeneutik I. Wahrheit und Methode*. Tübingen: J. C. B. Mohr (Paul Siebeck)

Gadlin, Howard (2000), "The Ombudsman: What's in a Name?", *Negotiation Journal*, January: 37-48

Garz, Detlef and Kraimer, Klaus (1991), „Qualitativ-empirische Sozialforschung im Aufbruch" in Detlef Garz and Klaus Kraimer (eds.), *Qualitative-empirische Sozialforschung. Konzepte, Methoden, Analysen.* pp. 1-34. Opladen: Westdeutscher Verlag GmbH

Gellhorn, Walter (1966a), *When Americans Complain: Governmental Grievance Procedures.* Cambridge, Mass.: Harvard University Press

Gellhorn, Walter (1966b), *Ombudsmen and Others: Citizens' Protectors in Nine Countries.* Camebridge, Mass.: Harvard University Press

Gerken, Jutta (1986), *Anstaltsbeiräte.* Frankfurt/Main: Lang

Giddings, Roy (2000), "The Future of the Ombudsman" in Roy Gregory and Philip Giddings (eds.), *Righting Wrongs. The Ombudsman in Six Continents,* pp. 459-73. Amsterdam: IOS Press

Giddings, Roy (2001), "Wither the Ombudsman?", *Public Policy and Administration* 16(2): 1-16

Glaser, Barney (1978), *Theoretical Sensitivity: Advances in the Methodology of Grounded Theory.* Mill Valley, CA: Sociology Press

Glaser, Barney (1992), *Emergence vs. Forcing: Basics of Grounded Theory Analysis.* Mill Valley, CA: Sociology Press

Glaser, Barney (1998), *Doing Grounded Theory: Issues and Discussions.* Mill Valley, CA: Sociology Press

Glaser, Barney and Holton, Judith (2007), "Remodeling Grounded Theory" in Günter Mey and Katja Mruck (eds.), *Grounded Theory Reader. Historical Social Research – Supplement No. 19,* pp. 47-68. Köln: Zentrum für Historische Sozialforschung

Glaser, Barney and Strauss, Anselm (1967), *The Discovery of Grounded Theory: Strategies for Qualitative Research.* New York: Aldine de Gruyter

Goffman, Erving (1961), "On The Characteristics of Total Institutions," in Erving Goffman *Asylums: Essays on the Social Situation of Mental Patients and Other Inmates.,* pp. 1-124. New York: Doubleday Anchor

Gottehrer, Dean (2000), "Designing an Ombudsman System" in Roy Gregory and Philip Giddings (eds.), *Righting Wrongs. The Ombudsman in Six Continents,* pp. 415-25. Amsterdam: IOS Press

Gottehrer, Dean (2009), "Fundamental Elements of an Effective Ombudsman Institution", The Stockholm 2009 Conference Papers. Available from http://www.theioi.org/ publications/the-stockholm-2009-conference-papers (last accessed June 6th, 2012)

Gottehrer, Dean and Hostina, Michael (2000), "The Classical Ombudsman Model" in Roy Gregory and Philip Giddings (eds.), *Righting Wrongs. The Ombudsman in Six Continents,* pp. 403-15. Amsterdam: IOS Press

Gottehrer, Dean et al. (2000), "Ombudsman Offices in the United States" in Roy Gregory and Philip Giddings (eds.), *Righting Wrongs. The Ombudsman in Six Continents,* pp. 355-73. Amsterdam: IOS Press

Graziadei, Michele (2006), "Comparative Law as the Study of Transplants and Receptions" in Mathias Reimann and Reinhard Zimmermann (eds.), *The Oxford Handbook of Comparative Law,* pp. 440-475. Oxford: Oxford University Press

Gregory, Roy (2000), "Types of ombudsmen" in Ludo Veny and Rita Passemiers (eds.), *Looking for Ombudsman Standards,* pp. 13-39. Gent: Mys and Breesch

Gregory, Roy and Giddings, Philip (2000), "The Ombudsman Institution: Growth and Development" in Roy Gregory and Philip Giddings (eds.), *Righting Wrongs. The Ombudsman in Six Continents,* pp. 1-21. Amsterdam: IOS Press

Gregory, Roy and Giddings, Philip (2000b), "The United Kingdom Parliamentary Ombudsman Scheme" in Roy Gregory and Philip Giddings (eds.), *Righting Wrongs. The Ombudsman in Six Continents,* pp. 21-47. Amsterdam: IOS Press

Groves, Matthew (2002) "Ombudsmen's Jurisdiction in Prisons", *Monash University Law Review* 28: 181-205

Groves, Matthew (2003), "Administrative Law and the Management of Prisons and Prisoners", PhD. Dissertation, Monash University, Victoria, Australi

Gutteridge, Harold (1946), *Comparative Law: an introduction to the comparative method of legal study and research.* Cambridge: Cambridge University Press

Gwyn, William (1976), "Obstacles within the Office of Economic Opportunity to the Evaluation of Experimental Ombudsman", *Public Administration* 177-97

Haas, Peter (1992), "Introduction: epistemic communities and international policy coordination", in Peter Haas (ed.), *Knowledge, power and international policy coordination,* pp. 1-36. Columbia, South Carolina: University of South Carolina Press

Hadi, Maher (1977), "L'extension de l'ombudsman: triomphe d'une idée ou déformation d'une institution?", *International Review of Administrative Sciences* 43: 334-44

Haller, Walter (1965), *Der schwedische Justitieombudsman.* Winterthur: Verlag P. G. Keller

Hansen, Jürgen (1972), *Die Institution des Ombudsman*. Frankfurt am Main: Athenäum

Harrison, Tyler (2004) "What is Success in Ombudsman Processes? Evaluation of a University Ombudsman", *Conflict Resolution Quarterly* 21(3): 313-35

Heede, Katja (2000), *European Ombudsman: redress and control at Union level*. The Hague: Kluwer Law International

Henham, Ralph (2000), "Some Alternative Strategies for Improving the Effectiveness of the English Prisons Ombudsman Scheme", *The Howard Journal of Criminal Justice* 39(3): 290-305

Hertogh, Marc (1998), "The Policy Impact of the Ombudsman and Administrative Courts: A heuristic Model", *The International Ombudsman Yearbook* 63-85

Hertogh, Marc (2001), "Coercion, Cooperation, and Control: Understanding the Policy Impact of Administrative Courts and the Ombudsman in the Netherlands", *Law & Policy* 23(1): 47-67

Heskamp, Brian (2007-2008), "The Prisoner's Ombudsman: Protecting Constitutional Rights and Fostering Justice in American Corrections", *Ave Maria Law Review*, 6(2): 527-57

Hill, Larry (1976), *The Model Ombudsman. Institutionalizing New Zealand's Democratic Experiment*, Princeton, New Jersey: Princeton University Press

Hoffmann, Klaus (2000), „Buchbesprechung: Krause, Thomas, Geschichte des Strafvollzugs: Von den Kerkern des Altertums bis zur Gegenwart", *Monatsschrift für Kriminologie und Strafrechtsreform* 4: 251-3

Hoffmann, Klaus (2003), "Der Strafgefangene als Subjekt der Behandlung – zum Spannungsverhältnis von Menschenwürde und Vollzugsziel", *Zeitschrift für Strafvollzug und Straffälligenhilfe*, 4: 207-212

Holt, George et al. (1980), "Panel Discussion: Evaluation of the Efficiency and Effectiveness of the ombudsman" in *Proceedings of the Second International Ombudsman Conference, 1980 Jerusalem and Alberta*, pp. 36-38 International Ombudsman Institute, Edmonton, Alberta

Home Office (1987), *A Review of Prisoners' Complaints* (Report by HM Chief Inspector of Prisons). London: HMSO

Home Office (1989), *An Improved System of Grievance Procedures for Prisoners Complaints and Requests*. (HM Prison Service). London: HMSO

Home Office (1991) *Custody, Care and Justice, the Way Ahead for the Prison Service in England and* Wales, Cm 1647. London: HMSO

Home Office (1992) *An Independent Complaints Adjudicator for Prisons: A Consultation Paper*, HM Prison Service, London: HMSO

Hopp, Helmut (1993), *Beauftragte in Politik und Verwaltung*, Bonn: Stiftung Mitarbeit

Hyson, Stewart (2006), "Ombudsman Research Project", Notes for a roundtable discussion at the Annual Meeting of the Canadian Political Science Association, York University, Toronto, Ontario, 1 June 2006)

Hyson, Stewart (2009a), "Ombudsman Research Project: The Provincial and Territorial Ombuds-Offices in Canada" in Stewart Hyson (ed.), *Provincial and Territorial Ombudsman Offices in Canada*, pp. 3-26. Toronto: University of Toronto Press

Hyson, Stewart (2009b), "Speciality Ombudsman Offices: The New Breed of Structural Heretics", Paper prepared for the Annual Meeting of the Canadian Political Science Association, Carleton University, Ottawa, 27 May 2009.

Ikenberry, G. John (1990), "The international spread of privatization policies. Inducements, learning and 'policy band wagoning' in Ezra Suleiman and John Waterbury (eds.), *The political economy of public sector reform and privatization*, pp. 88-112. Boulder, Colorado: Westview Press

Jacobs, Andrea (2004) "Prison power corrupts absolutely: exploring the phenomenon of prison guard brutality and the need to develop a system of accountability", *California Western Law Review* 41: 277-301

Jacoby, Daniel (1999), "The Future of the Ombudsman" in Linda C. Reif (ed.), *The international Ombudsman Anthology*, pp. 15-51. The Hague: Kluwer Law International

Jacoby, Wade (2000), *Imitation and Politics. Redesigning Modern Germany*. Ithaca: Cornell University Press

Jamieson, Robert (1997) The Ombudsman's Annual Report: Strengthening the Ombudsman Office in Africa", *The International Ombudsman Yearbook* 1:45-8

Jansen, Nils (2006), "Comparative Law and Comparative Knowledge" in Mathias Reimann and Reinhard Zimmermann (eds.), *The Oxford Handbook of Comparative Law*, pp. 305-38. Oxford: Oxford University Press

Jessar, Kevin (2005) "The Ombud's Perspective: A critical analysis of the ABA 2004 Ombudsman Standards", *Dispute Resolution Journal* August/October: 56-61

Johnson, Cedric (1988), "Complaints – Grievance Procedures for Prisoners", *The Ombudsman Journal* 123-37

JUSTICE (1977), *Our fettered Ombudsman*. London: JUSTICE

JUSTICE (1983), *Justice in Prison*. London: JUSTICE

Kaiser, Günther and Schöch, Heinz (2002), "Strafvollzug". Heidelberg: C. F. Müller Verlag

Kamann, Ulrich (1991), *Gerichtlicher Rechtsschutz im Strafvollzug*. Pfaffenweiler: Centaurus-Verlags-Gesellschaft

Kaminski, Andrea (2012), "Aus Beschwerden und anderen Eingaben lernen: für einen Strafvollzug im Geiste unserer Verfassung", *Betrifft Justiz* 110: 286-92

Kauß, Udo (1989), *Der suspendierte Datenschutz bei Polizei und Geheimdiensten*. Franfurt/Main; New York: Campus Verlag

Kelle, Udo (2005), "'Emergence' vs. 'Forcing' of Empirical Data? A Crucial Problem of 'Grounded Theory' Reconsidered", *Forum: Qualitative Research [Online Journal]* 6(2): Art. 27 http://www.qualitative-research.net/index.php/fqs/article/view/467 (last accessed June 6th, 2012)

Kempf, Udo (1976), *Bürgerbeauftragte. Eine vergleichende Studie unter besonderer Berücksichtigung des Bürgerbeauftragten des Landes Rheinland-Pfalz*. Mainz: Landeszentrale für politische Bildung Rheinland-Pfalz

Kempf, Udo and Mille, Marco (1993), "The Role and the Function of the Ombudsman: Personalised Parliamentary Control in Forty-Eight Different States", *The Ombudsman Journal* 11: 195-226

Kimweri, Mjemmas (1993), "The Effectiveness of an Executive Ombudsman" in Linda C. Reif et al. (ed.), *The Ombudsman: Diversity and Development*, pp. 37-65 Edmonton: International Ombudsman Institute

Kirkham Richard (2008), "Explaining the lack of enforcement power possessed by the ombudsman", *Journal of Social Welfare & Family Law* 30 (3): 253-263

Kirkham, Richard (2010), "Ombudsman section: lessons from devolution", *Journal of Social Welfare & Family Law* 32 (3): 325-34

Kirkham, Richard et al. (2008), "When Putting Things Right Goes Wrong: Enforcing the Recommendations of the Ombudsman", *Public Law* Autumn: 510-530

Kirkham, Richard et al. (2009), "Putting the Ombudsman into Constitutional Context", *Parliamentary Affairs* 62(4): 600-617

Klasen, Sepp (1991), *Das Petitionsrecht zum Bayerischen Landtag – eine Ombudsman-Einrichtung*. München: Bayerischer Landtag

Kleining, Gerhard (1982), „Umriß zu einer Methodologie qualitativer Sozialforschung", *Kölner Zeitschrift für Soziologie und Sozialpsychologie* 34: 224-253

Koeppel, Thordis (1999), *Kontrolle des Strafvollzuges: individueller Rechtsschutz und generelle Aufsicht; ein Rechtsvergleich*. Mönchengladbach: Forum Verlag Godesberg

Kreft, Adolf (1953), *Die Parlamentarische Kontrolle der Verwaltung*. Osnabrück: Dissertation Universität zu Münster

Krent, Harold (2000), "Federal Agency Ombuds: The Costs, Benefits, and Countenance of Confidentiality", *Administrative Law Review* 52(1): 17-60

Kretschmer, Joachim (2005), "Ergänzungen und Alternativen zum Strafvollzugsrechtlichen Rechtsschutzsystem", *Zeitschrift für Strafvollzug und Straffälligenhilfe*, 4: 217-23

Krey, Volker (2001), *Deutsches Strafrecht. Allgemeiner Teil. Band 1. Grundlagen, Tatbestandsmäßigkeit, Rechtswidrigkeit, Schuld*. Stuttgart: W. Kohlhammer

Kruse, Julia (2006), *Der öffentlich-rechtliche Beauftragte. Ein Beitrag zu Systematisierung der deutschen Variante des Ombudsmannes*. Berlin: Duncker & Humblot

Kucsko-Stadlmayer, Gabriele (2008), *Europäische Ombudsman-Institutionen*. Wien: Springer

Kühler, Hans (1970), "Brauchen wir einen Justiz- oder Strafvollzugsbeauftragten?", *Zeitschrift für Strafvollzug* 19: 323-37

Lamnek, Siegfried (2005), *Qualitative Sozialforschung* Weinheim: Beltz PVU

Lasser, Mitchel (2003), "The question of understanding", in Pierre Legrand and Roderick Munday (eds.), *Comparative Legal Studies: Traditions and Transitions*, pp. 197-239, Cambridge: Cambridge University Press

Laubenthal, Klaus (2008), *Strafvollzug*. Berlin: Springer

Laubenthal, Klaus (2011), *Strafvollzug*. Berlin: Springer

Lazarus, Liora (2004), *Contrasting Prisoners' Rights*. New York: Oxford University Press

LeBaron, Michele (2008) "Watchdogs and Wise Ones in Winter Lands: The Practice Spectrum of Canadian Ombudsman", Forum of Canadian Ombudsman (FCO) Liz Hoffman Research Award Paper Available from http://www.ombudsmanforum.ca/ en/?page_id=184/ (last accessed June 6th, 2012)

Legrand, Pierre (1995), „Comparative Legal Studies and Commitment to Theory", *The Modern Law Review*, 58(2): 262-73

Legrand, Pierre (1999), "John Henry Merryman and Comparative Legal Studies: A Dialogue", *The American Journal of Comparative Law* 27(3): 3-66

Legrand, Pierre (2003), "The same and the different" in Pierre Legrand and Roderick Munday (eds.), *Comparative Legal Studies. Traditions and Transitions*, pp. 240-311. Cambridge: Cambridge University Press

Lesting, Wolfgang (1993), "Vorschläge zur Verbesserung des Rechtschutzes von Strafgefangenen", *Kriminologisches Journal*. 48-55

Lesting, Wolfgang and Feest, Johannes (1987), "Renitente Strafvollzugsbehörden", *Zeitschrift für Rechtspolitik* 11: 390-3

Leyland, Peter (2002), "Oppositions and Fragmentations: in search of a formula for comparative analysis?" in Andrew Harding and Esin Örücü (eds.), *Comparative Law in the 21st Century*, pp. 211-33

Leyland, Peter and Anthony, Gordon (2009), *Administrative Law*. New York: Oxford University Press

Livingstone, Stephen et al. (2003), *Prison Law*. Oxford: Oxford University Press

Livingstone, Stephen et al. (2008), *Prison Law*. Oxford: Oxford University Press

Loucks, Nancy (2000), *Prison Rules: A working guide*. London: Prison Reform Trust

Lux, Marshall (1993), "Perspectives on Costs and Cost Effectiveness of Ombudsman Programs in Four Fields – Case 5: State Ombudsman Office Cost Effectiveness Estimates", *Journal of Human Health and Resources Administration* 15(3) : 306-12

Maccoby, Eleanor and Maccoby, Nathan (1974), „Das Interview. Ein Werkzeug der Sozialforschung" in René König (ed.), *Praktische Sozialforschung I. Das Interview. Formen, Technik, Auswertung.* pp. 37-86. Köln: Kiepenheuer & Witsch

Maguire, Mike (1985), "Prisoners' grievances: the role of the Boards of Visitors" in Mike Maguire, Jon Vagg et al. (eds.), *Accountability and Prisons. Opening up a closed world*, pp. 141-55

Majone, Giandomenico (1991), "Cross-national sources of regulatory policy making in Europe and the United States", *Journal of Public Policy* 11, 79-106

Male, Barbara (2000), "Assessing Ombudsman Performance", *The International Ombudsman Yearbook* 4: 59-77

Male, Barbara (1999), "Assessing Ombudsman Performance: Two case studies in North America", PhD. dissertation, University of Southern California.

Mamadouh, Virgine et al. (2002) "An introduction to institutional transplantation" in Martin De Jong et al. (eds.), *The Theory and Practice of Institutional Transplantation*, pp. 1-16. Dordrecht, Netherlands: Kluwer

Marsh, David and Sharman, Jason (2009), "Policy diffusion and policy transfer", *Policy Studies*, 30(3): 269-88

Marti, Hans (1961), „Die aufsehende Gewalt" in Max Imboden et. Al. (eds.), *Verfassungsrecht und Verfassungswirklichkeit. Festschrift für Hans Huber.* Bern: Stämpfli

Martynowicz, Agnieszka (2011), "Oversight of Prison Conditions and Investigations of Deaths in Custody: International Human Rights Standards and the Practice in Ireland", *The Prison Journal* 91(1): 81-102

Massey, Andrew (2009), "Policy mimesis in the context of global governance", *Policy Studies*, 30(3): 383-95

Matheson. I. D. (1982) "The Ombudsmen and prison complaints", *Victoria University of Wellington Law Review* 12: 265-76

Matthes, Hagen (1981), *Der Bürgerbeauftragte*. Berlin: Duncker und Humblot

May, Edgar (1975), "Prison Ombudsmen in America ... they listen to both sides", *Corrections Magazine* 1(3): 45-55, 58-60

McLeod, Ron (2003), "Administrative Justice – an Ombudsman's Perspective on Dealing with the Exceptional", *AIAL Forum*, 36: 58-67

Melissaris, Emmanuel (2004), "The more the merrier? A new take on legal pluralism", *Social and legal studies*, 13(1): 57-79

Menski, Werner (2006), *Comparative Law in a Global Context*. Cambridge: Cambridge University Press

Merten, Klaus (1996), *Inhaltsanalyse. Einführung in Theorie, Methode und Praxis*. Opladen: Westdeutscher Verlag

Meuser, Michael and Nagel, Ulrike (1991), „ExpertInneninterviews – vielfach erprobt, wenig bedacht" in Detlef Garz and Klaus Kraimer (eds.), *Qualitative-empirische Sozialforschung. Konzepte, Methoden, Analysen*. pp. 441-71. Opladen: Westdeutscher Verlag GmbH

Mey, Günter and Mruck, Katja (2007a), "Vorwort/Preface" in Günter Mey and Katja Mruck (eds.), *Grounded Theory Reader. Historical Social Research – Supplement No. 19*, pp. 5-7. Köln: Zentrum für Historische Sozialforschung

Mey, Günter and Mruck, Katja (2007b), "Grounded Theory Methodologie – Bemerkungen zu einem prominenten Forschungsstil" in Günter Mey and Katja Mruck (eds.), *Grounded Theory Reader. Historical Social Research – Supplement No. 19*, pp. 11-39. Köln: Zentrum für Historische Sozialforschung

Mey, Günter and Mruck, Katja (2007c), "Einführung in Teil I" in Günter Mey and Katja Mruck (eds.), *Grounded Theory Reader. Historical Social Research – Supplement No. 19*, pp. 43-46. Köln: Zentrum für Historische Sozialforschung

Michaels, Ralf (2006), "The Functional Method of Comparative Law" in Mathias Reimann and Reinhard Zimmermann (eds.), *The Oxford Handbook of Comparative Law*, pp. 339-382. Oxford: Oxford University Press

Moore, John (1968a), "Ombudsman and the Ghetto", *Connecticut Law Review* 1: 244-62

Moore, John (1968b), "State Government and the Ombudsman" in Stanley V. Anderson (ed.), *Ombudsmen for American Government?*, pp. 70-101. Englewood Cliffs, NJ: Prentice-Hall, Inc.

Moore, John (1975), "The Prison Ombudsman", *The Center Magazine*, November/December: 10

Moran-Ellis, Jo et al. (2006), „Triangulation and integration: processes, claims and implications", *Qualitative Research*, 6(1): 45-59

Morgan, Rod (1991), "Woolf: In Retrospect and Prospect", *The Modern Law Review* 54(5): 713-25

Morgan, Rod (1992), "Following Woolf: The Prospects for Prison Policy", *Journal of Law and Society* 19(2): 231-49

Morgan, Rod and Liebling, Alison (2007), "Comparing Criminal Justice" in Mike Maguire et al. (eds.), *The Oxford Handbook of Criminology*, pp. 1100-38. Oxford: Oxford University Press

Morris, Philip and Henham, Ralph (1998), "The Prisons Ombudsman: Critical Review", *European Public Law* 4(3): 345-78

Morris, Philip and Henham, Ralph (1999), "The Scottish Prisons Complaints Commission: A Preliminary Study", *The Anglo-American Law Review* 28(3): 365-95

Mossberger, Karen and Wolman, Harold (2003), "Policy Transfer as a Form of Prospective Policy Evaluation: Challenges and Recommendations", *Public Administrative Review*, 63(4): 428-40

Müller-Dietz, Heinz (1992), „15 Jahre Strafvollzugsgesetz. Reform oder Ruine?", *Neue Kriminalpolitik* 27-33

Müller-Dietz, Heinz (1994), „Menschenrechte und Strafvollzug" in Heike Jung and Heinz Müller-Dietz (eds.), *Langer Freiheitsentzug – wie lange noch?* pp. 43-63, Mönchengladbach: Forum Verlag Godesberg

Münchbach, Hans-Jörg (1973), *Strafvollzug und Öffentlichkeit unter besonderer Berücksichtigung der Anstaltsbeiräte.* Stuttgart: Ferdinand Enke Verlag

Neff, Stephen and Avebury, Eric (2000), "Human Rights Mechanisms in the United Kingdom" in Kamal Hossain et. al. (eds.), *Human Rights Commissions and Ombudsman Offices*, pp. 667-691. The Hague: Kluwer Law International

Nelken, David (1995), „Disclosing/Invoking Legal Culture: An Introduction", *Social and & Legal Studies* 4: 435-52

Nelken, David (1997), "Whom can you Trust? The Future of Comparative Criminology" in Piers Beirne and David Nelken (eds.), *Issues in Comparative Criminology*, pp. 469-90. Hants, England: Ashgate Publishing Limited

Nelken, David (2000), "Virtually There, Reseraching there, Living there" in David Nelken (ed.), *Contrasting criminal justice: getting from here to there*, pp. 23-46, Burlington: Ashgate

Nelken, David (2003), "Legal transplants and beyond: of disciplines and metaphors" in Andrew Harding and Esin Örücü (eds.), *Comparative Law for the 21st century*, pp. 19-34. Hague: Kluwer

Neubacher, Frank (2008), "Gewalt unter Gefangenen", *Neue Zeitschrift für Strafrecht*, S. 361-6

Neudek, Kurt (1991), "Federal Republic of Germany" in Dirk Van Zyl Smit & Frieder Dünkel (eds.), *Imprisonment Today and Tomorrow*, pp. 706-712. Deventer, The Netherlands: Kluwer Law and Taxation Publishers

Offe, Claus (1994), "Designing Institutions for East European Transitions", *IHS Reihe Politikwissenschaft*, 19

Oosting, Marten (1999), "The Ombudsman and his Environment: A Global View" in Linda C. Reif (ed.), *The international Ombudsman Anthology*, pp. 1-15. The Hague: Kluwer Law International

Örücü, Esin (2002), "Unde venit, quod tendit comparative law?" in Andrew Harding and Esin Örücü (eds.), *Comparative Law in the 21st Century*, pp. 1-17

Örücü, Esin et al. (1996), *Studies in legal systems: Mixed and Mixing.* The Hague: Kluwer Law International

Owen, Stephen (1993), "The Ombudsman: Essential Elements and Common Challenges" in Linda C. Reif et al. (ed.), *The Ombudsman: Diversity and Development*, pp. 1-21 Edmonton: International Ombudsman Institute

Owers, Anne (2004), "Prison Inspection and the Protection of Human Rights", *European Human Rights Law Review* 107-16

Owers, Anne (2006), "The Protection of Prisoner's Rights in England and Wales", *European Journal on Criminal Policy and Research* 12:85-91

Patterson, A. N. (1959-63), "The Ombudsman", *University of British Columbia Law Review* 1: 777-81

Pearce, Dennis (1992), „Minding the People's Minder", *Canberra Times*, March

Pearce, Dennis (2005), "The Jurisdiction of Australian Government Ombudsmen" in Matthew Groves (ed.), *Law and Government in Australia*, pp. 110-139. Sydney: The Federation Press

Player, Elaine (1992), "The Woolf Report on Prison Disturbances", *The King's College Law Journal* 137-140

Plessis, Jacques du (2006), "Comparative Law and the Study of Mixed Legal Systems" in Mathias Reimann and Reinhard Zimmermann (eds.), *The Oxford Handbook of Comparative Law*, pp. 477-512. Oxford: Oxford University Press

Pollitt, Christopher (2011), "Not odious but onerous: Comparative Public Administration", *Public Administration* 89(1): 114-27

Puchta, Josef (1986), "Funktion und Rolle des Ombudsmans in den parlamentarischen Demokratien" in Udo Kempf and Herbert Uppendahl (eds.), *Ein deutscher Ombudsman*, pp. 119-29. Opladen: Leske Verlag + Budrich GmbH

Radaelli, Claudio (2000), "Policy Transfer in the European Union: Institutional Isomorphism as a Source of Legitimacy", *Governance: An International Journal of Policy and Administration*, 13(1): 25-43

Radbruch, Gustav (1969), *Einführung in die Rechtswissenschaft*. 12th ed. Stuttgart: K.F. Koehler Verlag

Raphael, Adam (1975), "The European Experience", *Corrections Magazine* 1(3): 56-7

Redeker, Konrad (1967), "Notwendigkeit und rechtliche Gestaltungsmöglichkeiten von Parlamentsbeauftragten in Deutschland", *Neue Juristische Wochenschrift* 20(29): 1297-1301

Reif, Linda (2000), "Building Democratic Institutions: The Role of National Human Rights Institutions in Good Governance and Human Rights Protection", *Harvard Human Rights Journal* 1-69

Reif, Linda (2004), *The Ombudsman, Good Governance, and the International Human Rights System*. Leiden, Netherlands: Martinus Nijhoff Publishers

Reigrotzki, Erich (1966), „Der Ombudsmann ist in Gefahr", *Mensch und Staat* 3:39

Reigrotzki, Erich (1968), „Der Ombudsmann ist in Gefahr", *Mensch und Staat* 1:7-8

Reigrotzki, Erich (1970), "Die Verfälschung einer Idee", *Mensch und Staat* 6: 81-82

Ritter, Sebastian (2009), *National Institutions for the promotion and protection of human rights*. Norderstedt: Books on Demand GmbH

Rose, Richard (1993), *Lesson-Drawing in Public Policy. A Guide to Learning Across Time and Space*. Chatham, New Jersey: Chatham House Publishers

Rotthaus, Karl (2008), "Ein Ombudsmann für das deutsche Gefängniswesen", *Bewährungshilfe* 373-87

Rowat, Donald (1968), "Preface to Second Edition" in Donald C. Rowat (ed.), *The Ombudsman. Citizen's Defender*, pp. v-xxi

Rowat, Donald (1973), *The Ombudsman Plan: Essays on the World-wide Spread of an Idea*. London: McCalland and Stewart

Rowat, Donald (1985), *The Ombudsman Plan*. Lanham: University Press of America

Rowat, Donald (1993), "Why a Legislative Ombudsman is Desirable", *Ombudsman Journal* 127-37

Rowat, Donald (2007), "The American distortion of the ombudsman concept and its influence on Canada", *Canadian Public Administration* 50: 42-52

Roxin, Claus (1966), „Sinn und Grenzen staatlicher Strafe", *Juristische Schulung* 6(10): 377-87

Roxin, Claus (1997), *Strafrecht Allgemeiner Teil. Band I. Grundlagen. Der Aufbau der Verbrechenslehre*. München: C. H. Beck'sche Verlagsbuchhandlung

Ryan, Mick and Ward, Tony (1993), "A Prison Ombudsman of sorts: The long road to reform" in Neil Hawke (ed.), *The Ombudsman – twenty-five years on*, pp. 37-51. London: Cavendish Publishing Limited

Sanker, Friedhelm (2007), "Der Ombudsmann für den Strafvollzug hat seine Arbeit aufgenommen", *Der Vollzugsdienst* 6: 52-54

Sapers, Howard and Zinger, Ivan (2010), "The Ombudsman as a Monitor of Human Rights in Canadian Federal Corrections", *Pace Law Review* 30(4): 101-17

Schäfer, Karl (1985), *Anstaltsbeiräte – die institutionalisierte Öffentlichkeit?*, Ph.D. dissertation, University of Mainz, Germany

Schlaffer, Rudolf (2006), *Der Wehrbeauftragte 1951-1985*. München: Oldenbourg Wissenschaftsverlag

Schlesinger, Rudolf et al. (1998), *Comparative Law – Cases, Text, Materials*. 6th ed. New York: Foundation Press

Schwind, Hans-Dieter et al. (2009), "Strafvollzugsgesetz. Bund und Länder". Berlin: De Gruyter

Selke, William (1992), "Problem concepts of international corrections", *International Journal of comparative and applied criminal justice*, 16(1): 87-100

Selke, William (1993), *Prisons in Crisis*. Bloomington: Indiana University Press

Seneviratne, Mary (1994), *Ombudsmen in the Public Sector*. Buckingham: Open University Press

Seneviratne, Mary (2000a), "'Joining up' the ombudsman – the Review of the Public Sector Ombudsman", *Public Law* Winter: 582-91

Seneviratne, Mary (2000b), "Ombudsmen 2000", *Nottingham Law Journal*, 9(1): 13-24

Seneviratne, Mary (2001), "The Prisons Ombudsman", *Journal of Social Welfare & Family Law* 23(1): 93-101

Seneviratne, Mary (2002), *Ombudsmen. Public Services and Administrative Justice*. London: Butterworths

Seneviratne, Mary (2008), "Updating the Local Government Ombudsman", *Public Law* Winter: 627-35

Seneviratne, Mary (2010), "The Prisons and Probation Ombudsman: a review", *Nottingham Law Journal* 19(2): 1-21

Shaw, Stephen (1999), "The European Convention on Human Rights: the Human Rights Act and the prison service", *Prison Service Journal*, 121: 10-2

Shaw, Stephen (2004) "A specialist Ombudsman for Prisoners", *The International Ombudsman Yearbook* 8: 122-31

231

Skinner, Shera and Hyman, Carly (2006), "The Ombudsman Offices in Denmark and British Columbia, Canada: A Comparative Study", *The International Ombusman Yearbook* 10: 83-119

Smith, Philippa (1998), "Red Tape and the Ombudsman", Paper presented as a lecture in the Department of the Senate Occasional Lecture Series at Parliament House on April 17th 1998

Söderman, Jacob (2004), "How to be a good ombudsman", Occasional Paper #80, International Ombudsman Institute, Edmonton, Alberta

Steyvers, Kristof et al. (2009), "Towards a Multifaceted Approach to Assessing the Impact of an Ombudsman" in Rita Passesmiers et al. (eds.), *The impact of ombudsmen*, pp. 15-32. Brugge: Vanden Broele Publishers

Stieber, Carolyn (2000), "57 Varieties: Has the Ombudsman Concept Become Diluted?", *The Negotiation Journal* 6(1): 49-57

Stone, Diane (2000), "Non-Governmental Policy Transfer: The Strategy of Independent Policy Institutes", *Governance: An International Journal of Policy and Administration* 13(1): 45-62

Strauss, Anselm (2007), "Interview mit Heiner Legewie und Barbara Schervier-Legewie" in Günter Mey and Katja Mruck (eds.), *Grounded Theory Reader. Historical Social Research – Supplement No. 19*, pp. 69-80. Köln: Zentrum für Historische Sozialforschung Glaser, Barney (2007) (2007), "All is Data", *The Grounded Theory Review* 6(2): 1-22

Strauss, Anselm and Corbin, Juliet (1990), *Basics of Qualitative Research. Grounded Theory Procedures and Techniques*. London: Sage Publications

Strübing, Jörg (2007), "Glaser vs. Strauss? Zur methodologischen und methodischen Substanz einer Unterscheidung zweier Varianten von Grounded Theory" in Günter Mey and Katja Mruck (eds.), *Grounded Theory Reader. Historical Social Research – Supplement No. 19*, pp. 157-174. Köln: Zentrum für Historische Sozialforschung

Stuhmcke, Anita (2010), "'Each for Themselves' or 'One for All'? The Changing Emphasis of the Commonwealth Ombudsman", *Federal Law Review* 38: 143-67

Stuhmcke, Anita (2009), "An Empirical Study on the Systemic Investigations Function of the Commonwealth Ombudsman from 1977-2005", PhD. dissertation, The Australian National University

Sztompka, Piotr (1990), "Conceptual frameworks in comparative inquiry: divergent or convergent?" in Martin Albrow and Elizabeth King (eds.), *Globalization, Knowledge and Society*, pp. 47-60. London: Sage Publications

Taugher, Brian (1972) "The Penal Ombudsman: A Step Toward Penal Reform", *Pacific Law Journal* 3: 166-189

Taylor, John (2000), "The Role of Mediation in Complaints Handling: The Experience of the Office of the Commonwealth Ombudsman", in Finn C. (ed.), *Sunrise or Sunset? Administrative Law in the New Millennium*, pp. 188-205, AIAL, Canberra

Taylor, Richard (1984/1985), "Ombudsman Success in the Federal Republic of Germany: The Role of Specialized and General Ombudsmen in a Large Federation", *The Ombudsman Journal* 149-65

Thacker, Sara (2009), "Good Intentions Gone Astray: How the ABA standards Affect Ombudsmen", *Journal of the International Ombudsman Association* 2(1): 65-88

Tham, Henrik (2011), „Vilnius, Criminal Policy and Comparative Research", *Newsletter of the European Society of Criminology* 12(3): 12

Thulesius, Hans and Grahn, Brigitta (2007), *Reincentivizing Work: A grounded theory of work and sick leave* 6(2): 47-66

Tibbles, Lance (1971) "Ombudsmen for American Prisons", *North Dakota Law Review* 48: 384-441

Uppendahl, Herbert (1986), "Überlegungen zur Wirksamkeitskontrolle von Ombudsmännern" in Udo Kempf and Herbert Uppendahl (eds.), *Ein deutscher Ombudsman*, pp. 191-205. Opladen: Leske Verlag + Budrich GmbH

Van Roosbroek, Steven and van de Walle, Steven (2008), "The Relationship between Ombudsman, Government, and Citizens: A Survey Analysis", *Negotiation Journal* July: 287-302

Wagner, Joachim (1976), "Der Rechtsschutz der Strafgefangenen", *Monatsschrift für Kriminologie und Strafrechtsreform* 59(5): 241-67

Walker, Diane and Myrick, Florence (2006), "Grounded Theory: An Exploration of Process and Procedure", *Qualitative Health Research* 16(4): 547-59

Walter, Michael (2007), „Der Skandal von Siegburg und der künftige Umgang mit jungen Strafgefangenen", *Zeitschrift für Jugendkriminalrecht und Jugendhilfe* (1): 72-5

Walter, Michael (2009), „Der Häftlingsmord von Siegburg: Zu Formern seiner gesellschaftlichen Verarbeitung", *Zeitschrift für Jugendkriminalrecht und Jugendhilfe* (2): 149-53

Walter, Michael (2012), "Möglichkeiten der Gefängniskontrolle durch einen externen Beauftragten" in *Macht und Machtmissbrauch der Institutionen. Buchpublikation zum Workshop.* Wiesbaden: VS-Verlag Sozialwissenschaften (in print)

Warrington, Edward (1999), "The Ombudsman's oracle. Critic, Counselor, Champion – A Comparative Study of Ombudsman Report", *The International Ombudsman Yearbook* 3: 32-70

Watson, Alan (1974), *Legal Transplants. An approach to Comparative Law*. Edinburgh: Scottish Academic Press

Wener, Geoffrey (1983), *A legitimate grievance*. London: Prison Reform Trust

Whitman, James (2003), "The neo-Romantic turn" in Pierre Legrand and Roderick Munday (eds.), *Comparative Legal Studies: Traditions and Transitions*, pp.312-43 Cambridge: Cambridge University Press

Wild, Eberhard (1970), "Der Ombudsman in Deutschland", Dissertation, Bayerische Julius-Maximilians-Universität, Würzburg

Williams, J.E. Hall (1984), "The Need for a Prison Ombudsman", *The Criminal Law Review* Feb: 87-93

Williams, Theatrice (1975), "The Minnesota Corrections Ombudsman", *Social Work* November 488-90

Woolf, Harry and Tumim, Stephen (1991), *Prison Disturbances April 1990: Report of an Inquiry* London: Great Britain Home Dept Cm. 1456

Wyner, Alan (1975), "Executive Ombudsmen, and Criticisms of Contemporary American Public Bureaucracy" in Alan Wyner (ed.), *Executive Ombudsman in the United States*, pp. 1-17. Berkley: Institute of Governmental Studies

Yardley, David (1994), "The Ombudsman and the Protection of Human Rights in the United Kingdom" in Franz Matscher (ed.), *Ombudsman in Europe. The Institution.*, pp. 73-82

Zedner, Lucia (1995), "In Pursuit of the Vernacular: Comparing Law and Order Discourse in Britain and Germany", *Social and Legal Studies* 4: 517-34

Zweigert, Konrad and Kötz, Hein (1998), *An Introduction to Comparative Law*. Oxford: Oxford University Press

German Abstract

Jedes Jahr sterben in Nordrhein-Westfalen 20 bis 45 Strafgefangene. In England und Wales beruhen sogar 60 bis 100 Todesfälle pro Jahr auf unnatürlichen Todesursachen. Homizid und Suizid sind zwar Extremformen, aber die Verletzung von Individualrechten ist im Strafvollzug eine Alltagserscheinung. Derartige Rechtsverletzungen müssen dabei abgegrenzt werden von der bloßen Einschränkung von Individualrechten, denn Gefängnisse als „totale Institutionen" sind gerade dazu konzipiert, bestimmte Freiheitsrechte einzuschränken.

Seit der Zurückdrängung der Todesstrafe handelt es sich beim Freiheitsentzug um die einschneidendste Strafform, die von Staaten zur Ahndung von Straftaten eingesetzt wird. Daher erstaunt es umso mehr, dass die Gesellschaft als Ganzes sich so wenig für die Wirklichkeit hinter ihren Gefängnismauern interessiert und dass das Leben dort weitgehend unbeeinflusst von den üblichen gesellschaftlichen Kontrollmechanismen abläuft.

Trotz dieses gesellschaftlichen Desinteresses ist es mittlerweile einhellige Meinung, dass Rechtsstaatlichkeit nicht am Gefängnistor enden darf, sondern Bestrafung und Freiheitsentzug nur dann berechtigt und sinnvoll sind, wenn sie der Resozialisierung des Individuums dienen, indem sie Gelegenheit zur Selbstreflexion und zur Änderung des fehlerhaften Lebenswandels mit dem Ziel der vollständigen Wiedereingliederung in die Gesellschaft bieten. Diese Zielsetzung begrenzt die staatliche Freiheitsbeschränkung auf das geringst-notwendige Maß, so z.B. die Einschränkung der Fortbewegungsfreiheit, der Versammlungsfreiheit etc. Aber wo immer Menschen Macht über Andere ausüben, entsteht, ob begründet oder unbegründet, absichtlich oder unabsichtlich, Anlass zu Beschwerden. Diese erstrecken sich von Bedürfnissen bei der Körperpflege über Disziplinarfragen bis hin zu Eingriffen in die körperliche Unversehrtheit.

Angesichts dessen vermag die Bandbreite, mit der das Verwaltungsrecht den Strafgefangenen Beschwerdemöglichkeiten einräumt, kaum zu überraschen. Die Mehrheit der Gefangenenbeschwerden wird systemimmanent bearbeitet bzw. behoben. Dennoch bedarf es zusätzlich einer ständigen, unabhängigen Kontrolle, die eines der elementaren Grundprinzipien einer menschenrechtskonformen Strafvollzugspolitik ausmacht. Das gesteigerte Schutzbedürfnis von Gefangenen spiegelt sich auch in der Zahl der Urteile des Europäischen Gerichtshofs für Menschenrechte wider. So stellen z.B. britische Gefangene diejenige europäische Gruppierung dar, die diesen Gerichtshof am häufigsten angerufen und einen Großteil dessen zentraler Urteile zu Strafvollzugsfragen erstritten hat.

Neben den gerichtlichen Regresswegen, die die am weitesten verbreitete Form institutionalisierter, unabhängiger Kontrollmechanismen für den Strafvollzug darstellen, bestehen auch außergerichtliche Beschwerdemöglichkeiten bei Abgeordneten der Parlamente des Bundes und der Länder, Petitionsausschüssen etc. Diese Beschwerdewege sind Ausdruck der Ausdehnung des Begriffs *contre-rôle* über dessen ursprüngliche Bedeutung der Überprüfung abgeschlossener Vorgänge hinaus hin zur unterstützenden Begleitung noch laufender Verfahren. Die einflussreichste Variante dieser Form der außergerichtlichen Kontrolle stellt der Ombudsman dar, der in vielen Ländern als ein zusätzlicher Mechanismus in bestehende mehrgleisige Ansätze integriert wurde.

Bisher wurde stets der institutionelle Erfolg von Ombuds-Einrichtungen als ausschlaggebend für die rasche Verbreitung – gerne auch als „Ombudsmania" bezeichnet – angesehen. Hierbei handelt es sich aber mangels einschlägiger Forschung um eine bloße Vermutung. In Betracht der Einsatzmöglichkeit von Ombuds-Institutionen einerseits zur Behebung, andererseits zur Verschleierung von Problemen und angesichts der Tatsache, dass keine Institution so gut ist, dass sie nicht verbessert werden könnte, erscheint diese Forschungslücke eklatant. Diese Forschungslücke besteht in besonderer Form auch bei Strafvollzugsombudsleuten, die nicht nur im Hinblick auf Erfolge bisher kaum erforscht sind.

Die Kombination aus drohenden Menschenrechtsverletzungen, der Resozialisierungaufforderung an Gefangene, der Bedeutung des Freiheitsentzuges als Strafe und der finanziellen Aufwendungen für den Strafvollzug lässt es als nicht hinnehmbar erscheinen, dass die folgenden Fragen immer noch keine Antworten gefunden haben:

- Erfüllen Ombuds-Institutionen ihren Zweck?
- Sind sie als Kontrollmechanismen für den Strafvollzug zu empfehlen?
- Und falls dem so ist, wie sollten sie gestaltet sein?

Die vorliegende Untersuchung bezweifelt nun die Vermutung institutionellen Erfolges als Quell der Verbreitung von Strafvollzugsombudsleuten. Denn dazu wäre erforderlich, dass die staatlichen Organe, die selbige einführen, sich nach hinreichender Prüfung ausländischer Strafvollzugskontrollmechanismen auf ihre Zweckdienlichkeit im Hinblick auf lokale Probleme und Anwendbarkeit im Rahmen des bestehenden Tableaus bewusst für die Implementation einer Strafvollzugsombuds-Einrichtung entscheiden. Dies wurde aber bisher nicht erforscht, geschweige denn bewiesen.

Die vorliegende Studie beabsichtigt die Forschungslücke im Hinblick auf Strafvollzugsombudsleute dadurch zu verkleinern, dass sie das Warum und das Wie ihrer Verbreitung über Staatsgrenzen und Rechtskulturkreise hinweg erforscht. Die Untersuchung stellt die Fragen:

- Wie sind Strafvollzugsombudsleute entstanden?

- Was hat deren Verbreitung ausgelöst?

Es geht hierbei darum, welche Bedürfnisse staatliche Organe mit einer Einführung von Strafvollzugsombuds-Einrichtungen befriedigen wollen. Doch diese auf die Verbreitung fokussierte Perspektive erlaubt nur ein unvollständiges Verständnis insoweit, als dass sie die Fragen

- Wie laufen solche Neuerungen ab?
- Welche Rechtsformen werden gewählt?

bezüglich der von den Staatsorganen benutzten Strukturen unberührt lassen. Deswegen erstreckt sich diese Analyse auch auf die Implementierung von Strafvollzugsombuds-Einrichtungen. Erst diese Implementationsperspektive ermöglicht die Identifikation von und belegt das Vorkommen von Wissenstransfer. Das Wissenstransferkonzept entstammt dem Forschungsgebiet der internationalen Beziehungen, der Staatswissenschaften, der Politik und der Soziologie. Dementsprechend verfolgt diese Studie einen rechtsvergleichenden Ansatz, der Elemente dieser Wissenschaften mit denen der Kriminologie, Rechts- und Verwaltungswissenschaften verbindet.

Diese Untersuchung zweifelt die Annahme institutionellen Erfolges als Grund der Verbreitung von Strafvollzugsombudsleuten deswegen an, weil planvoll vorgehende Staatsorgane seltener die Einführung als sog. Exekutivombudsleute wählen sollten. Die vorliegende Untersuchung betrachtet daher folgenden drei Hypothesen:

- Strafvollzugsombudsleute werden nur in Zeiten akuten Drucks auf Strafvollzugssysteme eingeführt.
- Ihre Implementation erfolgt mittels als „cross-fertilization" bezeichneten inter-staatlichen Ideenaustausches.
- Dies mündet häufig in der Einführung als Exekutivombuds-Institutionen.

Die Überprüfung dieser Hypothesen erfolgt in der Studie, indem zunächst der aktuelle Forschungsstand zum Thema dargelegt und die in den Hypothesen verwendeten Fachbegriffe (Ombudsman, Exekutivombudsman, Strafvollzugsombudsman und cross-fertilization) operationalisiert werden. Grundsätzliche Fragen zum Ombudsman-Konzept werden vorab beantwortet. Daran schließt sich die Beschreibung von Definition, Amt und Praxis von Strafvollzugsombudsleuten an. In einem dritten Teil wird erkundet inwieweit die Geschichte des Prisons and Probation Ombudsman for England and Wales und des Justizvollzugsbeauftragten des Landes Nordrhein-Westfalen Prozesse staatlichen Ideenaustauschs aufweist.

Der Ombudsman wird heutzutage als eine Form des Ausdrucks der demokratischen Sehnsucht nach der Kontrolle durch den staatlichen Souverän verstanden und eingesetzt. Da diese Einrichtung trotz ihrer Verbreitung bisher kaum Echo im wissenschaftlichen und öffentlichen Diskurs gefunden hat, sei erwähnt, dass nicht alle Einrichtungen, die die Charakteristika von Ombuds-Institutionen aufweisen, auch eine entsprechende Bezeichnung im Titel führen. Während der Ursprung des Ombudsmans auf germanische Wurzeln zurückgeführt wird, leitet sich das Wort etymologisch von den schwedischen Wörtern „ombuds" oder „umbuds" ab, was so viel heißt wie Repräsentant oder Anwalt des Volkes oder einer speziellen Untergliederung des selbigen. Bei dieser Übersetzung handelt es sich natürlich bestenfalls um eine andeutende Beschreibung, keineswegs aber um eine echte Definition. Die Studie belegt, dass es jeglichen bisherigen Definitionen an hinreichender Präzision und Aktualität mangelt. Daher wird im Rahmen eines eigenen Ansatzes der Ombudsman als öffentlich-rechtliche Institution definiert, deren Aufgabe sowohl der Individualrechtsschutz, als auch die Verteidigung der freiheitlichen demokratischen Grundordnung mittels der Überwachung verwaltungsrechtlichen Handelns ist. Zu diesem Zweck sind sie von einem Parlament, einem Ministerium oder einer deren Untergliederungen bevollmächtigt – aus Eigeninitiative oder aus Anlass erhaltener Bürgerbeschwerden – unabhängige Nachforschungen bezüglich vorgenommenen oder unterlassenen Verwaltungsakten oder zugrundeliegender struktureller Probleme anzustellen. Mangels eigener Entscheidungsbefugnis stellen ihre persönliche Autorität, ausgesprochene Handlungsempfehlungen, vorgelegte Jahres- und Spezialberichte sowie Öffentlichkeitsarbeit die einzigen Möglichkeiten zur Einflussnahme dar.

Ombuds-Einrichtungen werden dabei als Möglichkeit betrachtet, auf ökonomische Weise Anlass und Aufwand einander anzugleichen und Korrekturen an insgesamt funktionstüchtigen Systemen vorzunehmen. Letztere können sich auf äußerst unterschiedliche Felder erstrecken. So umfasst der Aufgabenbereich vieler Ombuds-Institutionen zwar den Strafvollzug – explizit dafür geschaffen wurden sie aber nicht. Anders gestaltet sich das bei sog. Strafvollzugsombuds-Einrichtungen, die eine der zahlreichen Adaptierungen des Konzepts darstellen. Deren Verbreitung war bis 2007 auf den common law-Raum beschränkt, wo sie seit den 1970ern als Kontrollmechanismus für den Strafvollzug Anwendung finden.

Die Studie ermittelt den Bedarf für Strafvollzugsombudsleute durch einen Vergleich mit anderen strafvollzugsrechtlichen Kontrollmechanismen. Dabei werden einerseits die internen Mechanismen wie die Selbstkontrolle der Verwaltung, Anstaltsbeiräte und die Gefangenenmitverantwortung und andererseits die externen Kontrollorgane wie Parlamentarier, Petitionsausschüsse, Monarchen und andere Staatshäupter, fachübergreifende Ombudsleute, NGOs, Seelsorger, Medien, europäische und internationale Organisationen sowie Gerichte unterschieden. Im Hinblick auf ihre Leistungsfähigkeit bei Strafvollzugskontrolle und Gefangenenbeschwerdebearbeitung ergibt die Analyse, dass diese Einrichtungen häufig zu teuer, langsam, unbekannt, wirkungslos, ineffizient oder schlicht unzuständig sind. Dementsprechend wird der Strafvollzugsombudsman als ein sinnvolles alternatives Kontrollorgan betrachtet.

Die Studie weist nach, dass Strafvollzugsombudsleute entweder in der Form von Exekutiv- oder Legislativombuds-Einrichtungen vorkommen. Diese unterscheiden sich hinsichtlich ihrer rechtlichen Grundlagen – im ersten Fall sind es Exekutivakte wie Ministerialerlasse und im zweiten Fall Gesetze oder Verfassungsparagraphen. Derzeit existieren weltweit sieben Strafvollzugsombuds-Institutionen – vier in Nordamerika und drei in Europa. Davon sind zwei Legislativ- und fünf Exekutivombudsleute. Die exekutive Einführungsform gilt dabei als problematisch, da diese rechtliche Grundlage zwar einerseits eine rasche Einführung, andererseits aber auch eine ebenso rasche Abschaffung gestattet, wenn der Amtsinhaber das Missfallen der einsetzenden Minister, Gouverneure oder anderen staatlichen Stellen erregt. Dies reduziert sowohl die Legitimität, als auch die Effektivität dieser Ombudsleute.

Die Hypothese der Verbreitung von Strafvollzugsombudsleuten mittels cross-fertilization erfordert die Darstellung des Forschungsstandes bei zwischenstaatlichen Lernprozessen. Die Möglichkeit solchen Ideenaustauschs wird nicht einhellig akzeptiert. Im Rahmen des sog. culturalism wird vertreten, dass es nicht möglich ist, ein hinreichendes Verständnis einer fremden Rechtskultur zu erlangen, und daher die Transferierung von Rechtsinstitutionen als unerreichbar abgelehnt. Anhänger der universalistischen Position hingegen betrachten Recht als ein kulturunabhängiges Konstrukt, dessen Wesenskern sich in allen Rechtskreisen grundsätzlich ähnelt. Diese Ansicht erkennt zwar den Einfluss des lokalen Anwenders auf die rechtlichen Komponenten an, verweist aber darauf, dass selbst Gadamer kein totales Vorverständnis bei interkulturellem Austausch verlangt hat und Recht letztlich nur eine Form menschlichen Handelns und damit imitierbar ist.

Daher beschäftigen sich viele wissenschaftlichen Disziplinen mit der Erforschung zwischenstaatlichen Ideenaustauschs. Die vorliegende Studie verfolgt einen rechtsvergleichenden Ansatz, für den eine einheitliche Terminologie im internationalen und interdisziplinären Diskurs fehlt. Eine Betrachtung der bei staatlichem Ideenaustausch ablaufenden Prozesse führt zur Differenzierung von Akquise- und Implementationsphasen. Daher erfolgt eine dahingehende Begriffsklärung, dass diese Studie den technischen Begriff cross-fertilization als Umschreibung der Prozesse einsetzt und mit „legal transplant" das Produkt eines akkuraten Akquiseprozesses beschreibt, das bei umsichtiger Umsetzung der Implementation zu einem „ideal fit", einer idealen Passform der entliehenen Institution in das neue Rechtssystem führt.

Solche Prozesse zwischenstaatlichen Ideenaustauschs können aus unterschiedlichen Anlässen und auf unterschiedliche Weise angestoßen werden. Es werden gemeinhin drei wesentliche Faktoren als Auslöser von cross-fertilization genannt – nämlich prozessbegleitende Personen (sog. key-holders), Willenselemente (Freiwilligkeit oder Zwang) und zeitliche Komponenten. Key-holders können Politiker, Bürokraten, Think-Tanks, Bildungseinrichtungen, Wissenschaftler und andere Experten, sowie Interessenverbände, internationale Finanzinstitutionen, internationale Organisationen und supra-nationale Institutionen sein. Diese begründen oder befördern in ihren Heimatstaaten oder Drittländern den Wunsch, bestimmte Rechtsinstitutionen zu transferieren. Dies kann entweder aus Überzeugung und damit auf freiwilliger Basis oder aufgrund externen Drucks, z.B. über Auflagen zum Erhalt bestimmter (finanzieller) Begünstigungen, erfolgen. Zeitliche Komponenten sind insofern ausschlaggebend, als sich im Rahmen staatlicher und rechtlicher Entwicklung immer wieder Opportunitätsfenster öffnen und schließen, in denen besonderes Interesse an der Erkundung und Einführung neuer Institutionen besteht. Auslöser solcher zeitlich begrenzter Gelegenheiten wiederum können generell Unzufriedenheit, staatsinterne oder – externe Routineüberprüfungen oder Konflikte und Krisen sein.

Im Anschluss an diese Beschreibung des Forschungsstandes wird die Methodenauswahl und -durchführung dargelegt. Aufgrund der bisher nur geringen Erforschung von Ombuds-Einrichtung im Allgemeinen und Strafvollzugsombudsleuten im Besonderen wurde für diese Studie grounded theory als ein Ansatz gewählt, mit dem möglichst viele neue Einblicke in das studierte Phänomen erzielt werden können. In der Studie wird die von Strauss und Corbin entwickelte Form der grounded theory angewendet. Dabei werden mittels induktiver Prozesse Hypothesen generiert. Die Ergebnisse von grounded theory verstehen sich gerade nicht als Tatsachenberichte, sondern es handelt sich vielmehr um Wahrscheinlichkeitsaussagen über den bestehenden Zusammenhang von Konzepten oder um einen integrierten Satz konzeptueller Hypothesen, entwickelt aus empirischen Daten. Da grounded theory zwar heutzutage vor allem in englischsprachigen Raum eine anerkannte Forschungsmethode ist, aber gerade in Deutschland noch wenig Verbreitung erfahren hat, wurden die mit Hilfe der grounded theory-Methode erlangten Ergebnisse in einem klassischen Forschungsdesign präsentiert.

Diese Untersuchung konzentriert sich auf die Analyse zweier Strafvollzugsombuds-Einrichtungen, nämlich des Prisons and Probation Ombudsman for England and Wales und des Justizvollzugsbeauftragten des Landes Nordrhein-

Westfalen. Diese wurden als Beispiele zur Hypothesengenerierung ausgewählt, weil damit sowohl der Rechtskulturkreis des common law und civil law repräsentiert sind und dennoch ihre Vergleichbarkeit als Exekutivombuds-Einrichtungen in Staaten der Europäischen Union, mit ähnlichen Strafgefangenenzahlen, aber sehr unterschiedlichen Beschwerdezahlen und personeller bzw. finanzieller Ausstattung gegeben ist. Ausschlaggebend war nicht zuletzt auch ihre räumliche Nähe und die damit gegebene Erforschbarkeit durch einen Einzelnen.

Die Analyse der beiden Untersuchungssubjekte gestaltet sich dabei wie folgt: Zunächst wurde jeweils deren institutionelle Einbettung in ihre rechtlichen lokalen Gegebenheiten, gegliedert nach Forschungsstand, Strafvollzugsgeschichte, Strafgefangenenzahlen und -spezifika, Rechtsgrundlage der Inhaftierung, Strafvollzugsgestaltung und externe wie interne Kontrollmechanismen betrachtet. Daran schließt sich jeweils eine Untersuchung der Abläufe und Ergebnisse der Implementationsprozesse an. Die empirischen Daten wurden mittels qualitativer Forschung einerseits an vorhandenen Schriftquellen und andererseits in drei Experteninterviews erhoben.

Die Ergebnisse der Untersuchung lauten wie folgt: Schon geraume Zeit vor der Einführung des Prisons and Probation Ombudsman for England and Wales wurde im lokalen wissenschaftlichen Diskurs über den Nutzen einer solchen Einrichtung dahingehend diskutiert, dass eine solches Amt die Missstände im Strafvollzug zu beheben geeignet wäre. Angestoßen wurde der Einführungsprozess dann konkret durch den im Nachgang zu den schwersten Gefängnisrevolten in England und Wales öffentlich in Auftrag gegebenen Untersuchungsbericht von Woolf und Tumim. Der von diesen vorgeschlagene „independent complaints adjudicator" wurde 1994 im Nachgang zu politischen Beratungen als Prisons Ombudsman eingeführt.

Diese kurze Institutionengeschichte wird in die Darstellung der Forschungsergebnisse einbezogen, da auf ihr die Beweisführung bzgl. der Qualität des Prisons and Probation Ombudsman als das Produkt eines cross-fertilization-Prozesses fußt. Als Auslöser des Einführungsvorgangs kommt zunächst Unzufriedenheit mit dem strafvollzugsrechtlichen *status quo ante* in Betracht. Diese Unzufriedenheit produziert mittels des durch Wissenschaftler und Interessenverbände, insbesondere JUSTICE, aufgebauten Diskurses einen systemischen Veränderungsdruck. Letzterer führte aber nie zur Implementation eines Strafvollzugsombudsmans. Allein die Implementation liefert jedoch den Beweis für erfolgten staatlichen Ideenaustausch. Erst durch die hinzukommende Krise des englischen Strafvollzugs, ausgelöst durch die sog. Strangeways-Revolten, wurde dieser latente Druck akut. Obwohl in England und Wales schon vor der Einführung des Strafvollzugsombudsmans Ombudsleute wie der Parliamentary Commissioner for Administration operierten, generierten einzelne Wissenschaftler wie Interessenverbände in der Akquisephase Datenmaterial über die bestehenden ausländischen Strafvollzugsombudsleute, insbesondere den Canadian Correctional Investigator, als ein entsprechendes, innerhalb des Commonowealth operierendes Kontrollorgan des Strafvollzugs. Diese key-holder wurden nun in der Implementationsphase von Politikern und weiteren Interessenverbänden (the Association of the Members of the Boards of Visitors and the Prison Reform Trust) unterstützt. Gerade in der Missachtung des von Woolf und Tumim vorgeschlagenen Adjudicator-Titels zu Gunsten des letztlich eingeführten Prisons Ombudsman kommt zum Ausdruck, dass eine Beeinflussung des Implementationsprozesses eines unabhängigen Kontrollorgans für den Strafvollzug durch in der Akquisephase gesammeltes Material erfolgt ist. Ein zwischenstaatlicher Ideenaustausch ist also erfolgt. Die Analyse des Implementationsergebnisses zeigt, dass die Implementation des Prisons and Probation Ombudsman durch den Home Secretary mittels seiner Bevollmächtigung im Prison Act von 1952 als Exekutiverlass erfolgt ist. Trotz wiederholter Bemühung um eine gesetzliche Grundlage beschränkt sich die rechtliche Verankerung des englischen Strafvollzugsombudsmans bis heute auf eine sog. Rahmenvereinbarung und ein Terms of Reference-Dokuments des Justizministeriums. Bei dem Prisons and Probation Ombudsman handelt es sich also um einen Exekutivombudsman.

Die Institutionengeschichte des zweiten gewählten Beispiels, des Justizvollzugsbeauftragten des Landes Nordrhein-Westfalen, muss sinnvollerweise auch die Geschichte dessen Vorgängers, des Ombudsmanns für den Justizvollzug Nordrhein-Westfalen miteinbeziehen. Selbiger verdankte seine Einführung einem als „Siegburger Foltermord" bekannt gewordenen Justizskandal, bei dem drei Insassen der Siegburger Jugendvollzugsanstalt den vierten Zelleninsassen über mehrere Stunden folterten und im Anschluss zum Selbstmord zwangen. Die rasch in der Kritik der parlamentarischen Opposition stehende damalige Justizministerin reagierte darauf mit einem Maßnahmenbündel, das als langfristige Maßnahmen die Einführung eines Ombudsmannes für den Justizvollzug Nordrhein-Westfalen vorsah. Im Nachgang hierzu wurde die Mittelbereitstellung umgehend in den Haushaltsplan für das Jahr 2007 eingepasst und der Ombudsmann mittels Allgemeinverfügung eingeführt. Nach dem Regierungswechsel im Jahre 2010 ersetzte die an die Regierung gekommene damalige Opposition die Allgemeinverfügung durch eine weitere Allgemeinverfügung, mit der der Justizvollzugsbeauftragte des Landes Nordrhein-Westfalen eingeführt wurde. Im Rahmen der Überarbeitung der rechtlichen Grundlage fügte das Ministerium die geschaffene Institution durch die Namensgebung bewusst in die deutsche Beauftragtenkultur (vgl. Wehrbeauftragter, Bürgerbeauftragte, Datenschutzbeauftragte) ein.

Entsprechend dieser Institutionengeschichte findet die Analyse der Institutionen im Hinblick auf erfolgte cross-fertilization-Prozesse zweigeteilt statt. Durch den „Siegburger Foltermord" entstand für den nordrhein-westfälischen Justizvollzug eine akute Drucksituation, die nach Bekunden der Justizministerin den Einführungsprozess nicht unwesentlich beschleunigte. Dieses Bewusstwerden des Drucks als Katalysator hat den Implementationsprozess aber nicht soweit rationalisiert, als das cross-fertilization-Prozesse ausgeschlossen worden wären. Vielmehr führte der entstandene Druck dazu, dass sich die Ministerin aus Gründen der Selbstverteidigung, parteipolitischer Strategie und Gesichtswahrung zu raschem Handeln gezwungen sah. In der kurzen Akquisephase orientierte sich das Justizministerium lose an Ombudseinrichtungen des deutschen Privatsektors sowie an skandinavischen und englischen Ombudsleuten. Die Ideensammlung bei ausländischen Ombudsinstitutionen blieb dabei aufgrund der Zeitnot sehr reduziert, d.h. ohne tatsächliche Kontaktaufnahme oder Besuche. In der Implementationsphase führte die zeitliche Komponente in Verbindung mit dem oppositionellen Widerstand gegen die Idee trotz der persönlichen Präferenz der Justizministerin für eine legislative Verankerung zur Einführung des Ombudsmannes mittels Exekutiverlass. Beim Ombudsmann für den Justizvollzug Nordrhein-Westfalen handelt es sich also um einen Exekutivombudsman. Eine nachträgliche gesetzliche Verankerung erfolgte beschränkt auf den Jugendstrafvollzug im später erlassenen Jugendstrafvollzugsgesetz. In beiden Phasen des cross-fertilization-Prozesses waren ausschließlich Politiker und Bürokraten als key-holder aktiv, die einschlägige wissenschaftliche Befassung kann aufgrund ihres geringen Umfangs und des Alters mehrerer Jahrzehnte keinen Einfluss, z.B. in Form eines latenten Drucks, ausgeübt haben.

Als Rechtsnachfolger des Ombudsmanns handelt es sich bei dem Justizvollzugsbeauftragten zwingend ebenfalls um das Produkt eines cross-fertilization-Prozesses. Dennoch vernachlässigt die Studie nicht zu prüfen, ob der Justizvollzugsbeauftragte auch aus eigener Kraft als ein cross-fertilization-Produkt zu klassifizieren ist. Dabei ist der Umstand der raschen Überholung der Institution einerseits und des dadurch begrenzten Ideenaustauschs andererseits zu berücksichtigen. Im Falle des Ombudsmannes für den Justizvollzug hat die Justizministerin die Möglichkeit einer raschen Überholung ganz bewusst schon bei Einführung angedeutet, um so die Opposition zur Wahl einer permanenteren Verankerung entsprechend der von der Justizministerin präferierten gesetzlichen Grundlage zu inspirieren. 2008 unternahm diese tatsächlich einen entsprechenden Versuch, der nach dem Regierungswechsel 2010 in einem entsprechenden Überarbeitungsverfahren, wenn auch unter Verzicht auf eine legislative Implementierung, mündete. Dieser Verzicht verweist auf die Begrenztheit des Ideenaustauschs in Überarbeitungsprozessen. Im vorliegenden Fall fürchtete die neue

Regierung ebenfalls ein mögliches Scheitern einer Gesetzesinitiative im Parlament, wodurch die rasche Einführung mittels einer Allgemeinverfügung ungleich attraktiver erschien als noch zu Oppositionszeiten derselben Parlamentarier. Auch die Wiederaufnahme des Beauftragtentitels passt in das Konzept der Begrenzung des Ideenaustauschs bei der Überarbeitung staatlicher Institutionen. Die Existenz eines Vorgängers sowie die Wiederaufnahme des Beauftragtenbegriffs könnten dabei als Ausdruck fehlenden interstaatlichen Wissenstransfers angesehen werden. Im Falle des Justizvollzugsbeauftragten liegen aber Anhaltspunkte dafür vor. So zitiert die Opposition schon 2008 den Prisons and Probation Ombudsman for England and Wales als best-practice-model für eine Überarbeitung des Ombudsmannes für den Justizvollzug und weist auf die Ungeeignetheit des exekutiven Implementierungsmodus hin. Es hat also eine vom Ombudsmann unabhängige, eigene Akquisephase für den Justizvollzugsbeauftragten stattgefunden, in der Politiker als key-holder tätig waren. Auslöser für die Implementation war der interdisziplinäre Diskurs mit Beteiligung von Politikern und Wissenschaftlern. Letztere steuerten in Zusammenarbeit mit Bürokraten des Justizministerium auch die Neuauflage der Allgemeinverfügung und damit die Implementation selbst. Bemerkenswert ist dabei der erhebliche Einfluss, den der anvisierte neue Amtsinhaber noch als Wissenschaftler auf die Ausgestaltung seines späteren Amtes nehmen konnte. Auch eine zeitnahe Schaffung einer gesetzlichen Grundlage erscheint aber in Anbetracht der Andeutung des selbigen Amtsinhabers und der anstehenden Einführung eines nordrhein-westfälischen Strafvollzugsgesetzes nicht unrealistisch. Dann würde der Justizvollzugsbeauftragte des Landes Nordrhein-Westfalen vom Exekutivombudsman zum ersten europäischen Strafvollzugsombudsman legislativer Ausprägung.

Beide Untersuchungssubjekte sind damit durch systemischen Druck bzw. interdisziplinären Diskurs ausgelöste cross-fertilization-Prozesse entstanden und als Ombudsleute mit exekutiver Ausgestaltung eingeführt worden. Damit erscheint die Aufstellung der dieser Arbeit zu Grund liegenden Hypothesen, dass

- Strafvollzugsombudsleute nur in Zeiten akuten Drucks auf Strafvollzugssystem eingeführt werden,
- ihre Implementation mittels als „Cross-fertilization" bezeichneten interstaatlichen Ideenaustausch erfolgt, und
- dies häufig in der Einführung als Exekutivombuds-Institutionen mündet,

gerechtfertigt. Aufgrund der Anwendung von grounded theory als Untersuchungsmethode ist allein die Aufstellung von geeigneten Hypothesen, nicht aber deren Überprüfung Untersuchungsziel. Die aus forschungsökonomischen Gründen indizierte Begrenzung der Studie auf zwei ausgewählte Beispiele wird dadurch ein wenig ausgeglichen, als die dem letzten Teil der Analyse angefügte

Tabelle über alle existierenden Ombudsleute, gegliedert nach Implementations-anlass und -ergebnis, die gebildeten Hypothesen zwei und drei weiter zu stützen vermag. Dies gilt, obwohl mit den Strafvollzugsleuten Michigans und Kanadas zwei legislative Einrichtungen vorliegen. Deren Existenz belegt jedoch nur, dass eine legislative Ausgestaltung von Strafvollzugsombuds-Institutionen grundsätz-lich möglich ist.

Angesichts dieser Untersuchungsergebnisse kann das Untersuchungsziel dieser Studie als erreicht betrachtet und der institutionelle Erfolg als Quell der Verbreitung von Ombudsleuten zumindest in ihrer Ausprägung als Strafvollzug-sombuds-Institutionen zu Recht bezweifelt werden. Im Zuge der von der groun-ded theory methodisch geleiteten Untersuchung wurden Strukturen, Ausprägun-gen und Verbreitungsformen von Strafvollzugsombuds-Einrichtungen in einem bisher nicht vorhandenen Ausmaß zusammengetragen und übersichtlich darge-stellt. Der induktive Prozess ergab dabei ein integriertes Verständnis von Straf-vollzugsombudsleuten als evolutionäre Unterform von bereichsübergreifend tä-tigen Ombuds-Institutionen. Die vorliegende Forschung ergab dabei, dass Straf-vollzugsombuds-Einrichtungen zur Ausfüllung des für moderne Strafvollzugs-systeme spezifischen Bedarfs an unabhängiger Kontrolle entwickelt wurden. Ein Bedarf, der besonders dann augenfällig wird, wann immer sich Strafvollzugssys-teme Zeiten akuten Drucks ausgesetzt sehen. Zu diesen Zeiten benutzen Trans-feragenten Strafvollzugsombuds-Institutionen als vorhandene ausländische Antworten auf lokale Probleme, wodurch es zu Prozessen zwischenstaatlichen Ideenaustauschs mittels cross-fertilization kommt. Die begleitende zeitliche Komponente begünstigt die Präferenz lokaler staatliche key-holder für die Aus-wahl exekutiver Implementationsformen. Dies beweist, dass die Vermutung in-stitutionellen Erfolges als Quell der Verbreitung von Strafvollzugsombudsleuten von dieser Studie zu Recht bezweifelt wurde. Key-holder werden vorwiegend von lokalen Gegebenheiten wie Druck auf das heimische Strafvollzugssystem beeinflusst, während der auswärtige Erfolg der Institutionen weder gefordert, noch vor der Implementation selbstständig geprüft wird. Wäre dem nicht so, wä-re eine exekutive Einführung aller Wahrscheinlichkeit nach nicht die häufigste Implementationsform.

Künftig empfiehlt sich auf einer speziellen Ebene eine vergleichende Evalu-ation des Kostenaufwandes von Strafvollzugsombuds-Einrichtungen und Ge-richten ebenso wie Analyse des Nutzens der Ausweisung dieser Einrichtungen als National Preventive Mechanisms im Rahmen des OPCAT. Auf einer grund-sätzlichen Ebene bedarf es weiterhin der Entwicklung eines allgemeingültigen Katalogs zur Leistungsmessung von Ombudsleuten.

Publications

Carl, Sabine (2012) Toward a Definition and Taxonomy of Public Sector Ombudsmen. Canadian Public Administration 55(2): 203-20

-,- (2012) Ombudsman und Strafvollzug. Eine Übersicht über die weltweit tätigen Justizvollzugsbeauftragten. Forum Strafvollzug 61(2): 106-8

-,- (2012) Review: The Ombudsman Enterprise and Administrative Justice, The Modern Law Review 75(2): 305-6

-,- (2012) Buchbesprechung: The Ombudsman Enterprise and Administrative Justice, Forum Strafvollzug 61(2): 126

Würzburger Schriften
zur Kriminalwissenschaft

Herausgegeben von Klaus Laubenthal

Band 20 Susanne Werner-Eschenbach: Jugendstrafrecht. Ein Experimentierfeld für neue Rechtsinstitute. 2005.

Band 21 Stefanie Röhrs: Vergewaltigung von Frauen in Südafrika. Primäre, Sekundäre und Tertiäre Viktimisierung. 2005.

Band 22 Andrea Lindner: 100 Jahre Frauenkriminalität. Die quantitative und qualitative Entwicklung der weiblichen Delinquenz von 1902 bis 2002. 2006.

Band 23 Michael Steiner: Der Strafgefangene im System der gesetzlichen Sozialversicherung. 2006.

Band 24 Simone Kleespies: Kriminalität von Spätaussiedlern. Erscheinungsformen, Ursachen, Prävention. 2006.

Band 25 Caroline Vöhringer: Tötung auf Verlangen. Die Abgrenzung des § 216 StGB zur straflosen Beihilfe zum Suizid sowie das Verhältnis von privilegierenden zu qualifizierenden Tötungsumständen. 2008.

Band 26 Jörg Weddig: Mittelbare Täterschaft und Versuchsbeginn bei der Giftfalle. Eine Auseinandersetzung mit dem „Passauer Apothekerfall" (BGHSt 43, 177 ff.). 2008.

Band 27 Isabel Albert: Innerfamiliäre Gewalt gegen Kinder. Eine kriminologische und rechtliche Betrachtung der Erscheinungsformen, Ursachen und Möglichkeiten der Bekämpfung. 2008.

Band 28 Nina Nestler: Churning. Strafbarkeit der Spesenschinderei nach deutschem Recht. 2009.

Band 29 Leonie Ackermann: Die Altersgrenzen der Strafbarkeit in Deutschland, Österreich und der Schweiz. 2009.

Band 30 Annika Flaig: Die nachträgliche Sicherungsverwahrung. 2009.

Band 31 Simona Markert: Der bayerische Jugendstrafvollzug in Theorie und Praxis. Betrachtet vor dem Hintergrund der Entscheidung des Bundesverfassungsgerichts vom 31.5.2006. 2012.

Band 32 Klaus Jünemann: Gesetzgebungskompetenz für den Strafvollzug im föderalen System der Bundesrepublik Deutschland. Eine Analyse anlässlich der Föderalismusreform 2006 unter besonderer Berücksichtigung der Ziele und Aufgaben des Strafvollzugs. 2012.

Band 33 Lars Firchau: Das fachgerichtliche Rechtsbehelfssystem der Untersuchungshaft sowie die Regelung des Vollzuges. Unter Einbeziehung des Bayerischen Untersuchungshaftvollzugsgesetzes. 2013.

Band 34 Sabine Carl: Proliferation and Implementation of Prison Ombudsmen. Comparative Analysis of the Prisons and Probation Ombudsman for England and Wales and the Justizvollzugsbeauftragter des Landes Nordrhein-Westfalen. 2012.

Band 35 Maximiliane Friederich: John Howard und die Strafvollzugsreformen in Süddeutschland in der ersten Hälfte des 19. Jahrhunderts. 2013.

www.peterlang.de